"I'm gonna make you an offer you can't refuse..."

Now listen closely, 'cause I'm only gonna say this once. This ain't no negotiation. It's a one-time deal. I'm gonna do something those of us who live in the world of organised crime don't usually do and let you in. You'll see things you never even thought were possible, and you better be prepared to meet people you couldn't dream up in your worst nightmares. This ain't for the faint-hearted, all right?

First up we got the likes of the Peaky Blinders of Birmingham and the crooks who used to run the Big Apple. You might even call them pioneers, for they were some of the first to form into what the cops like to call gangs. Me, I don't like the phrase. I don't run a gang – I run an organisation, and don't you forget. Anyway, next we'll meet a few of my old friends from the Mob and some of the most formidable dames you ever did see. Assuming you survive all that, we'll be heading out east to see what the yakuza have been up to in Japan and find out why the Russian Mafia seems to be doing so well. And if you think these guys are scary, wait until you meet the real weirdos. I'm talking people who will cut your hair off for a few bucks or steal your dinner plates. After them we'll take a ride with the Hells Angels and the Mongols. No, not together! Are you crazy?!

Now where was I? Oh yes, last but certainly not least, we got the real ruthless types. Some of 'em are in the slammer, some ain't, but whether it's the Mexican Mafia, the Crips or MS-13, I suggest you don't look 'em in the eye. We'll finish with a rundown of the best mobster flicks. Don't breathe a word of this to anyone. We don't like snitches. Capiche?

Contents

08
BRITAIN'S FIRST GANGS

12
THE REAL PEAKY BLINDERS

16
GANGS OF NEW YORK

24
INTERVIEW WITH A MAFIA EXPERT

26
PROHIBITION AND THE MOB

34
BOSS OF BOSSES

42
TOP DONS

50
WOMEN OF THE UNDERWORLD

58
YAKUZA FAMILY

64 THE 14K TRIAD

70 THE RUSSIAN MAFIA

76 THE WORLD'S WEIRDEST GANGS

82 THE HIGHWAY TO HELL

88 MEET THE MONGOL HORDE OF AMERICA

96 THE ARYAN BROTHERHOOD

102 BANGED-UP BANDITS

108 SCOURGE OF 18TH STREET

114 THE BATTLE OF LOS ANGELES

118 AMERICA'S MOST LETHAL GANG

124 MOBS AND THE MOVIES

6

Industrial Violence

8
BRITAIN'S FIRST GANGS

12
THE REAL PEAKY BLINDERS

16
GANGS OF NEW YORK

Britain's First Gangs

BEFORE THE PEAKY BLINDERS, A ROGUES' GALLERY OF LESSER-KNOWN CROOKS TERRORISED NUMEROUS CITIES AND TOWNS IN BRITAIN

WORDS JAMES SEAGAL

Gangs have always been amongst us, the twin notions of strength in numbers and might makes right as old as civilisation itself. But while many latter-day criminal crews became immortalised by popular culture – from the Peaky Blinders to the Kray twins' infamous Firm – some of Britain's most brutal but less-storied outfits hailed from the lawless hinterlands of history, exploiting the chaos of a time before coordinated policing, forensics and witness protection. From the smoke-blackened estates of the urban inner-city to the impoverished wilds of the deep countryside, any backdrop could provide a fertile breeding ground for Britain's first gangs, and these were six of the most feared and respected ever to rule their patch.

Scuttlers
MANCHESTER AND SURROUNDING AREAS
LATE 19TH CENTURY

To walk through the slums of Manchester and its satellite towns in the dying days of the 19th century was to risk being caught in the crossfire between rival scuttling gangs. Every area had its own mob of bored, angry, unemployed working-class youths, all finding an outlet and a community of sorts among their fellow exponents of street violence and petty crime.

From the Bengal Tigers and the Meadow Lads to the Grey Mare Boys and the Terrace Lads, the battle lines were drawn in blood across the North, but the rival scuttlers did share some common philosophies, typically dressing in bell-bottoms, scarves and cruel brass-capped clogs (the better for shattering an opponent's shin bones). For weaponry, they favoured knives and a makeshift whip created by removing the belt and lashing adversaries with the buckle, but the more imaginative street fighter might enter the fray with a cutlass, fire poker or bottle tied with string, whirled above the head like a lasso.

At its peak in 1890, scuttling was an epidemic, with 500-strong clashes between gangs not uncommon and Strangeways Prison struggling to contain those rounded up by the police. And while a handful of pivotal social advancements – from the advent of youth clubs to the clearing of the slums – defanged the movement in the early 20th century, the influence of this proto-street violence can still be felt in modern football hooliganism.

BRITAIN'S FIRST GANGS

Hawkhurst Gang SOUTHEAST ENGLAND **1735–1749**

Woe betide the lost soul who ventured into the Oak and Ivy Inn in Hawkhurst. Taking their name from the unassuming Kent village from which the gang masterminded a smuggling racket across the South Coast (supposedly through a labyrinthine warren of tunnels), the loaded weapons brazenly displayed by Hawkhurst foot soldiers on the tables of their pub headquarters left no doubt as to the nature of their sideline: ultra-violence.

At the peak of their powers in the early 1740s – and with their ranks bolstered by savage young toughs like Jeremiah Curtis – any interruption to Hawkhurst's slick operation was met by brutal reprisal. Just some of the entries on their spiralling rap sheet saw the gang shooting dead the riding officer who intercepted a shipment of stolen tea, whipping to death a farm labourer suspected of dipping the merchandise, swaggering into local pubs firing guns in the air, and even throwing rivals down wells or burying them alive.

Hawkhurst's infamy was sealed by their audacious 1747 night raid on Poole's Custom House (making off with over 3,000 pounds of tea). But the gang's iron fist proved their undoing, with the communities they governed rising up against them; that same year, a militia formed of Goudhurst townsfolk routed Hawkhurst, and in their weakened state the authorities moved in, executing kingpins Arthur Gray and Thomas Kingsmill, then hanging and gibbeting countless underlings. The pub still stands, but the gang that used it as their base is long confined to the past.

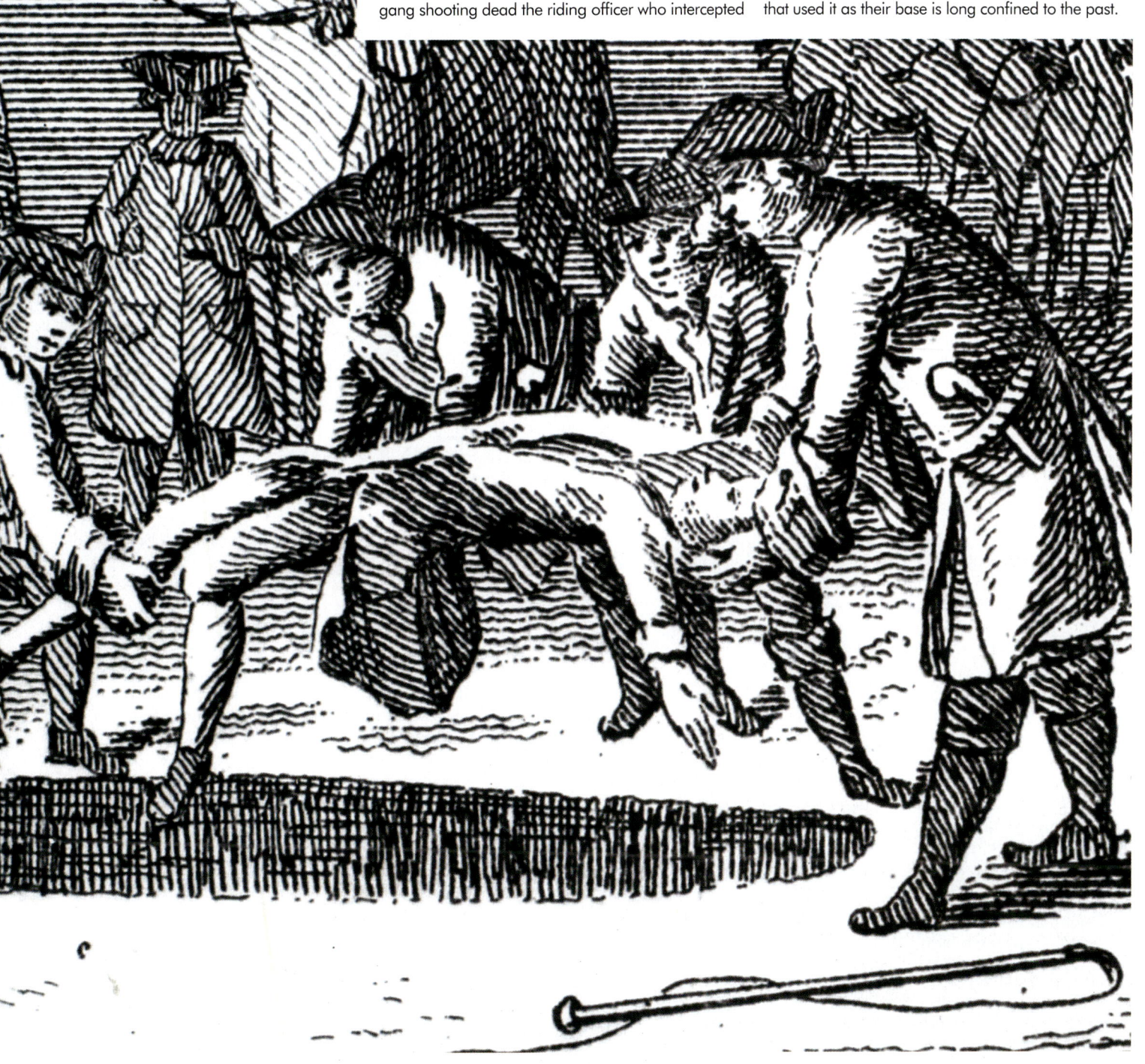

A FEMALE SHOPLIFTER.

The Forty Elephants
📍 LONDON **1870S–1950S**

By the late 19th century, the department stores of London's West End were held in a state of paralysis, helpless prey to a merciless and near-militaristic shoplifting campaign unrivalled in British history. From the mean streets of South London, the ladies of the Forty Elephants arrived smartly dressed in hats, cummerbunds and muffs – before loading the pockets of their adapted coats with loot that was instantly spirited away onto the black market.

This was a tightly organised racket, with gang members operating in cells and assigned their own turf (while rival thieves were ordered to either pay a toll or suffer the consequences). Working hand-in-glove with the Elephant and Castle Mob, these female thieves were often the family breadwinner. As Brian McDonald, author of *Gangs of London*, explains, "Many a husband lounged at home while his missus was out at work, and many an old lag was propped up by a tireless shoplifting spouse. Some of these terrors were as tough as the men they worked for and protected."

Ruling the Forty Elephants from the age of 20, none came tougher than Alice Diamond, who both masterminded the operation and got her own hands dirty on occasion, notorious for a punch sharpened by a fistful of glittering rings. Under Diamond, the gang's activities spread across Britain, while their lavish lifestyles and glamorous parties made a mockery of the old lie that crime doesn't pay.

The Cock Road Gang
📍 SOUTH GLOUCESTERSHIRE **LATE 1700S–1815**

While authorities perceived most gangs of the 18th and 19th centuries to be a by-product of urban blight, one of the era's most feared exponents emerged from the bucolic countryside of Gloucestershire. Deep within the lawless Kingswood Forest, the Bristol hamlet of Cock Road carried a fearsome reputation, earned by a cabal of powerful pan-generational families whose activities reportedly spanned from burglary, horse theft, highway robbery and counterfeiting to a tiered protection racket that saw local farmers charged based on the acreage of their land.

As the reverend and historian H.T. Ellacombe wrote, "They kept the neighbourhood in so much dread that people used to pay them an annual stipend not to rob them. Some paid 10s, some 6d, some 5s, which was regularly collected at Lansdown Fair."

The Cock Road Gang's stranglehold seemed unbreakable, with even the hanging of Joseph Fry and Samuel Ward for robbery in 1786 doing little to slow their campaign. But the mob grew too bold: when gang member Isaac Crib was arrested in 1815, his comrades stormed the lock-up on Bitton High Street that held him and had to be fought back by constables. The uprising could not go unanswered and that same year authorities struck back with a coordinated raid by police, watchmen and Bristol city guards that rounded up the entire gang and saw them hung, jailed or transported to the colonies.

The Penny Mob
📍 GLASGOW **1870S**

Not for nothing has Glasgow been dubbed 'Little Chicago' – and the city's gangland narrative can be traced all the way back to the 1870s. With tensions raised by the spike in Irish-Catholic immigration following the mid-century potato famines and young working-class men choosing their side of the battle lines on a religious or territorial basis, the Penny Mob emerged as a force that briefly seemed unstoppable. The gang's monicker was earned from the court's ultimatum whenever a member was arrested: pay a stiff fine or serve a jail sentence (at which point the gang would have a whip-round from those on their turf, demanding they cough up a penny apiece to secure their comrade's release).

Hailing from Glasgow's tough East End, the Penny Mob's organisation was as sharp as their dress code, with the gang employing a structured hierarchy and even electing chairmen to control the flow of funds. When it came to physicality, these ferocious fighters didn't shrink from a challenge, with terrifying battles (known as 'square-gos') against rival outfits like the Tim Malloys unfolding under cover of darkness on ancient Glasgow Green or the banks of the River Clyde.

While control of Glasgow passed on to rolling generations of powerful new forces, the Penny Mob remains one of Scotland's trailblazing crime organisations, its brand of lethal intelligence setting the template for the century to come.

BRITAIN'S FIRST GANGS

The High Rip Gang
LIVERPOOL 1880S

Around the same period the Peaky Blinders rose to become lords of Birmingham, the streets of Liverpool's North End belonged to the High Rip – and God help anyone who walked them at night. Preying on foreign seamen who strayed from the safety of their ships, the High Rip Gang first hit the headlines with the shocking Blackstone Street murder of 1884, which saw Spanish sailor Exequiel Rodriguez Nuniez slashed across the neck (a crime for which 18-year-old gang members Michael McLean and Patrick Duggan were hung at Kirkdale prison).

Violence could erupt any time the High Rip darkened your path – and it was not reserved for rival gangsters. Harrowing tales in Michael Macilwee's book *Tearaways* tell of babies being punched in the face, shops being savagely turned over, strangers being beaten to death for refusing to cough up 'ale money' and even of gang members raining blows upon their own parents. The High Rip's formidable reputation and the ferocity of their turf wars were such that Liverpool's police were loathe to break up the melee (one clash involving over 2,000 toughs raged for more than half an hour).

But their reign was too brutal to last. The pushback by the Logwood Gang – a vigilante group of dockers armed with wooden batons – combined with harsh sentencing and flogging for apprehended gang members depleted the High Rip, and by the decade's end their influence was on the wane.

The Real Peaky Blinders

HOW THE GANG KNOWN AS THE PEAKY BLINDERS CAME TO DOMINATE THE CRIMINAL UNDERWORLD IN TURN-OF-THE-CENTURY BIRMINGHAM

WORDS NEIL CROSSLEY

Few period crime dramas in recent decades have come close to matching the style, exhilaration and sheer audacity of *Peaky Blinders*. The BBC One drama first aired on 12 September 2013 and went on to spawn a cult following around the globe.

Created by screenwriter and film director Steven Knight, the series was inspired by the stories his mother and father told him about growing up in the Small Heath area of Birmingham. *Peaky Blinders* is a stylish and exquisitely compelling series in which revenge, betrayal and wrong footings abound. The accents are questionable at times and the violence is gaudy and exploitative, but there's a glorious swagger to the series, anchored by strong storylines and the powerful, charismatic performances of its stars, such as Cillian Murphy (Thomas Shelby) and the late Helen McCrory (Polly Gray).

Peaky Blinders is based only loosely on fact. There was no Thomas Shelby or Shelby family, for example. But there was certainly a Birmingham gang known as the Peaky Blinders. They might not have quite had the visual dynamism of the Irish-Romani-descended gang depicted in the TV series, but all evidence suggests that they were equally as violent and ruthless.

The harsh economic deprivations of working-class Victorian Britain formed the breeding ground for the gang that became known as the Peaky Blinders. Poverty was rife in the late 19th century, with over 25 per cent of the population living at or above the subsistence level. Industrialisation had created a divided society, and it has long been argued by historians that poverty was responsible for the criminal underclass that emerged in Britain in the 19th century.

In the large and burgeoning city of Birmingham, disenfranchised young men from the slums were forming a separate culture of their own. The origins of this subculture can be traced back to the 1850s when the police, due to pressure from the upper and middle classes, cracked down

THE REAL PEAKY BLINDERS

ABOVE The ruthless Shelby brothers, around which Steven Knight's stylish and pacey BBC One series *Peaky Blinders* was centred

on gambling dens and rough street sports taking place in Birmingham's inner city. The youth fought back, banding together in what became known as 'slogging gangs'.

By 1890, the Peaky Blinders had emerged from Small Heath and gained dominance by fighting for territory with rival slogging gangs. The name of the gang derives from the peaked caps worn by its members. One commonly held view suggests that gang members would stitch disposable razor blades into the peaks and headbutt their enemies in a bid to blind them, or use the peaks to slash foreheads so that blood ran down into their enemies' eyes. But as the first disposable razor blades weren't manufactured in Britain until the early 1900s, some doubt has been cast on this theory. Birmingham historian Professor Carl Chinn has suggested that the name is actually more to do with the gang's sartorial elegance.

Whatever the reason, the Peaky Blinders became the most vicious gang to emerge from the slums of late-19th-century Birmingham. Writing in the *Birmingham Mail* in 2019, Professor Chinn noted that the Peaky Blinders and other gangs were "infamous for their violence and fighting with metal-tipped boots, stones, belt buckles and sometimes knives".

While the BBC One series is set largely in the 1920s, historical accounts state that the real gang held control for just 20 years, from approximately 1890 until 1910, although it seems likely that the term 'Peaky Blinders' prevailed for decades, passed into generic usage as a term for any street gang in Birmingham.

Steven Knight, the creator of the TV series whose family lived in Small Heath for generations, said that his aunts, uncles and grandparents recalled the term 'Peaky Blinders' being in common usage well into the 1930s.

Knight was inspired to write the TV series following a story his father told him. His father's uncles, the Sheldons – a name that influenced the fictional Shelbys – were bookmakers and part of the Peaky Blinders heritage. His father told him of being eight or nine years old and being asked by his own father to deliver a message to his uncles at an address in the city's Artillery Street.

> **THE REAL PEAKY BLINDERS MIGHT NOT HAVE QUITE HAD THE VISUAL DYNAMISM OF THE GANG DEPICTED IN THE TV SERIES, BUT ALL EVIDENCE SUGGESTS THAT THEY WERE EQUALLY AS VIOLENT AND RUTHLESS**

Dressed to Kill

Members of the Peaky Blinders gang flaunted their illicitly won wealth via their overtly stylish clothes. Unlike other Birmingham gangs, almost all of the Peaky Blinders wore tailored suits, long-lapelled coats, button waistcoats, bell-bottomed trousers, leather boots and peaked caps. Some of the wealthier members were even more sartorially dynamic, sporting penny collared shirts with starched collars, metal tie buttons and silk scarves.

Their wives, girlfriends and mistresses were equally striking, wearing lavish clothing, pearls, silks and colourful scarves. The distinctive dress of the Peaky Blinders and their entourage made them easily recognisable to the police, rival gang members and the general public.

> **THE DISTINCTIVE DRESS OF THE PEAKY BLINDERS WAS EASILY RECOGNISABLE TO THE POLICE, RIVALS AND THE PUBLIC**

"My dad was told to go and deliver this message," he told *BBC History* magazine in 2016, "so he ran through the streets barefoot, knocked on the door, the door opened and there was a table with about eight men sitting around it, immaculately dressed, wearing caps and with guns in their pockets. The table was covered with money – at a time when no one had a penny – and they were all drinking beer out of jam jars because these men wouldn't spend money on glasses or cups. Just that image – smoke, booze and these immaculately dressed men in this slum in Birmingham – I thought, that's the mythology, that's the story, and that's the first image I started to work with."

The origins of the Peaky Blinders gang are slightly hazy, but they were certainly formed in Small Heath, possibly by a man named Thomas Mucklow. The first report of the gang appeared in the *Birmingham Mail* on 24 March 1890 and centred on their violent, unprovoked attack on a young man from Small Heath called George Eastwood, who left a pub called the Rainbow Public House in Adderley Street after buying a bottle of ginger beer. Eastwood was beaten viciously with belt buckles. "A murderous outrage at Small Heath, a man's skull fractured," ran the newspaper report.

The gang focused on the acquisition of favourable land in Small Heath and Cheapside, extreme slum areas of Birmingham. Their expansion was noted by rival gang the Cheapside Sloggers, who battled against them in an effort to control land. The Sloggers had originated in the 1870s and were known for engaging in street fights in the Bordesley and Small Heath areas.

The Peaky Blinders prevailed, gaining control of territory and expanding their criminal enterprise. This included protection rackets, fraud, land grabs, smuggling, hijacking, robbery and racketeering. The gang became notorious for its violence against innocent civilians, rival gangs and the police. The Peaky Blinders deliberately attacked police officers, which became known as 'constable baiting'. In 1897, a police constable called George Snipe was killed by the gang, and four years later another constable, Charles Philip Gunter, also had his life taken. Hundreds more police officers were injured and the level of violence prompted some to leave the force.

By far the most powerful member of the Peaky Blinders was a man known as Kevin Mooney, whose real name was Thomas Gilbert. Other prominent members were David Taylor, Earnest Bayles, Stephen McNickle and Harry Fowles, who was known as "Baby-faced Harry". The gang used an assortment of weapons, such as belt buckles, fire irons, metal-tipped boots, canes and knives. Firearms like Webley Revolvers were also used, such as in the shooting and killing of a Summer Hill gang member by Peaky Blinder William Lacey in September 1905.

Despite their fearsome reputation, there was no real organised strategy to the Peaky Blinders. In a lecture at Leeds Samuel Beckett University in 2013, academic Dr. Heather Shore argued that the real Peaky Blinders were more focused on street fighting, robbery and racketeering, as opposed to organised crime. It's a view reinforced by Professor Chinn. "Peaky Blinders gangs were not big-time criminals," he told Express.co.uk in April 2020. "They were backstreet thugs and petty criminals, whose main objective was to show off their fighting prowess."

The Peaky Blinders ruled the Birmingham streets for two decades, but by 1910 they had lost power to a rival gang known as the Birmingham Boys, led by former Peaky Blinder Billy Kimber. The Peaky Blinders' audacious expansion into racecourses had prompted a violent backlash from the Birmingham Boys.

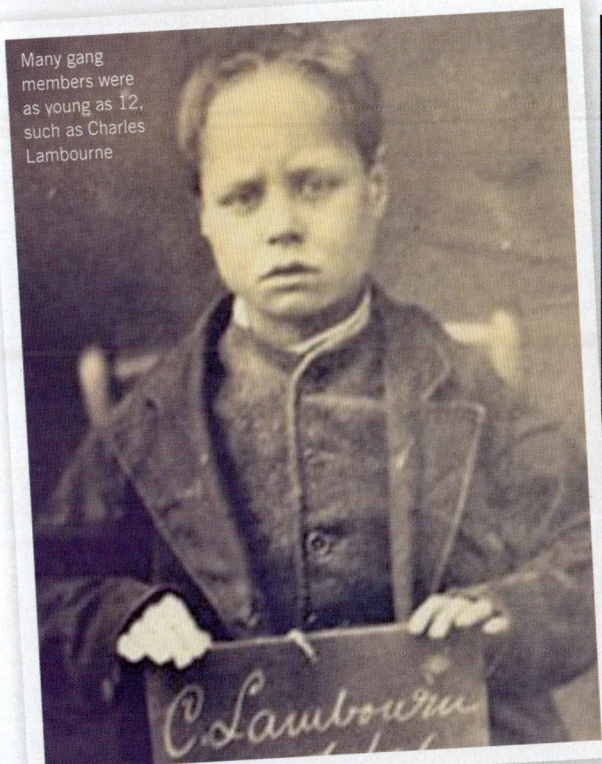

Many gang members were as young as 12, such as Charles Lambourne

The Peaky Blinders emerged from extremely poor areas such as Small Heath and Cheapside

THE REAL PEAKY BLINDERS

Police mugshots of prominent Peaky Blinders: (from left to right) Harry Fowler (a.k.a. "Baby-faced Harry"), Earnest Bayles, Stephen McNickle and Thomas Gilbert (with and without peaked cap)

Over time, Peaky Blinder families moved to the countryside, distancing themselves from Birmingham's centre and its criminal underworld. By the end of the 1920s, a London gang called the Sabinis had ousted the Birmingham Boys and claimed all of the Peaky Blinders' former Birmingham territories.

In truth, the very existence of Birmingham's ruthless gangs had been under threat since 1899, when police chief constable Charles Haughton Rafter was appointed with the task of turning the nation's second city around. He embarked on a "rapid recruitment campaign of fit and young men", hiring up to 500 additional police officers. "They asked three things: Can you read? Can you write? And can you fight?" Professor Chinn told Express.co.uk. "They needed to have a certain standard of education but also had to be tough lads with lots of physical training."

The police were no longer outnumbered and stood a chance of being able to arrest gang members. The presence of more police on the streets encouraged more people from the area to report crimes. "Before, they were reluctant and some were too scared to come to the police as the Peaky Blinders would attack them," says Chinn.

Rafter also secured longer sentences, which deterred younger people from joining gangs. By the second decade of the 20th century more children were attending school, while social changes and increased leisure activities for children made a dent in the number of people that gangs could actually recruit.

Over a century on, the legacy of the Peaky Blinders in most people's eyes will be immortalised in the high production values and riveting, fast-paced drama that played out across the six series of the hugely successful BBC TV show.

For series creator Steven Knight, the existence of such a turbulent, dramatic past on the very Small Heath streets where he grew up came as something of a revelation, as did the fact that his family had a direct link to the gang. He recalls the old tenements before they were knocked down, and the Garrison pub – recreated as a pivotal Peaky Blinders HQ in the TV series – where his grandfather would bang out a tune on the piano in exchange for free beer and whiskey after the horses he had bet on that day failed to win.

Knight would often have to coax the stories out of his relatives. But the more he heard, the more it fired his imagination.

ABOVE *Peaky Blinders* creator Steven Knight was inspired to write the series after hearing stories of the gang from his parents as a child

"It was reluctantly delivered, but my family did give me little snapshots, of gypsies and horses and gang fights and guns, and immaculate suits," Knight told *GQ* magazine in September 2019. "This was mad, wild stuff that most writers wouldn't dare put into a work of fiction because it was too far out, but it was true – all of it. It was our history."

Thanks to his endeavour, it is a history that will live on forever, immortalised by the irrepressible Thomas Shelby.

Gangs of New York

MEET THE CUT-THROAT KILLERS WHO ONCE PROWLED THE STREETS OF THE BATTLEGROUND THAT WAS THE 19TH-CENTURY FIVE POINTS AREA

WORDS CALLUM MCKELVIE

New York, New York. So good they named it twice. But America's most famous city wasn't always a welcoming tourist hotspot where anyone with a dream could make it big. Far from it. In the 19th century it was a different world to the bustling metropolis we know today. Back then, one area in particular, the neighbourhood of Five Points in Lower Manhattan, was a poverty-stricken warren where vice and criminality reigned. European immigrants who had fled to America seeking a better life ended up living in squalor within its streets. Yet for all the tales of destitution and corruption, it is for the fearsome gangs that stalked its alleys and saloons that the Five Points remains notorious. With names such as the Bowery Boys and the Whyos, they were said to have flamboyant dress senses and a taste for violence. Much about them remains unknown, with historians disagreeing about events and in some cases whether specific gangs even existed at all. So just who were the real gangs of New York?

The Five Points earned its name due to the fact it centred on the intersection of three streets, which formed five corners, or 'points'. This notorious den of squalor was built on top of a pond that was known as the Collect. Over time, the Collect had become increasingly contaminated with filth and was filled in with dirt. As a result the houses often sank at odd angles and disease was a regular occurrence. Charles Dickens, who visited the area during a five-month tour of North America in 1841, noted that "poverty, vice and wretchedness are rife enough" and that "here too are lanes and alleys, paved with mud knee deep, underground chambers where they dance and game… all that is loathsome, drooping and decayed is here". Yet any visitor hoping to follow in Dickens' footsteps will be sorely disappointed. "It is now covered over by a court and other state and federal buildings," explains Wilbur Miller, author of *The Social History of Crime and Punishment in America: An Encyclopedia*. "Columbus Park, built in the early 20th century, was constructed over Mulberry Bend, a particularly notorious part of the points."

Desperate immigrants, including many Irish who were escaping the hardships of the potato famine, made their way to New York. In fact, according to *The New York Times*, by 1860, 69 per cent of the city's voters were foreign-born. Many of these immigrants, unable to afford adequate housing, ended up in the Five Points. "It was very mixed," says Miller. "Most residents were Irish, but there were also African-American and Italian immigrants, as well as American-born workers."

Legends of the area's destitution began to spread, and with it tales of violence and crime. Some accounts state

---

EXPERT BIO

WILBUR MILLER

Wilbur Miller is an emeritus professor at Stony Brook University, New York. He is the editor of the five-volume encyclopaedia *The Social History of Crime and Punishment in America* (2012) and the author of *Cops and Bobbies* (1977), *Revenuers and Moonshiners* (1991) and *A History of Private Policing in the United States* (2019).

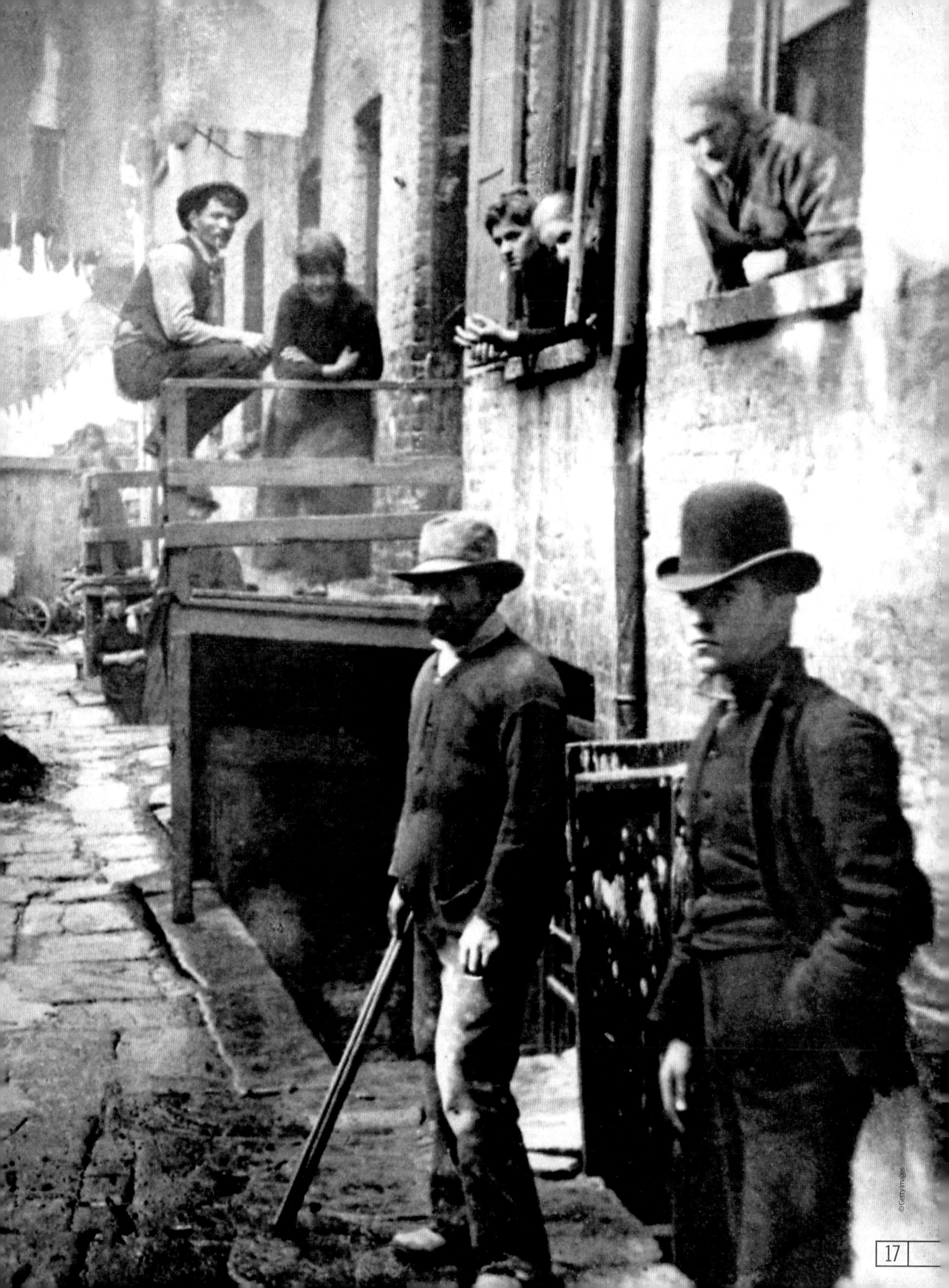

> **THE FORTY THIEVES WERE EVEN SAID TO HAVE ACQUIRED AND TRAINED AN OFFSHOOT GROUP OF CHILD CRIMINALS, THE FORTY LITTLE THIEVES**

that 15 murders were committed in the Five Points every night, and the Old Brewery was said to have been witness to one homicide a day for 15 years. However, as with many impoverished areas, it's argued that the danger of the Five Points has been exaggerated. Historian Tyler Anbinder, who worked on revising the *Gangs of New York* (2002) film script, was quoted by National Geographic as stating, "I looked at the statistics, and other than public drunkenness and prostitution, there was no more crime in Five Points than in any other part of the city."

Perceived criminality aside, if the Five Points is remembered today it is for its infamous gangs, each with their own colourful sense of dress and a formidable reputation. "Gangs offered a route of mobility, especially into politics," says Miller. "They provided outlets for young men (not teenagers) who were out of work or worked in occupations like butchers and had afternoons off after the morning markets." Unlike some gangs, many of the Five Points crews were more political in nature, and although their activity was sometimes dubious, it was not strictly criminal.

"They mostly engaged in turf fights with each other, serving as 'shoulder hitters' and 'repeaters' at elections, starting riots at elections," Miller explains. "Although sometimes gang members would beat and/or rob a well-dressed man who wandered into the wrong place."

However, the first gang known in the area, and perhaps even in New York itself, most certainly was criminal. The Forty Thieves began inauspiciously enough in the back rooms of a 'grocery' store. Opened by Rosanna Peers in 1825, the store was in fact a front for an illegal bar and soon became a favourite haunt for pickpockets, crooks and other villains. The Forty Thieves leader, Edward Coleman, formed the gang from the best scoundrels Peers had to offer. He was notoriously tough and enforced a strict quota system: members who were unable to return to the store with a specific value of stolen goods were quickly thrown out. Coleman had a separate business, recruiting attractive young women, known as 'hot corn girls', to sell corn on the street. His own wife was part of this racket, but when she consistently failed to meet her targets he beat her to death. Coleman was hanged for his crime in 1838, but the Forty Thieves continued. They were even said to have acquired and trained an offshoot group of child criminals, the Forty Little Thieves.

As a result of the high number of immigrants in the Five Points area, many of the gangs that were formed had predominantly Irish members. One of the first of these gangs was the Roche Guard. This group was formed at the beginning of the 1850s by saloon owner Walter Roche, though some sources state their leader was in fact called Ted Roach. Legend has often stated that another Irish group, the fearsome Dead Rabbits, was formed from wayward Roche gang members. As a result the two groups were deadly enemies. The Rabbits' distinctive name has a rather colourful history. "The Dead Rabbits were said to carry a dead rabbit hanging from a pole," Miller tells us. But despite the folklore surrounding the gang, there is now a question as to whether the Dead Rabbits existed at all. Anbinder says there is little evidence that the gang existed and posits that 'Dead Rabbits' may have been a nickname used by the Bowery Boys to demean Irish gangs.

Who were the Bowery Boys? Only the most infamous of the Five Points gangs. Although the name was applied to a variety of groups at different times, they all appear to have had a Nativist ideology, which was staunchly anti-immigrant and anti-Catholic. In his book *The Bowery Boys: Street Corner Radicals and the Politics of Rebellion*, historian Peter Adams

BELOW An 1857 sketch of a member of the so-called Dead Rabbits gang

The Five Points area of New York was home to many notorious gangs

ABOVE Charles Dickens visited the Five Points in 1841 and commented on the widespread poverty that he witnessed

states that many belonged to professions such as shipbuilders, carpenters, butchers and printers. The Bowery Boys were noted for wearing stovepipe hats and, particularly in later years, their increasingly dapper style of dress. Adams notes that a haircut described as short at the back, slicked down at the front and with distinctive ringlets pasted down in front of the ears (known as 'soap locks') became a characteristic Bowery Boy look. "The gangs often affected the dress, swagger and slang of the Bowery B'hoy, a type who became a celebrated stage character 'Mose' who is an urban version of the American 'tall tale' tradition like Paul Bunyan or Pecos Bill," says Miller.

The man most associated with the Bowery Boys is without a doubt Bill 'The Butcher' Poole, memorably portrayed by Daniel Day-Lewis in Martin Scorsese's *Gangs of New York*. Of the real Poole much is shrouded in mystery, and there are a number of conflicting accounts of his life. Born on 24 July 1821 in New Jersey, Bill was ten years old when his family moved to New York City. His father owned a butcher's shop and the young man soon followed in his footsteps. Under his rule the Bowery Boys clashed frequently with their Irish rivals the Dead Rabbits. Poole enforced the nativists' cause during elections and became known as a particularly vicious fighter.

By 1855 Poole had become the leader of the political movement the Know Nothings. Tom Hyer, who headed up the Know Nothings' sporting fraternity, got into an altercation with a rival political group that led to increasing animosity between them. On 18 February this would result in Poole being shot during a bar fight. Herbert Asbury, the author of *The Gangs*

ABOVE A contemporary depiction of the vicious 1857 riots between the Dead Rabbits and the Bowery Boys

Draft Riots

FOR FOUR NIGHTS IN 1863, NEW YORK CITY ERUPTED IN A MAELSTROM OF BLOODSHED

Between 11–14 July 1863, angry New Yorkers took to the streets to oppose the Civil War draft. As the bloody conflict between the North and the South raged on, New Yorkers faced new strict laws in the effort to find men to join the fight. However, affluent draftees could, for the princely sum of $300, avoid being conscripted. This caused widespread discontent among the working population. For many people $300 was an entire year's wages and they were angered by the blatant inequality.

Black people became the target of much of the violence. President Abraham Lincoln's Emancipation Proclamation in September 1862 had caused anger in New York, where some did not wish to see slavery abolished but wanted to preserve the Union. Many who were against the war feared that emancipation of the slaves would cause mass unemployment among the impoverished whites in the city. What's more, as Black men were not considered American citizens, they were exempt from the draft. At one point during the carnage a group of rioters descended on an African-American orphanage housing some 200 children.

The riot was eventually quelled and the draft went ahead as planned. The resultant damage from the disorder is said to have cost some $1,500,000.

The Legend of Piker Ryan

THIS VICIOUS CRIMINAL WAS RUMOURED TO CHARGE $15 TO CHEW OFF A MAN'S EAR

As with other gangs, legends of the Whyos' ferocity were perpetuated by Herbert Asbury in his 1928 book *The Gangs of New York*. One member of the gang, known as Piker Ryan, became infamous after he purportedly listed the prices he would charge for certain hit jobs. These ranged from punching a man for $2 to shooting them in the leg for $25. One of the most savage was his offer to chew off a man's ear for $15. Ryan was said to have kept a list of the various attacks he had undertaken.

However, as with a number of his claims, questions have been raised about Asbury's stories of Piker Ryan. For example, he includes what he claims is a picture of the notorious criminal, but in fact it's of a different gentleman, Patrick Ryan, who had nothing to do with the Whyos. Asbury also notes that Piker Ryan was active around 1900, whereas the Whyos are thought to have ceased operating around 1890. Perhaps most damning is the appraisal of historian John Oller who, in *Rogues' Gallery: The Birth of Modern Policing and Organized Crime in Gilded Age New York*, observes, "Why would a hoodlum put such an incriminating, easily memorised list in writing and keep it in his possession?"

> **"THE BOWERY BOYS WERE NOTED FOR WEARING STOVEPIPE HATS AND, PARTICULARLY IN LATER YEARS, THEIR INCREASINGLY DAPPER STYLE OF DRESS"**

of New York, stated, "Poole lived for 14 days after the shooting, to the vast amazement of his doctors, who declared vehemently that it was unnatural for a man to live so long with a bullet in his heart." But even Poole was not invincible, and on 8 March he finally succumbed to his wounds. Purportedly his final words were, "Good-bye boys, I die a true American!"

Despite his notoriety, Poole was not the only leader of the Bowery Boys, and one faction under the direction of Mike Walsh became a political force to be reckoned with. At one point Walsh's Bowery Boys were so powerful that they were even able to provide the bail for their leader when he was arrested and sent to jail for a second time. In 1839, Walsh's political skill paid off and he was elected to the state assembly. In 1843 he founded the Spartan Association, described by author Luc Sante as being "equally of the political club, the fraternal order, and the gang, although it had… a deliberately proletarian cast to it". The Association was a formidable force that used brute strength to attack Whig (a conservative party) headquarters and even storm the stage at Tammany Hall, one of the political centres in the city.

Other Bowery Boys groups were content to protect their turf and pick fights with the Dead Rabbits. The two gangs clashed regularly, but on 4 July 1857 they had their most infamous skirmish, resulting in a riot, eight deaths and hundreds of injuries. The violence began when the Dead Rabbits (or possibly members of the Roche Guard) sought to raid a clubhouse occupied by the Bowery Boys. The New York City

BELOW No quarter was given during the so-called 'Dead Rabbits riot' of 1857

GANGS OF NEW YORK

Police were at the time in disarray and still reeling from their own riot on 16 June. As such the police were not dispatched. Matters were not helped when another gang, the Five Pointers, returned with the Dead Rabbits to attack a different Bowery Boys haunt the following morning. The violence continued over the following two days.

While the Bowery Boys and the Dead Rabbits were content to engage in street violence, a new gang with an even more formidable reputation quickly became the most prominent in the Five Points. The Whyos were formed at some point in the 1860s and dabbled in crimes far more serious than their predecessors, including prostitution, racketeering and counterfeiting. According to Miller, they were known for communicating via a variety of bird and animal noises. In fact, the name 'Whyo' was intended to be derived from an owl's distinctive 'hoo-hoo'.

At one point the gang was led by Danny Driscoll and Danny Lyons. Driscoll met his end after accidentally shooting his friend Bridget Garrity, having intended to murder his rival John McGarty instead. However, the remnants of the Whyos were not kept idle for long. The enterprising Paul Kelly incorporated them, as well as any leftovers from other gangs, into a new group called the Five Points Gang. With a primarily Italian and Italian-American membership, Kelly's operation was immensely successful and he is said to have commanded a crew of 1,500. According to historian Humbert S. Nell, this powerful gang "literally controlled the area between the Bowery and Broadway, Fourteenth Street and City Hall Park". Reputedly, among Kelly's followers was an aspiring young crook called Al Capone.

Between 1898 and 1904 Kelly's gang fought for control of the area against the Eastman Gang, a predominantly Jewish gang led by Monk Eastman. Eastman was arrested and his successor Max Zwerbach was later killed by the Five Points Gang. With his own gang in disarray, Kelly was pressured to keep a low profile and eventually became a labour racketeer.

By now the Five Points area itself had begun to disintegrate. In the 1890s photographer Jacob Riis showcased the poverty of the Five Points in a series of images that shocked the general public. The most infamous area, Mulberry Bend, was demolished and the rest of Five Points was slowly replaced over time. Yet the legends of gangs such as the Bowery Boys and the Dead Rabbits continue to fascinate, primarily thanks to the work of one man – the aforementioned Herbert Asbury.

Born in 1891, Asbury enjoyed a prolific career as a journalist before he turned to long-form writing during the 1920s. Although he dabbled in fiction (including *The Devil of Pei-Ling*, which *The New Yorker* described as "a gory horror show") it was for his non-fiction that he was best known. In 1928 he authored *The Gangs of New York*, the book that Scorsese loosely adapted into the 2002 film. Although the book certainly remains an important source, historians have pointed out that there are obvious flaws in Asbury's presentation of the facts. In an interview with the *Gotham Gazette*, Anbinder stated, "Asbury is very good at finding material. The problem is that he lacked judgement, so he missed obvious lies and falsehoods about the neighbourhood, and New York in general."

Yet thanks to Asbury the interest in the gangs of 19th-century New York continues. The hit movie, while largely fictionalised, presented these violent men to a whole new audience. Due to this and the work of numerous historians, the stories of these merciless marauders lives on.

ABOVE Bill 'The Butcher' Poole, the infamous leader of the Bowery Boys

BELOW The Bowery Boys were known for their dapper dress sense

Martin Scorsese's 2002 film *Gangs of New York* drew attention to the 19th-century gangs and was acclaimed for Daniel Day-Lewis' (centre) depiction of Bill 'The Butcher' Poole

Making the Mob

24
INTERVIEW WITH A MAFIA EXPERT

26
PROHIBITION AND THE MOB

34
BOSS OF BOSSES

42
TOP DONS

50
WOMEN OF THE UNDERWORLD

23

Interview with a Mafia Expert

WE SPOKE TO ANTONIO NICASO, AUTHOR AND ADVISER TO LAW-ENFORCEMENT AGENCIES THE WORLD OVER, ABOUT A LIFE DEDICATED TO EXPOSING THE TRUE NATURE OF ORGANISED CRIME

WORDS CHARLES GINGER

What inspired you to pursue a career dedicated to studying and teaching about organised crime? How have you managed to discover so much about it?
I was born and raised in an area of southern Italy known for its high density of mafia activity. There, I first encountered the grim realities of organised crime when the 'Ndrangheta tragically murdered my schoolmate's father. This heartbreaking event catalysed my lifelong dedication to understanding and combating this pervasive issue. I started collecting newspaper clippings in a notebook, then worked as a crime reporter for a daily newspaper, and later travelled, studied, and interviewed police officers, mobsters, informants and mafia victims. I have published over 40 books and have never stopped dealing with this phenomenon since 1971.

When did the first mafia crime syndicates emerge in Italy, and what were the catalysts for their formation?
As Ferdinand Braudel wrote in the 16th century, "no Mediterranean region" was immune to thieves, outlaws, criminals, and bandits. The bandits of that era had many characteristics in common with vagabonds; both were "brothers of misery" linked to unfavourable economic circumstances. However, while in many European countries they lived on the fringes of society, in the southern regions of Italy, where privilege continued to prevail over rights, the violent individuals were helpful to those who did not want to accept the overthrow of feudalism. The protection of personal safety suggested to the barons the use of covert force, the same recruited between 1840 and 1860 by those who had set out to remove the ancient regime. It was, in fact, the revolutionary fever that incubated what would become the Mafia in Sicily and the 'Ndrangheta in Calabria. In Naples,

EXPERT BIO

Antonio Nicaso is widely regarded as one of the leading authorities on mafias in the world. He has authored over 40 books, and he teaches social history of organised crime at Queen's University in Ontario, Canada. One of his books was even adapted into a television series called *Bad Blood*, which was also broadcast on Netflix. He serves as a consultant to many governments and law enforcement agencies in numerous countries.

on the other hand, it was the prison that conceived the Camorra, which, already in the first half of the 19th century, had its organisational structure extended to almost all city neighbourhoods. The term 'Camorra' had appeared much earlier, precisely in an official document in 1735. The code of this criminal organisation, known as 'frieno', literally 'brake', was published in 1842. It consisted of 26 rules likely written by a certain Francesco Scorticelli, described as a "contaiuolo", a role that in the Camorra of the 19th century was assigned to those who could read, write and do accounts.

Detention in the Bourbon prisons was essential in forming many criminal organisations. Some criminals in contact with political dissidents understood the importance of secrecy, founding myths and all the symbolic apparatus that legitimises and ritualises violence. This mechanism transformed brutal criminals into heirs of legendary sects, such as the Beati Paoli (Blessed Paulists), born to counter the abuse and oppression of the nobility, or the three mythical knights Osso, Mastrosso and Carcagnosso, who fled from Toledo, Spain, in 1412 after executing an aristocrat who had raped and killed a young woman.

The three main criminal organisations in Italy are 'Ndrangheta, Camorra and Cosa Nostra. What are the main similarities between these groups, and are there any key differences other than their respective territories?
They are different in terms of history and organisational structure. They are similar in their adaptability and their ability to create a system to establish a network of trusted people. The Camorra originated in Naples in an urban context, while the Sicilian Mafia [Cosa Nostra] and 'Ndrangheta are

more rural in their origins, although they have also gained prominence in urban settings. The organisational structure is different. The Mafia is hierarchical, with a structure similar to military armies. 'Ndrangheta, while having a coordinating body, has a more horizontal structure with many clans, called 'locali', that are dominant in their respective territories. The Camorra began as a unified structure, present in various neighbourhoods of Naples with a head, a boss, but over time it has become more fragmented, resembling the typical urban gangsterism. In reality, one should speak of 'camorre'; the one in Naples is more visible and present in the streets. The one in the provinces, as in the case of Caserta, is much more similar to the Mafia and 'Ndrangheta, less visible and more tied to centres of economic and political power.

Another aspect that distinguishes them is their structure. The 'Ndrangheta is based on familial ties, while the Camorra and the Mafia are based on functional friendships. Over time, the blood tie has become a protective shield for the 'Ndrangheta. It is much more difficult to find informants and turncoats in the 'Ndrangheta, which is tightly bound by blood ties, than in the Camorra and the Mafia.

How have these groups come to dominate the Italian underworld? What methods do they deploy to accrue and protect their wealth and how damaging are they to Italian society as a whole?
They have been underestimated for a very long time. Born in the 19th century, they have always managed to maintain excellent relationships with political and economic forces. For over a century the Mafia was considered a behaviour rather than an organisation. Many mafiosi managed to escape justice precisely because it was difficult to prove that the Mafia did exist as an organisation and not just as the behaviour of some Sicilians who did not let the fly land on their noses. They enjoyed the support of a portion of the population that always saw them as conflict solvers and mediators in the relationship between workers and landowners. In reality, they have always taken advantage of managing social relationships, contributing to making the territories of origin subject to compromise logic. Those who have nothing are forced to ask, and those who ask become bound.

What do you make of rumours of these three groups joining forces, and why do you think Milan is now apparently a key base of operations for them?
I don't think there can be a shared leadership in managing the three main Italian mafias. They are too identity-driven to answer to a single boss. It is possible, and it has happened in the past, that the three mafias can handle typical businesses in a joint venture, such as cigarette smuggling and drug trafficking. There isn't a mafia-like Spectre. These are images that evoke movies like the 007 or John Wick series.

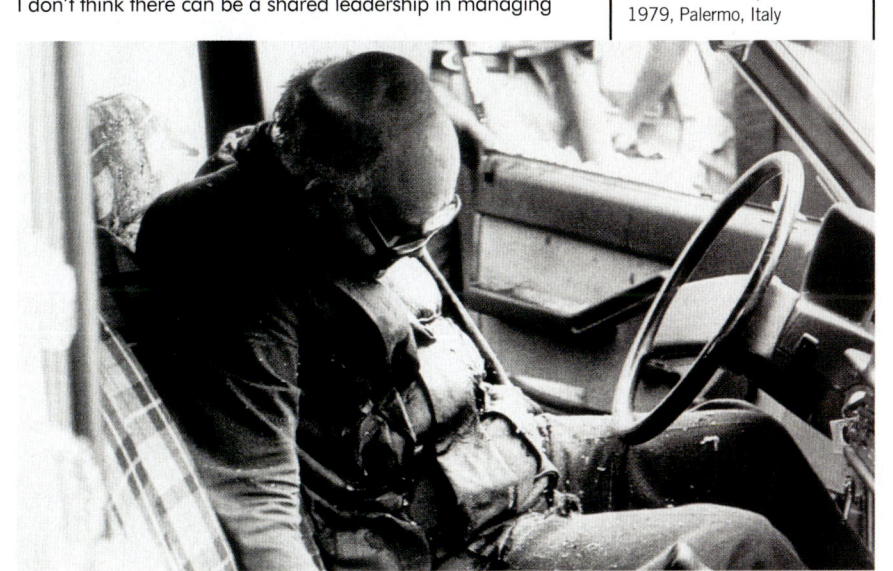

ABOVE A handcuffed Calogero Lo Piccolo is escorted by Carabinieri officers in the wake of raid that saw several high-profile members of the Cosa Nostra arrested, January 2019

In the book *Made Men* you expose the lie that is the idea that members of the Mafia follow a code of honour and valiantly defend tradition. Why do you think the media so often portrays organised criminals as lovable rogues, and is this misconception harmful?
We must debunk the myth of the old mafia that never really existed, except in the minds of novelists and filmmakers. The mafias are pathologies of power and have never been on the side of the weak against the strong or the poor against the rich. The romantic portrayal in movies like *The Godfather* has nothing to do with reality, which is less poetic, less respectful of women and children and much more cynical and ruthless.

How is Italian law enforcement working to combat the likes of the 'Ndrangheta?
In Italy, a lot is being done to combat the mafias. Since the introduction of the first anti-mafia law in 1982, it has not only been possible to arrest tens of thousands of mafiosi but also to seize the assets illegally acquired by them. The problem is not so much Italy, which could do much more if there were a more attentive political class in the fight against the mafias, but the rest of the world, where not enough is being done, especially now that the mafias have started using violence only when strictly necessary. Today, there is reason to believe that mafia money enters the legal economy with astonishing ease, thanks in part to unscrupulous professionals who facilitate money laundering operations.

BELOW The bullet-ridden body of anti-Mafia judge Cesare Terranova slumped in the chair of his Fiat, 25 September 1979, Palermo, Italy

Can you envisage a future in which organised crime in Italy is brought to heel? If so, what more could be done to bring the destruction of these groups about?
Implementing regulatory changes is crucial to deter delinquency and make it inconvenient for those involved. However, the problem is not solely a matter of repression. Handcuffs and sentences are not enough; there is a need to invest in education and culture. We must free the territories from fear and need. A Sicilian writer once said that to combat the mafias we need an army of elementary school teachers. He was not wrong.

INSET Arguably the most famous gangster of them all, Al Capone ran an underworld empire in the city of Chicago during Prohibition

Prohibition and the Mob

PROHIBITION PROVIDED EXTRAORDINARY OPPORTUNITIES FOR AMERICAN GANGSTERS TO PROFIT FROM THE ILLEGAL BOOTLEGGING TRADE IN BANNED ALCOHOL AND EMPOWERED THE CRIMINAL ORGANISATION KNOWN AS 'THE MOB'

WORDS MARC DESANTIS

Prohibition played a crucial role in the rise of the American gangster. There were certainly gangsters in America before Prohibition, and there would be gangsters after it was repealed, but the banning of alcohol gave underworld criminals a lucrative product to sell that many were willing to pay a high price for and break the law to get.

That alcoholic beverages could be banned in America must at first glance seem surprising, even shocking. Americans had a long history of alcohol consumption and had enthusiastically produced their own spirits, such as rum and whiskey. But for a long time there had been voices who had spoken out against alcohol, or at least too much of it. One famed Puritan preacher from early American history, Increase Mather, proclaimed, "Wine is from God, but the drunkard is from the devil."

Social factors also gave impetus to the drive for reform. In the late 19th century, the United States had been transformed into an industrial, urban nation. Millions of Americans had migrated from their farms to the cities to find work in factories. The introduction of rural America to the often unwholesome conditions of city life was an uneasy one. Many Americans fresh from the country blamed urban ills on alcohol.

Another disquieting aspect of the cities to the minds of rural folk was the presence of many millions of 'alien' immigrants from non-English-speaking nations. The late 19th and early 20th centuries were the heyday of immigration from Eastern and Southern Europe. Many of these immigrants came from countries where alcohol was not only drunk but embedded in the national culture. Many were also Catholic, and this was a source of suspicion for the more established Protestant Americans. The temperance movement was itself largely Protestant in its support.

The advent of World War I also had a powerful impact on energising the move for Prohibition. Most breweries in the country were owned by German-Americans. Once the United States entered the war against Germany alcohol could be tarnished by its association with the enemy, making it seem unpatriotic. Politically, the Prohibition movement gained strength in the early 20th century, with the Anti-Saloon League exemplifying its growing power and confidence. A Prohibition constitutional amendment bill was brought before the U.S. Senate for a vote in July 1917. It was approved, and the House of Representatives did the same in December. For it to become enacted law, it would have to be ratified by at least

The Tommy Gun

As the saying goes, war is the mother of invention, a maxim proven by the creation of the Thompson submachine gun in response to the need for a firearm well-suited for trench fighting. After the U.S. had entered World War I, the full-sized, bolt-action Springfield rifle, otherwise an excellent weapon, was found to be less than ideal for close combat. The U.S. Army desired something handier, with a high rate of fire that could sweep clear an enemy entrenchment.

General John T. Thompson came up with the fast-firing submachine gun in response. It spat a chunky .45 ACP cartridge packing an enormous punch that could reliably knock a man down, a big benefit in combat. Dubbed the Thompson submachine gun, it was not ready until 1919, after the war had ended.

The 'Tommy gun', as it was nicknamed, gained notoriety as the signature weapon of the American gangster during the Prohibition years. The Chicago gangsters who used it in their gun battles became known as 'Tommy men'. The Thompson was also called the 'Chicago Piano' due to its association with the Mob. It figured prominently in the infamous 1929 St. Valentine's Day Massacre. From a gunman's point of view, the Tommy gun was close to perfect, largely thanks to its ability to fire a devastating 700 rounds per minute, enabling the shooter to lay down a curtain of lead.

As a result of its underworld popularity and its appearance in cinematic portrayals of gangsters, the weapon became wedded in the minds of many Americans with organised crime and gangland shootouts. However, during World War II, the Thompson was used to equip U.S. troops and supplied in huge numbers to numerous Allied forces. The soldiers battling Axis tyranny greatly appreciated the Thompson's lethal stopping power.

The Purple Gang of Detroit was notoriously violent and known for hijacking other gangs' shipments of bootleg liquor

---

three-quarters of the then 48 states. In just 13 months, 36 states had ratified the proposal, which went into effect as the 18th Amendment in 1920.

Prohibition's advocates had won a long battle fought against massive odds over many decades. The 18th Amendment would bear bitter fruit, however. A terrible menace, one worse than the problems caused by the consumption of alcohol, would soon arise, fuelled by the insatiable thirst for the liquor that, even though now illicit, Prohibition could never dispel: the Mob.

When liquor had been made illegal, organised criminal gangs stepped in to provide Americans with what they wanted, for a hefty price of course. The cost to America of this flourishing of organised crime was not merely money. The sheer amount of cash to be made through illegal means was so great that gangs would fight pitched battles over the right to supply liquor.

American cities became the domains of gun-toting, bootlegging gangsters, all striving and killing and dying because they had a product that could not be legislated out of existence. In acknowledgement of the utter failure of Prohibition, in 1933 the 18th Amendment was repealed (13 years after it had gone into effect) by another amendment, the 21st. By then, however, the damage had been well and truly done. Prohibition meant that the Mob had become a force far larger and more powerful than what it had ever been before.

Arguably the most famous of all Prohibition-era mobsters was Al Capone. He was not alone or even the first in his criminal activities, and he initially had a patron under whom he learned much about the world of organised crime. Capone got his start as an underling in Chicago running brothels on behalf of Johnny Torrio. Torrio had moved to Chicago from New York and had craftily bought up breweries that had been put out of business by Prohibition. Hard liquor was smuggled from Canada. These banned substances became part of the attraction of the gambling parlours, bordellos and speakeasies (illegal bars that served alcohol) that Torrio controlled. Since these were all illicit enterprises, protection was bought by paying generous bribes to politicians, judges and police officers.

However, the direst threat to Torrio, whose criminal empire was based in Chicago's south, came from other gangsters. Just as modern corporations compete for market share, so too did Chicago's gangsters for the underworld business, and theirs was a bloody contest indeed.

Torrio was 17 years Capone's senior, and quite unlike his brutal young acolyte. He was quiet and exuded a mild aura. He may not have been vicious like Capone, but he was no angel either. He certainly employed other men to do his dirty work when necessary. One major hit authorised by Torrio was the murder of another gangster, Dean O'Banion. O'Banion's North Side Gang had been hijacking Torrio's alcohol shipments and also had a hand in getting Torrio arrested for an alcohol-related offence. Since this was Torrio's second, he could potentially be sent to prison. Torrio, and another gang that had a grievance against O'Banion, the Terrible Gennas, who ran an illicit industrial alcohol production racket, teamed up to have him killed. On 10 November 1924, a trio of men walked into the flower shop that O'Banion ran. When O'Banion extended his hand in greeting, one of the men gripped it and would not let go. His two companions took out handguns and shot O'Banion dead.

It was Torrio's turn next. Surviving members of the North Side Gang caught up with Torrio three months later and shot him three times. Astonishingly, Torrio survived the

PROHIBITION AND THE MOB

> **JUST AS CORPORATIONS COMPETE FOR MARKET SHARE, SO TOO DID CHICAGO'S GANGSTERS FOR THE UNDERWORLD BUSINESS, AND THEIRS WAS A BLOODY CONTEST INDEED**

assassination attempt, but his days as a gangster were over. He decamped for Italy and handed over the reins of his Chicago outfit to his protégé.

After Al Capone, perhaps the most famous gangster to emerge from the Prohibition era was Charles 'Lucky' Luciano. Born in a poor village in Sicily in 1897, Luciano was brought to America by his mother in 1906, settling in New York City on Manhattan's Lower East Side. He was a school dropout at 14 and was soon involved in small-scale criminal activities, including robberies and muggings. From an early age he was an admirer of the local gangsters he saw around him. "[T]hey were rich," he explained later, "and rich was what counted, because the rich got away with anythin'."

He took up with other young gangsters who would become dark legends in their own right, including Bugsy Siegel, Frank Costello and Meyer Lansky. The enactment of the 18th Amendment would give such ruthless, enterprising criminals unparalleled opportunities to make fortunes. Luciano became a stalwart of the bootlegging business in New York.

Luciano was very eager to project an image of himself that was markedly different from the older generation of mobsters who were variously called 'Mustache Petes' or 'greaseballs'. He took care to dress well but not flamboyantly. In his outward appearance he was more akin to a respectable businessman than that of a stereotypical gangster.

He came to the attention of older Mob bosses who were eager to recruit him into their own organisations. In 1927 he joined with Joe 'the Boss' Masseria, serving as his right-hand man. In 1929 he was captured by one of Masseria's bitter enemies, Salvatore Maranzano. Maranzano's men worked over Luciano badly, with Luciano taking serious knife cuts to his face. He was left with a permanent droop to his right eye, but he lived. For his unexpected survival he was dubbed "Lucky" by fellow gangster Meyer Lansky.

Luciano was repelled by the wasteful fights between gangs that disrupted the otherwise lucrative business of the criminal underworld. He believed that there was enough for everyone and that crime should be run as if it were a legitimate business; efficiently and with as little friction as possible. The feuds of the older generation of Mob bosses, such as Masseria and Maranzano, were not at all to his liking. He had especially disliked what the so-called 'Castellammarese War' had done to the underworld business.

To Luciano, and other younger mobsters, the older generation was too hidebound, too set in their ways and too antiquated in their notions of a twisted code of honour to see which way the business of organised crime was actually heading. He had a hand in the 1931 murder of his old boss, Masseria, and also in the subsequent killing of Maranzano.

Luciano, at the urging of Johnny Torrio, then instituted the Commission in 1931, an umbrella organisation for the Mob in which each group (or family) ran its own businesses on their own turf, but the heads of each would meet periodically to manage relations between them. Luciano was adamant that they had to co-operate for the good of all. "I told 'em jealousy was our biggest enemy," said Luciano. "In our kind of business there was so much money to be made that nobody had the right to be jealous of nobody else."

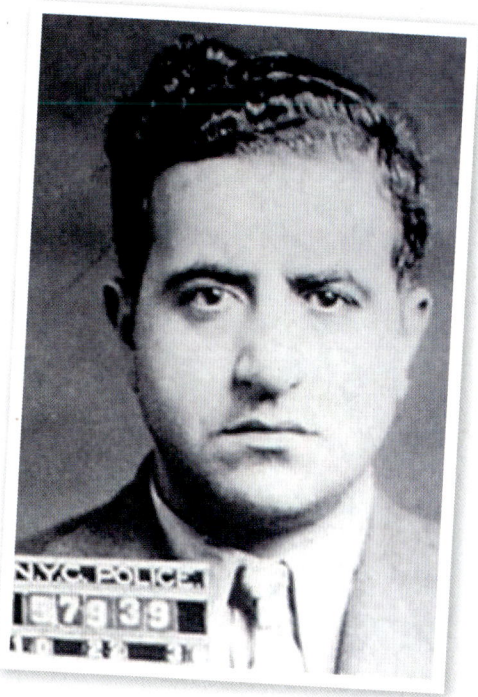

ABOVE Along with Joe Adonis, Albert Anastasia was one of the founders of Murder, Inc.

BELOW 'Big Jim' Colosimo was a Chicago underworld boss engaged in gambling and prostitution. He was assassinated in 1920 by Johnny Torrio

Luciano in 1948 after his release from prison

In modern business terms, Luciano had organised the criminal syndicates into a cartel that would eliminate needless competition. Luciano was the Commission's first chairman, and the heads of the others families were similar to a corporate board of directors.

Luciano's considerable luck, like that of so many mobsters, would eventually run out. In 1936 he was convicted on prostitution charges. He had built his empire on prostitution as well as bootlegging, and at his trial there came a stream of women from his operation who testified against him. That June he was given a sentence of 30 years in prison. For a man just shy of 40, it was effectively a life sentence.

Luciano's later years were not as dramatic as those of the Prohibition era, but he did still manage to find himself embroiled in events nonetheless, and he always made sure to use it to his advantage. Though still in prison in the early 1940s, Luciano dominated the Longshoreman's Union, which included men who worked at the docks. With America's entry into World War II, there was a real fear that German saboteurs would hurt port operations. The U.S. Navy requested Luciano ensure that the docks remained secure. In 1946, on account of his aid, his prison sentence was commuted and he was deported to Italy. Though he tried to remain relevant to the organised criminal underworld from various perches outside the United States, his influence declined and he died in Italy in January 1962.

Almost half a century earlier a 12-year-old Meyer Lansky (who was born in 1902 in Grodno in what was then part of the Russian Empire) became friends with an older youth who would later go on to become better known as "Lucky" Luciano. Lansky and Luciano became associates in New York's early 20th-century criminal underworld. Before that, while still a youth, Lansky formed a gang with another young Jewish gangster, Benjamin 'Bugsy' Siegel, called the Bugs and Meyer Gang. Their specialities were gambling and protection rackets. One of the more famous members of their outfit was Dutch Schultz.

Lansky was invited to have his gang, a mixed group of Jews and Italians, work for Arnold Rothstein, one of the most prominent bosses of New York's organised criminal syndicates. Rothstein recognised Lansky's ambition and wanted his help in moving liquor.

Rothstein's instincts regarding Lansky were correct. Under his guidance Lansky and his youthful Mob associates built the biggest bootlegging operation in the United States. Lansky would later go on to establish a portfolio of gambling casinos, which proved popular because the games played there were fair. In the 1940s Lansky became involved in the development of Las Vegas as a centre of legal gambling.

Knowing Luciano from an early age was also a plus. Lansky became an important member of the national criminal organisation that would come to dominate America in the 1930s. Lansky could not escape justice forever though, and in 1953 he was brought up on multiple charges of illegal betting. After pleading guilty to some of the charges he was given a sentence of only three months.

Lansky would later become a leading underworld figure in Cuba, where he was involved with casinos on the island. However, the Cuban Revolution of the 1950s saw the communists come to power, expel the mobsters and close the casinos. Lansky lived in Florida during the 1960s and '70s. Expecting to be eventually charged with tax evasion, he fled to Israel in 1970, but he was ordered to leave by the Israeli Government in 1972. Ironically, Lansky would in fact be acquitted in 1974 and died in 1983 in Miami Beach.

Meyer Lansky, one of the greatest of the Prohibition gangsters, lived to be 80, dying in 1983

❝ THE U.S. NAVY REQUESTED LUCIANO ENSURE THAT THE DOCKS REMAINED SECURE. IN 1946, ON ACCOUNT OF HIS AID, HIS PRISON SENTENCE WAS COMMUTED AND HE WAS DEPORTED TO ITALY ❞

PROHIBITION AND THE MOB

BELOW Police with an intercepted cargo of moonshine stand beside a damaged automobile

When it comes to the more colourful characters the Prohibition period, few were more vibrant than Bugsy Siegel, Meyer Lansky's close associate from an early age. In his younger days during Prohibition, Siegel was a hot-headed gunman who took contracts from the likes of Joe Masseria and Salvatore Maranzano. He was nicknamed "Bugsy", which he detested, supposedly because he was judged unstable and other gangsters would say he was 'going bugs' when he became agitated.

In 1937, after Prohibition had ended, he headed out west to Hollywood, where he set up a gambling operation. By 1946, Siegel was overseeing the building of the Flamingo Hotel in Las Vegas. The Flamingo was his biggest undertaking and entirely above-board, because gambling was legal in Nevada. Unfortunately, it turned out to be a huge money-loser, suffering from enormous cost overruns and delays. A project that had initially been budgeted at $1 million ended up costing about six. The Flamingo opened in late 1946 but was plagued with troubles. His investors, many of them other mobsters, were very unhappy and not an understanding bunch. Siegel was assassinated in 1947 at the home of his girlfriend, with nine shots fired, two of which found their mark. Suspicion naturally fell on his disappointed gangster investors, but there were any number of people who would have wanted Siegel dead.

One of the Mob's foremost assassins during the Prohibition era was Albert Anastasia. Anastasia has been placed as part of the group of gunmen who murdered Joe

Dean O'Banion, chieftain of Chicago's North Side Gang, was assassinated by Mob rival Johnny Torrio in 1924

Generational Conflict

The relations between the various gangs of the American underworld were always fraught with suspicion and deadly violence. One especially awful conflict between rival gangs was the so-called 'Castellammarese War' of 1930–1931, which took its name from the Sicilian town of Castellammare del Golfo in west Sicily, birthplace of leading American crime boss Salvatore Maranzano.

The Castellammarese War, which began in February 1930, was a lethal power struggle between Maranzano and Joe 'the Boss' Masseria for control of the Mob, but it has also been portrayed as a generational conflict in which younger mobsters, 'Young Turks' or 'Americans', overthrew the older 'Mustache Petes', with their luxurious facial hair, who represented the traditional Mafia in America. The younger group of gangsters was exemplified by Lucky Luciano, who had grown up in America. Luciano had been deeply involved in the rubout (murder) of Masseria at a Coney Island restaurant on 15 April 1931, which brought the Castellammarese War to a close. This allowed Maranzano to declare himself to be the 'boss of all bosses' of the New York Mafia. Luciano was also behind the 10 September 1931 murder of Maranzano himself, just a few months after Maranzano's faction claimed to have 'won' the war. Masseria and Maranzano were no innocents, of course. Luciano was simply striking first once he had learned that each man wanted him dead too.

As with almost all Mob-related history, the actual facts are murky and it is often impossible to separate truth from fiction. Traditional accounts have held that the war involved hundreds of gangsters across America and that around 60 perished in the merciless struggle for power. Others say the fighting was much less bloody, holding that the death toll was closer to around 14. Either way, it wasn't the end of the killing.

Joe Masseria was Lucky Luciano's boss during Prohibition and was a casualty of the Castellammarese War

31

> **"CANADA BECAME THE PLACE WHERE LIQUOR COULD BE OBTAINED AND SMUGGLED INTO THE U.S."**

ABOVE In the show *Peaky Blinders* the gang enlist the help of Al Capone to outsmart fictional Mob boss Luca Changretta (played by Adrien Brody, pictured)

Masseria. One of the men who was said to have gone along with him on the hit headed up Murder, Inc. with Anastasia. Murder, Inc. was a Brooklyn-based outfit of assassins who would eliminate any target for a price. The advantage of using Murder, Inc.'s services, from a Mob boss's point of view, was that the order to kill was sent from him to his lieutenant and then to the hitmen of Murder, Inc. The assassins did not know who was actually paying for the hit, and so there was little to connect the bosses to the murders they commissioned.

One of the most prominent victims of Murder, Inc. was a mobster named Dutch Schultz. Schultz had made a request to the Commission that it authorise the murder of Thomas Dewey, a federal prosecutor who had indicted Schultz twice for tax evasion. Schultz, knowing that Dewey would never give up, wanted him dead. The Commission saw matters very differently. Killing Dewey would only serve to increase federal attention on the Mob and it turned Schultz down. Schultz unwisely then declared that he would do the job himself. To forestall a murder that would bring nothing but trouble, Luciano authorised a hit on Schultz. On 23 October 1935, two Murder, Inc. gunmen mowed down Schultz and his bodyguards at a New Jersey restaurant.

Attention falls mainly on Chicago and New York as hotspots of underworld activity during Prohibition, but there were gangs in other cities too. Detroit was the domain of the Purple Gang. Standing atop the pyramid of the Detroit underworld, it was a Jewish gang with a penchant for murder, with 500 deaths being attributed to its members. This figure is

A timeline of Prohibition and the American Mob

1920 – PROHIBITION BEGINS
The 18th Amendment, banning the production and sale of alcoholic beverages, goes into effect in January 1920. American organised crime scrambles to supply it to thirsty customers.
17 January 1920

1920 – JOHNNY TORRIO ASSASSINATES 'BIG JIM' COLOSIMO
In Chicago, Johnny Torrio has 'Big Jim' Colosimo assassinated. One of Torrio's underlings is Al Capone, who will later take over his Chicago operations.
11 May 1920

1929 – ST. VALENTINE'S DAY MASSACRE
In a mass murder organised by Chicago crime boss Al Capone, four men, including two posing as police officers, gun down seven unsuspecting members of the rival North Side Gang in a garage.
14 February 1929

Detroit police raid an illegal brewery during Prohibition years

1931 – LUCKY STRIKES
Joe Masseria is assassinated on Lucky Luciano's orders, bringing the Castellammarese War between him and Salvatore Maranzano to a violent end.
15 April 1931

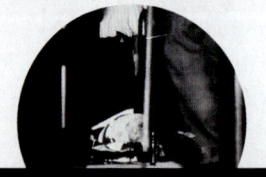

The body of Salvatore Maranzano following his assassination on 10 September 1931

1931 – COLLINGWOOD MANOR MASSACRE
The Purple Gang slaughters the Third Avenue Terrors at a Collingwood Avenue apartment in Detroit but a witness survives and goes on to testify against them. Several Purple Gang members are convicted and given life sentences.
16 September 1931

1931 – THE COMMISSION
Luciano sets up the 'Commission' to resolve disputes among the Mob's Five Families and a handful of other criminal groups. It relies on the services of Murder, Inc. to enforce discipline on unruly mobsters.
1931

PROHIBITION AND THE MOB

ABOVE Johnny Torrio, a leading gangster of the early Prohibition years and mentor of Al Capone

ABOVE RIGHT California police destroy confiscated liquor, 1932

even higher than those that were perpetrated in super-violent Chicago. A large number of the Purple Gang's members had emigrated from Eastern Europe in the late 19th century. It was led by the Bernstein brothers: Raymond, Joseph, Abe and Izzy. After coming to New York, they settled in Michigan.

Starting out as small-time criminals as youngsters, they graduated to bigger things as adults. Prohibition provided them with extraordinary opportunities. Detroit, the capital of American automobile manufacturing, was America's fourth-largest city and had a population of around 1 million. Importantly for the role it would play during Prohibition, Detroit lay on the U.S.-Canadian border. This was significant because Canada became the place where liquor could be obtained and smuggled into the United States to quench the thirst of American drinkers. When the Detroit River froze over in the winter, American bootleggers' trucks would roll over with cargoes of Canadian spirits.

The Purple Gang had a hand in extortion rackets, truck hijackings, prostitution, illegal gambling and armed robberies. The bulk of the gang's funds came from bootlegging alcohol. The money they earned was used to pay bribes to police and other government officials to look the other way. In the mid-1920s, the Purple Gang fought tooth and nail with Italian and Irish gangsters over territory. Such was their power and propensity for violence that they were able to dissuade Al Capone, who was hardly reluctant to use violent tactics himself, to keep out of Detroit.

Eventually, the Purple Gang's brutal ways brought about its downfall. In 1931, a hit gone wrong resulted in a survivor who testified against the gangsters and several of its leading members, including Raymond Bernstein, were given life sentences without the possibility of parole. The Purple Gang was mortally wounded and soon faded from the scene.

Prohibition came to an end in 1933 with the repeal of the 18th Amendment. The Mob, which had profited so enormously from Prohibition, had become far stronger than it otherwise might have been by having the opportunity to sell liquor for huge amounts of cash. It would go on to find other sources of revenue, now that alcohol was legal again, and prosper.

Federal prosecutor Thomas E. Dewey, the target of mobster Dutch Schultz's murderous wrath

LUCIANO GETS OUT
Lucky Luciano's lengthy prison sentence is commuted and he is released from prison because of the help he gave in securing American ports from Axis sabotage.
3 January 1946

A New York Police Department mugshot of Lucky Luciano, taken in 1931

Bugsy Siegel was gunned down at the age of 41

1935
ASSASSINATION OF DUTCH SCHULTZ
After antagonising the Commission with his dangerous plan to kill Thomas Dewey, a federal prosecutor, Murder, Inc. hitmen shoot rogue mobster Dutch Schultz at the Palace Chop House, a Newark, New Jersey restaurant. He dies the next day.
23 October 1935

1936
TRIAL OF LUCIANO
Lucky Luciano goes to trial on prostitution-related charges. He is later convicted and is sentenced to 40 years in prison.
13 May 1936

1947
BUGSY SIEGEL IS ASSASSINATED
Bugsy Siegel meets his end when a hail of bullets tears through the home of his girlfriend. Disgruntled Mob investors in his Flamingo Hotel are likely behind the hit.
20 June 1947

1962
LUCIANO'S END
Lucky Luciano suffers a heart attack in Naples, Italy, and dies at the age of 64.
26 January 1962

BOSS of BOSSES

IN THE HEYDAY OF THE AMERICAN DREAM, THE GOVERNMENT DIDN'T WANT TO ADMIT THE U.S. HAD AN ORGANISED CRIME PROBLEM, BUT IN 1957, THE NATION MET THE MOB ANYWAY

WORDS CHRISTIAN CIPOLLINI

They scattered like roaches when a light is turned on. Sixty or more scurrying scoundrels, some of them senior citizens, running from the cops as though they had just been caught tagging a store front. Some tried to flee in fancy Lincolns and Cadillacs; others opted for the scenic route – jogging through the muddy wooded environment, littering the land with large bills and anything else that may appear 'suspicious' if it was to be found on their person. Still others crawled into any dark crevice they could find within the compound. This was the almost-comical scene that unfolded on the afternoon of 14 November 1957 when two police officers decided to investigate the unusual number of out-of-state vehicles parked at a reputed mobster's estate in the normally quiet area of Apalachin, New York.

1957 proved to be a tumultuous year for the American gangster. A shift in ideology, a widening gap between old guard and new – these were just a few of the rumblings that had come to a stark and violent climax. First was the attempted assassination of Frank Costello in May 1957. From nearly point-blank range, a gunman ambushed the Mob's 'prime minister' as he was entering his Central Park West apartment building. "Somebody tried to get me," said Costello shortly after the .32-calibre round grazed his scalp. The 65-year-old gangster survived, refused to name the assailant (though it is widely believed future Mob boss Vincent "The Chin" Gigante pulled the trigger) and promptly took retirement from running what was once called the 'Luciano Family'. Then in October, the brutal barber shop slaying of infamous Murder, Inc. boss (and long-time ally of Costello, Luciano and Lansky) Albert Anastasia was the real turning point.

To put the convoluted mess into some perspective, suffice to say a power-hungry, one-time pal of the aforementioned Anastasia named Vito Genovese wanted to control the Luciano family and much more. He had plenty of rising Mob bosses on his side too. However, the thorn in his side was Costello – who was protected by the conservative faction some believe was still controlled by the exiled Lucky Luciano, along with Meyer Lansky and all his loyalists. Anastasia was the one remaining 'physical' obstruction to Genovese's goal.

Now to be clear, Anastasia's murder was probably not something even his old friends were losing sleep over. The hot-headed "Mad Hatter" was a loose cannon and in 1952 called for the murder of a guy he saw in the news because said guy (24-year-old Arnold Schuster) simply identified another known criminal to police. The entire scenario had nothing to do with Anastasia, but his anger at any perceived 'snitch' was uncontrollable. This sort of 'off-the-wall' behaviour didn't do his pals any good

" THE WHOLE GANG REMAINED VERY RESPECTFUL DURING THE INQUIRY BUT KEPT THE COPS IN THE DARK AS MUCH AS POSSIBLE "

either. That said, he was still a problem for Genovese until permanently removed, which, along with Costello forced into handing over control, made the transition to 'boss' much easier. The next step, however, required bringing all the important people on board, in which case a grand meeting would need to be scheduled.

Large-scale underworld meetings had taken place from time to time, but generally only when something really big was on the table. The risk, as we will see, was far too great for the frequent assembly of top Mob honchos. That said, this is the tale of the one 'major' Mob meeting that went terribly awry.

It all commenced with preparations worthy of visiting royalty. On 10 November 1957, more than $400 ($3,400 today) worth of meat was delivered to the $100,000 hilltop pad of Joseph Barbara, Sr., located at 625 McFall Road. 90 kilograms (198 pounds) of the finest cuts – veal, pork and beef – were unloaded by a wholesaler's delivery truck. Although the estate was certainly large enough to accommodate a respectable number of overnight guests, the list of visitors was far too large, and therefore special arrangements were made. Barbara, Sr., had been ill for some time, so much of the hands-on preparations were taken on by his son. The 21-year-old Joseph, Jr., secured a slew of rooms at two hotels in nearby Vestal, New York.

All of this activity was being noticed. Joseph Barbara, Sr., was a top-ranking affiliate of the Buffalo Mob (contrary to assumptions he was a Pennsylvania/Lower New York State boss), former bootlegger and suspected murderer. The large estate he owned was situated just a bit north of the Pennsylvania border in a region called Apalachin, pronounced 'Ap-ah-lake-in'. The town of Oswego is nearby to the west; Binghamton, where Barbara, Sr., operated a brewery, lies to the east. The 52-hectare property was, as gangland lore tells, the perfect location for a much-needed 'sit down' of all the major Mob entities from across the United States and beyond.

As with most underworld history, there will always be debate or conjecture regarding the elusive facts that will only ever be known to the privy few involved individuals. Nevertheless, data does suggest that the actual meeting was arranged by Buffalo crime boss Stephano Magaddino. This was an action in response to a direct request made by Tommy Lucchese (head of his namesake Mafia family) on behalf of Gambino family boss Carlo and the new boss of the Luciano faction – Vito Genovese.

The subjects to be discussed were (supposedly) the division of Anastasia's kingdom, other racketeering endeavours and the issue of narcotics. Interestingly, there is a bit of conflict within the stories regarding the dope. Some say the meeting was intended to make agreements for distancing away from the dope trade, but, as it turned out, Genovese had been watched by authorities for some time because of the heroin market he and others were very much in control of. Furthermore, the newly crowned family capo was eventually put in prison (and died there) for dealing in narcotics.

The fun began on the eve of the big barbecue at the Barbara house. Arriving from everywhere, the cars flowed into town, some bearing licence plates from Florida, California and the Midwest, but the majority were from New York and New Jersey. Checking into local hotels that Barbara, Jr., had reserved, the out-of-towners soon piqued the attention of local law enforcement – two in particular. This was quite unusual activity for a non-touristy locale.

On 14 November, invitees began arriving at the Barbara estate. The event was scheduled to kick off on a relaxed note, with mingling to start, followed by a cookout luncheon. Shortly before 1 p.m., as well-dressed men were feasting on the charcoaled steaks, Joseph Barbara's wife noticed two individuals in the driveway area jotting something down on notepads. These were not guests, and it became apparent they were taking down licence plate numbers, which meant only one thing – cops.

By the time guests realised the party was under scrutiny, Sergeant Edgar Croswell and his partner Vincent Vasisco had called in the State Police. Roadblocks had been set up and troopers converged on the property. The exodus, or attempt thereof, was under way. The first escapees actually made it through the roadblock. Intentionally or not, the police allowed that one vehicle to pass. Mobsters who witnessed that 'free pass' felt confident in driving to freedom. Such confidence was quickly dashed as troopers stopped all fleeing vehicles and took the occupants into

ABOVE An aerial view of the property located at 625 McFall Road, Apalachin, New York. This was the large complex where mobsters lunched then either hid within or ran like the wind from to evade the pursuing police officers

RIGHT TOP Frank Costello survived the assassination attempt against him, suffering only a scalp wound after a point-blank shot to the face

RIGHT CENTRE The body of Albert Anastasia lies on the floor of a barber shop in New York's Park Sheraton Hotel after his murder in 1957

BOSS OF BOSSES

SEIZE 62 MAFIA CHIEFTAINS IN UPSTATE RAID

Double-edged Sword

IN THE AFTERMATH OF THE MEETING THE SMALL VILLAGE HAD TO DEAL WITH BEING THRUST INTO NATIONAL HEADLINES

The Mob raid uproar certainly wasn't embraced with open arms by many of the local residents. Media, police and, of course, rubbernecking tourists were becoming a bit annoying. "We've kept our sense of humour about it," said Morris Cope, the head of a nearby school. "We know here the meeting didn't happen because Apalachin is a bad community." Then there were those who saw the ordeal as engaging, particularly from a 'profit' standpoint. "People stop in and ask how to get to the mansion," tavern owner Milo Kirch told reporters of the tourists. "I guess the publicity helped business."

> **THIS ENSEMBLE OF CHARACTERS WAS FOUND TO BE A PROLIFIC CAST INDEED**

It's thought some party-goers managed to remain hidden inside the Barbaras' grand estate during the raid

Family Affair

The majority of 'most noteworthy' Mob affiliates detained were from the reigning Five Families based in New York, followed by Pennsylvania, New England and so down the line. The presence of Tampa's Santo Trafficante, Jr., was also quite a big deal. Many of the families and offshoots sent at least two to three representatives, and three of the actual 'bosses' of New York families were present.

One of the many buildings on the property where Mob chieftains were mingling just before police converged

GENOVESE FAMILY
(FORMERLY THE LUCIANO FAMILY)

VITO GENOVESE (CAPO)
Crowned the new boss of the exiled Lucky Luciano's family, Don Vito was the primary guest and subject for the Apalachin meeting attendees to discuss.

MICHELE 'BIG MIKE' MIRANDA (CONSIGLIERE)

GAMBINO FAMILY

CARLO GAMBINO (CAPO)
Head of the Gambino family, he and the future boss – Paul Castellano – were netted in the Apalachin sting.

JOSEPH 'STATEN ISLAND JOE' RICCOBONO (CONSIGLIERE)

PAUL CASTELLANO (CAPOREGIME & EVENTUAL SUCCESSOR)

CARMINE 'THE DOCTOR' LOMBARDOZZI (CAPOREGIME)

JARMAND 'TOMMY' SIMONETTI (CAPOREGIME)

TAMPA/HAVANA

SANTO TRAFFICANTE, JR. (BOSS)

SALVATORE 'CHARLES' CHIRI (CAPOREGIME)

GERARDO 'JERRY' CATENA (UNDERBOSS)

---

custody. While those in cars were trying to escape in vain, other guests took to the surrounding landscape. The fall season in Apalachin provided a damp, muddy and highly uncooperative route for anyone adorned in patent leather shoes and tailored suits. One runner was found hooked on barbed wire. Antonio Maggadino, brother to the man who set the whole convention in motion, was so out of breath upon apprehension in an open field he could not speak for some time. In all, law enforcement personnel took 59 people into custody. There were more guests at the party (upwards of 100 it is believed), so indeed there were a number of successful escapes and/or hideaways within the estate complex itself.

Rounded up and taken in groups of four to a State Police substation, each party-goer was questioned. Not one of the apprehended had any identification on their person, though a few were found with cash rolls ranging from $100 to several thousand. They were a tight-lipped lot. The whole gang remained very respectful during the inquiry but kept the cops in the dark as much as possible.

> **AMONG THE BADDIES BROUGHT IN WERE VITO GENOVESE, PAUL CASTELLANO, CARLO GAMBINO AND SANTO TRAFFICANTE, JR.**

The single most prominent and scripted response to the question, "What were you doing there?" was simply, "To pay our respects to an ailing friend." And Barbara, Sr., himself, well, he had nothing to say to police. In turn, the weight of interrogation fell firmly on Joseph, Jr., who was a bit more antagonistic than the elder Mob statesmen.

This was not the first time a 'meeting' had taken place at Barbara's home. Police took note of a much smaller meeting a year earlier. This ensemble of characters was found to be a prolific cast indeed. Not only had the sting netted known criminals from as far away as Cuba and San Francisco, but among the baddies brought in were Vito Genovese, Paul Castellano, Carlo Gambino and Santo

BOSS OF BOSSES

LUCCHESE FAMILY
- VINCENT 'NUNZIO' RAO (CONSIGLIERE)
- GIOVANNI 'BIG JOHN' ORMENTO (CAPOREGIME)
- JOSEPH 'JOE PALISADES' ROSATOI (CAPOREGIME)

BONANNO FAMILY
- GIOVANNI 'JOHN' BONVENTRE (CAPOREGIME)
- ANTHONY 'TONY' RIELA (CAPOREGIME)
- NATALE 'JOE DIAMONDS' EVOLA (CAPOREGIME)

BUFALINO FACTION
(PITTSTON/SCRANTON)
- ROSARIO 'THE QUIET DON' BUFALINO (BOSS)
- JAMES OSTICCO (CAPOREGIME)
- DOMINIC ALAIMO (CAPOREGIME)

PROFACI FAMILY
(RENAMED COLOMBO FAMILY IN 1962) 
- JOSEPH 'DON PEPPINO' PROFACI (BOSS)
- JOSEPH 'FAT JOE/JOE MALYAK' MAGLIOCCO (UNDERBOSS)
- SALVATORE 'SAM' TORNABE (CAPOREGIME)

BUFFALO NY FACTION
- JOHN C. MONTANA (UNDERBOSS)
- ANTONIO MAGADDINO (CAPOREGIME) (STEPHANO MAGADDINO'S BROTHER)
- ROSARIO 'ROY' CARLISI (CAPOREGIME)

JOSEPH 'THE BARBER' BARBARA, SR.
HOST (CAPODECINA)
Born in Sicily, Barbara, Sr., entered the U.S. in 1931. He owned the estate where the Mob convention was held.

- JOSEPH BARBARA, JR., HOST
- JAMES 'JIMMY' LADUCA (CAPOREGIME)
- SAMUEL 'SAM' LAGATTUTA (CAPOREGIME)
- DOMINICK D'AGOSTINO (CAPOREGIME)

Trafficante, Jr., just to name a few of the 'big name' crime lords in custody.

Further disrupting the tranquillity of Apalachin, the media congregated in considerable numbers, eager to get the scoop on this unusual party-crashing incident. "We haven't a thing on them," a disheartened Sergeant Croswell told reporters. Despite the stunning array of criminal masterminds before them, Sergeant Croswell and company could do little more than issue a verbal warning and watch the caravans pull out of town. "We made it clear we wanted them out of the area," the sergeant said.

The bust at Apalachin was pie in the face to the bewildered and embarrassed lot of Mob bosses, but it was also a slap in the face to law enforcement. Though all of the 'captured' party-goers were released shortly after the raid, 20 of them were later indicted on obstruction of justice charges. It seems everyone knew that some or all of these fellows were career criminals, racketeers, even murderers, yet when all was said and done, none of the indictments stuck. There really wasn't any law

SMALLER REPRESENTATION

DECAVALCANTE FACTION (NEW JERSEY)
Frank Majuri (Underboss)
Louis 'Fat Lou' LaRasso (Caporegime)

PITTSBURGH FACTION
Michael 'Mike' Genovese (Caporegime)
Gabriel 'Kelly' Mannarino (Caporegime)

PHILADELPHIA FACTION
Joseph 'Joe' Ida (Boss)
Dominick Olivetto (Underboss)

CLEVELAND FACTION
John Scalish (Boss)
John DeMarco (Consigliere)

PATRIARCA FAMILY (NEW ENGLAND)
Frank 'The Cheeseman' Cucchiara (Consigliere)

CHICAGO OUTFIT
Frank Zito (Boss)

DALLAS FACTION
Joseph 'Joe' Civello (Boss)

COLLETTI FAMILY (COLORADO)
James 'Black Jim' Colletti (Boss)

LOS ANGELES FACTION
Frank DeSimone (Boss)
Simone Scozzari (Underboss)

broken in the first place. Moreover, the fact that the men apprehended at the Barbara estate were prominent, recognised national and international criminal top dogs further forced the one and only J. Edgar Hoover to finally 'admit' there was indeed a national organisation of criminals (a.k.a. the Mob).

New York's U.S. Attorney Paul W. Williams minced no words in describing what kind of 'association' the nation was dealing with, telling the media, "What we know of the ramifications of the various criminal syndicate operations in dope, in gambling, in shakedown rackets would indicate that the syndicate takes annually, from the pockets of the people, approximately 2 billion, 280 million dollars."

Now, the question of why Hoover had been so resistant in publicly stating such a thing is a complex and hotly debated story in and of itself and one for another day. The Apalachin incident proved that all these questionable characters were in cahoots; a sentiment loudly proclaimed by other government officials. At last, the FBI officially began recognising this criminal underworld faction as 'the Mob'. This also ushered in Robert Kennedy's direct involvement into further investigating the Mob as a whole.

Back to Sergeant Croswell and his 'happening upon' the Apalachin Mob conclave, there was an effort to further rub some salt in the Mob's wound. Croswell and Vasisco told the same story until their respective deaths, which implied the raid was a product of some less-than-bright mobsters with big mouths. The two cops claimed that a day or two before the big barbecue they had responded to a hotel's complaint over some 'bad cheques' when, in the lobby, they listened as a group of men rambled on about the gang convention at Barbara, Sr's. Whether this was truly how it all went down or not is subject to debate. Was the story an attempt to save face for police? A little more egg on the Mob's face? Thomas Hunt, historian and author of *Dicarlo: Buffalo's First Family of Crime*, said Croswell certainly put the bust in motion, but it probably didn't happen just because of a bounced cheque.

"Croswell was already quite familiar with Joseph Barbara at that time," Hunt explained. He said that while the cops may have indeed overheard some out-of-towners chatting, records show Croswell had been eyeing – and even wiretapping – Joseph Barbara, Sr., since 1944. "This wasn't a stumble, it was the result of a personal crusade."

Historians, researchers and of course government investigative bodies have also long since debated the reasons for noteworthy 'no shows' at the meeting. Although bosses came from around virtually everywhere, a handful of prominent people were either not invited or chose to not attend. Among those not present were Meyer Lansky and Frank Costello, and some writings mention that there was no representation from New Orleans, which was run by Carlos Marcello, but in reality there was one representative present: Paul Scarcelli.

According to Joseph "Doc Stacher" Rosen, a close ally of Meyer Lansky and other prominent Jewish gangsters of the era, the 'raid' on Apalachin was not only something he and his associates were aware of but something they themselves had a hand in. Stacher claimed, "Meyer and I were invited, but he sent word it was November and he didn't want to make the journey north from Miami." Lansky's explanation was that he had the flu, but Stacher also told biographers (years after the actual raid) a deal had been struck to get a man named Nelson Cantellops out of prison, which in turn would give the Federal Bureau

ABOVE One of the 20 party-goers that was indicted, the one-time Profaci Family (later Colombo Family) boss enters court in 1959

of Narcotics (FBN) all the ammo necessary to go after Genovese. "He gave exact details of where and how the drugs were imported." This, Stacher claimed, also led to Genovese's later conviction on narcotics charges.

What truly kick-started the 'tip off' conspiracy theory, however, was the public statement made by George H. Gaffney in 1960. The then district supervisor of narcotics in New York said the information leading to the Apalachin raid had come from "the underworld" and he had felt at the time it was indeed "reliable".

Even though affirmation of such gangland payback came from both a prominent player in the underworld and the FBN, this theory is still very much a debated conspiracy. Hunt said, "It probably would be far more interesting

❝ **HISTORIANS AND INVESTIGATIVE BODIES HAVE LONG DEBATED THE REASONS FOR THE NOTEWORTHY 'NO SHOWS' AT THE MEETING** ❞

All Downhill From Here

APALACHIN OPENED THE DOOR FOR THE MOST SCANDALOUS REVELATIONS YET

"If soldiers got arrested in a meet like that, you can imagine what the bosses would have done. There they are, running through the woods like rabbits, throwing away money so they won't be caught with a lot of cash, and some of them throwing away guns. So who are they kidding when they say we got to respect them?"

In the words of Mob whistle-blower Joe Valachi, a former member of the Genovese crime family, Apalachin put a nail in the coffin of respect. It was Valachi who shocked the world with his inside account of Mob history, told and televised during the 1963 McClellan Hearings. The congressional committee on organised crime, helmed by Senator John McClellan, was essentially created from concern over Mob-related activities.

ABOVE Mobster turned informant Joseph Valachi testifies before the Senate Rackets Committee, in Washington, D.C. He was the first Mob member to publicly acknowledge the existence of the organised crime families

to say that Luciano and Lansky somehow initiated the Apalachin raid, but I don't see any good reason to believe that's true." He explained that while the Anastasia and/or Costello incidents could have strained relationships with Genovese, these guys wouldn't have put the screws to basically the 'entire' roster of Mob bosses that suffered from the raid.

"With Croswell hounding Barbara for years, information from Luciano and Lansky would have been unnecessary. I also do not believe that the relationships involving Luciano, Lansky and Genovese actually were what most people think they were. I think the last testament [of Lucky Luciano] may be responsible for a lot of the confusion, and Valachi's hatred as well as natural perceptions of the conflict between Genovese and Costello probably contributed. From what I have seen, Genovese was well respected in the underworld, and he appears to have been a valuable Lansky ally."

Joseph Barbara, Sr., became a household name thanks to the Apalachin raid. His large estate was quickly put up for sale and the ailing gangster moved to nearby Endicott, New York, where he died of a heart attack on 17 June 1959 at the age of 53.

That same year, the total number of individuals listed on the 'Apalachin Indictment' was 63. Of those mobsters, 20 were convicted on charges of obstructing justice. Two years after the raid all 20 found themselves free and clear. The convictions were overturned in appeals court, where three presiding judges made a unanimous decision, stating, "Bad as many of these alleged conspirators may be, their conviction for a crime which the government could not prove... and on evidence which a jury could not properly assess, cannot be permitted to stand."

Vito Genovese, however, was persistently dogged by investigators and convicted of selling large quantities of narcotics in April 1958, along with over a dozen other underworld brethren, including Vincent "The Chin" Gigante, who would go on to become the capo of the Genovese crime family following Vito's death in 1969.

As for the rest, the escapades in Apalachin proved to be a close call. Yet while they ultimately recovered from the shock, arguably the reputation of the Mob never did.

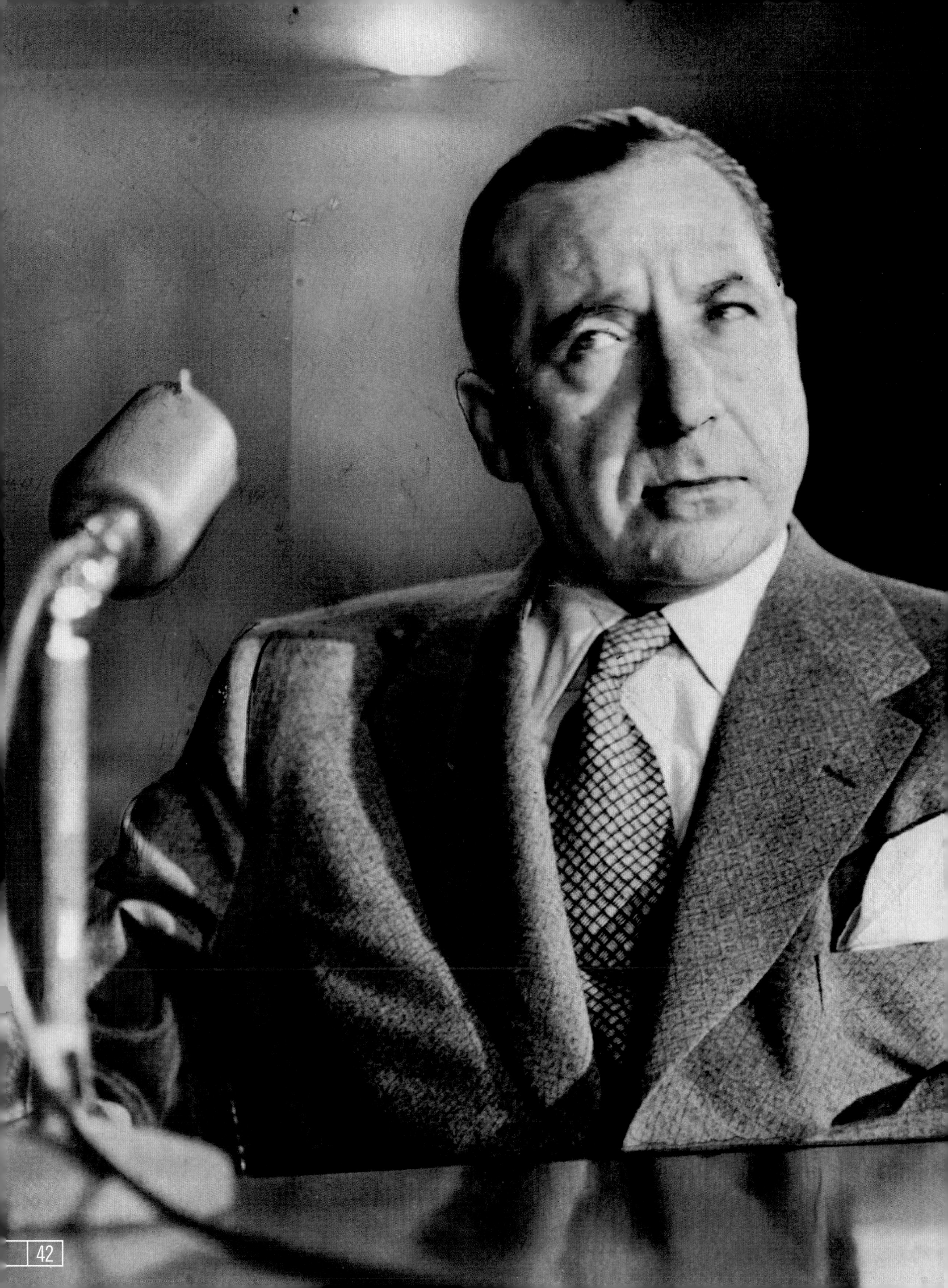

Top Dons

MEET SOME OF THE MOST FORMIDABLE GODFATHERS OF ORGANISED CRIME

WORDS SCOTT REEVES

Crime gangs are typically hierarchical organisations with a strict structure culminating in a single mastermind. These individuals hold ultimate power in the crime world and have the ability to snuff out a rival's life with a simple word or gesture. Yet it's a dangerous living, and many crime lords have been toppled by ambitious underlings. Many ended their lives in a hail of bullets, but a lucky few died peacefully – which is more than can be said for their many victims. Discover what it takes to be a true kingpin with our selection of the underworld's top bosses.

Frank Costello
LUCIANO CRIME FAMILY 1891-1973

Frank Costello rose to prominence during Prohibition after tying his fortunes to Charles 'Lucky' Luciano. When Luciano became the city's most powerful Mob boss in 1931, Costello was named Luciano's consigliere, or top adviser. Costello contributed more than anybody to the gang's coffers through his slot machine and bookmaking operations and expanded Luciano's influence into the state of Louisiana by agreeing a deal with Governor Huey Long.

But Costello wasn't Luciano's only right-hand man. After Luciano was sentenced to decades in prison in 1936, control of the crime family passed to his underboss, Vito Genovese. The following year, Genovese fled to Italy to avoid prosecution for murder. That left Costello in charge of the Luciano gang, but Genovese returned to New York in 1945 and was a threat to Costello's authority.

After years of stable leadership, Costello finally fell victim to a plot he'd long been expecting. Genovese ordered a hit on Costello in 1957. Luckily for Costello, the bullet wound to his head was superficial, but he took the hint and retired from the top spot, ceding control to Genovese. Costello lived out the rest of his life in comfortable retirement, a respected gangster who happily dished out advice to those who asked.

Santo Trafficante, Jr.
TRAFFICANTE CRIME FAMILY 1914–1987

After inheriting his father's operations in 1954, Santo Trafficante was the premier Mob leader in Florida. The Trafficante family operated nightclubs and casinos across the water in Cuba and used the offshore island to smuggle drugs into the U.S., but Trafficante's profitable trades came to a sudden end in 1959 when the Cuban Revolution brought Fidel Castro to power. The new communist government nationalised foreign-owned properties in Cuba, including those run by American organised crime gangs.

Annoyed by the damage to his bank account and reputation, Trafficante searched for an ally to help take Castro down. An unusual partnership was born when Trafficante began to work with the CIA, conspiring with the American intelligence agency to hatch several plans to assassinate Castro. None worked, but another supposedly Trafficante-backed assassination did. Rumours circulated that Trafficante was aware of plans to kill John F. Kennedy, but Trafficante testified before Congress that he had no knowledge of plots against the unfortunate President.

Though law enforcement took a keen interest in his diverse interests, Trafficante never served a day in prison. He weathered Mob violence, assassinations, revolution and conspiracy theories to die in a Texas heart hospital at the age of 72.

James "Whitey" Bulger
WINTER HILL GANG 1929–2018

Whitey Bulger rose to prominence in the Winter Hill Gang – an Irish American outfit based in Massachusetts – after he turned on his own leaders in an early 1970s turf war. Bulger switched to a rival outfit and helped them take full control of the Winter Hill neighbourhood. In 1979, the boss and deputy of the Winter Hill Gang were arrested for fixing horse races, leaving Bulger to take over. Bulger only avoided arrest because of a secret he'd kept for at least the last five years – he was an FBI informant, recruited by an old school friend to provide information on the activities of opposing mobsters.

Bulger's FBI handler turned a blind eye to the Winter Hill Gang's lucrative rackets. Bulger's underlings shook down drug dealers, trafficked arms to the IRA and ran illegal bookmaking and loansharking operations. In 1994, Bulger was warned that warrants were out for his arrest. He spent the next 16 years on the run until he was finally tracked down in Santa Monica, California. Bulger was sentenced to life in prison in 2013 and killed behind bars by vengeful mobsters in 2018. The FBI handler who tipped off Bulger about his arrest warrant was given a 40-year sentence for his part in aiding Bulger's life of crime.

TOP DONS

Vincent "the Chin" Gigante
GENOVESE CRIME FAMILY 1928–2005

A former professional boxer, Vincent Gigante became the protégé of Vito Genovese and was entrusted by the ruthless mobster to assassinate Frank Costello in 1957. Although Costello survived, Gigante rose through the ranks and inherited the outfit in 1981.

Many outsiders had no idea that Gigante wielded such power. He was best known for wandering the streets in a dressing gown, mumbling incoherently as though a madman. Instead, Anthony 'Fat Tony' Salerno was commonly thought of as the gang's top dog – but Salerno was just a front to fool the cops. Behind the scenes, it was Gigante who built a network of bookmakers, loan sharks and protection outfits.

Gigante was arrested in 1993 for the murder of six rival mobsters and conspiracy to kill three others. He unveiled the defence that he'd spent decades carefully cultivating – his lawyers argued that Gigante was unfit to face trial due to insanity. It almost worked, but after years of legal wrangling, a judge finally ruled that Gigante must answer for his actions in court. He was found guilty and sentenced to 12 years in prison, later increased by another three for obstruction of justice. He was still behind bars when he died in 2005.

The Kray Twins

THE FIRM 1933–1995 (RONNIE), 1933–2000 (REGGIE)

Many gang bosses shy away from the spotlight, but Ronnie and Reggie Kray were happy to be pictured in the papers. They established a front of legitimate business interests in 1950s London, but behind their legal activities they were also involved in armed robbery, black market trading and protection rackets. The Krays weren't to be messed with. When they bought the Regal Billiard Hall, a Maltese gang foolishly tried to shake them down for protection money and were sent packing by Ronnie wielding a cutlass.

After a three-year sentence for violent assault, Ronnie reached out to the American Mob for advice on how to refine their business model. Soon, The Firm's growing nightclub empire and illegal activities brought the Krays into conflict with the Richardson Gang. Ronnie ended up conducting a point-blank execution of a Richardson rival in a crowded pub, but thanks to The Firm's intimidating reputation no witnesses came forward. The police eventually caught up with the Krays after they brutally stabbed fellow Firm member Jack "The Hat" McVitie to death after he'd foolishly made several threats to kill the twins. Other members of The Firm gave evidence against them and the Krays were sentenced to life in prison in 1969.

Salvatore Riina
CORLEONESI MAFIA 1930–2017

Riina became head of the Corleonesi in 1974, and once in charge he began to purge any threats to his power. Riina began the Second Mafia War in 1981, triggering thousands of murders as different mafiosi jockeyed for position. The bloodbath ended in 1984 after Riina and the Corleonesi all but wiped out the Inzerillo, Bontate and Badalamenti families.

The slaughter drew the attention of the authorities. The police and judiciary tried to crack down on organised crime, but Riina gave any lawmen who got too close the same treatment as his Mafia rivals. His gangsters assassinated Pio La Torre, a politician who introduced new anti-Mafia laws, and Carlo Alberto dalla Chiesa, a Carabinieri general tasked with tracking down organised criminals in Sicily. In a break from usual Mafia conventions, Riina didn't seem to care if innocents were caught in the crossfire and even ordered terror attacks to draw resources away from the anti-Mafia investigation. Sixteen people were killed when Riina's gang planted a bomb on a passenger train in 1984.

After evading arrest for 23 years, Riina was captured in 1993 after one of his mobsters snitched on him. It led to fresh outbreaks of violence from the Corleonesi who wanted to intimidate potential witnesses, but Riina was found guilty and remained behind bars for the rest of his life.

Frank Lucas
LUCAS ORGANISATION 1930–2019

According to Frank Lucas' own account, he was robbed of his childhood innocence when he witnessed the killing of his 12-year-old cousin by the Ku Klux Klan in North Carolina. That murder made Lucas realise that a Black man like him would never make a fortune on the right side of the law. Instead, he'd carve a life for himself in the criminal underworld.

Lucas served a criminal apprenticeship under drug dealer Bumpy Johnson in New York. After Johnson died in 1968, Lucas stepped into Johnson's shoes and expanded the business. Rather than buy his drugs in the U.S., Lucas would find the best product and import it himself. Lucas sourced a pure form of heroin (which he called Blue Magic) and allegedly smuggled it from Vietnam in the coffins of dead American soldiers. He claimed to have smuggled drugs worth over $50 million.

Lucas came to the attention of federal investigators when he was spotted at a Muhammad Ali boxing match wearing a $100,000 chinchilla fur coat. Nobody was able to explain where he got the money for such an extravagant purchase. After his crimes were uncovered Lucas was jailed, freed early after informing on his fellow drug runners, only to be arrested again for resuming his trafficking career. He died at home at the age of 88.

John Gotti
GAMBINO CRIME FAMILY 1940–2002

When John Gotti's crew were arrested and charged with narcotics offences in 1985, Gotti's future hung in the balance. He'd broken the Gambino crime family's edict to never deal drugs and worried that his punishment would be a bullet in the head. Rather than wait to face the consequences, Gotti launched a preemptive strike by ordering the killing of boss Paul Castellano and then taking over the business.

Gotti had an eye for the camera and was happy to be pictured in the newspapers, confident that he would always get away with his crimes thanks to jury tampering and witness intimidation. The media nicknamed him the "Teflon Don" for his ability to beat federal charges – but the FBI didn't give up. They placed wiretaps in the Gotti's favourite hangout, the Ravenite Social Club, and eventually got the evidence they needed to lock the boss up.

Investigators cleverly arrested Gotti's subordinates and played tapes of Gotti criticising them, encouraging them to turn on him. It worked, and he was arrested and charged with racketeering and five murders. He was found guilty on all counts; in the words of the FBI, the Teflon Don had become the Velcro Don. He died ten years into a life sentence.

Frank Matthews
MATTHEWS ORGANISATION 1944–UNKNOWN

In the 1960s, Matthews was an up-and-coming drug dealer who wanted to work with New York's established crime families, but the mafiosi wanted nothing to do with him. Instead, Matthews opted to go it alone. It proved to be a lucrative choice. By the 1970s, Matthews' network of Black and Latino underbosses stretched across 21 states. He paid air crew to carry drugs in their personal bags and smuggled more than 100 kilograms (220 pounds) of heroin into New York a year.

Matthews was identified as a drug kingpin by his neighbour, a detective who grew suspicious of Matthews' affluent lifestyle and the number of dubious characters who called at his house. When Matthews' visitors were identified as known drug dealers, the investigation against him began to escalate.

Matthews was arrested in January 1973 on a money-laundering trip to Las Vegas and released on bail. He was never seen again. Some think he fled abroad; others think he was assassinated by the Mafia. Maybe he's still alive more than 50 years after vanishing without a trace, living off the fortune he earned in the illegal drugs trade.

TOP DONS

Sammy "The Bull" Gravano
GAMBINO CRIME FAMILY 1945–PRESENT

Ten-year-old Sammy was given his nickname by local gangsters who watched him challenge a bunch of older kids who'd taken his bike. One of the men said that he'd "fought like a bull" and the name stuck.

Gravano was recruited into the Mob as soon as he was old enough and developed a reputation as a ruthless enforcer, committing his first murder in 1970. Eight years later, Gravano was ordered to kill his brother-in-law, Nicholas Scibetta, a drug-addicted mobster said to have gravely insulted a superior's daughter. Gravano initially gave his relative a beating, hoping that would be enough. When his bosses said it wasn't, Gravano killed him.

In 1985, Gravano participated in the killing of Gambino family boss Paul Castellano on behalf of John Gotti. For years Gravano was Gotti's principal associate – until Gotti pinned numerous murders on Gravano during police interviews. Gravano duly turned on his boss, testifying against Gotti at trial before entering witness protection. He soon discarded his new identity and gave a number of media interviews about his past before slipping back into a life of crime. He was arrested in 2001 for leading a drug-running operation in Arizona. He was released in 2017 and now fronts a podcast and YouTube channel.

Revolver in hand, Bonnie Parker poses on the front of a motorcar

Women of the Underworld

WHOEVER SAID CRIME WAS A MAN'S WORLD NEVER CROSSED PATHS WITH THESE RUTHLESS LADIES

WORDS BEE GINGER

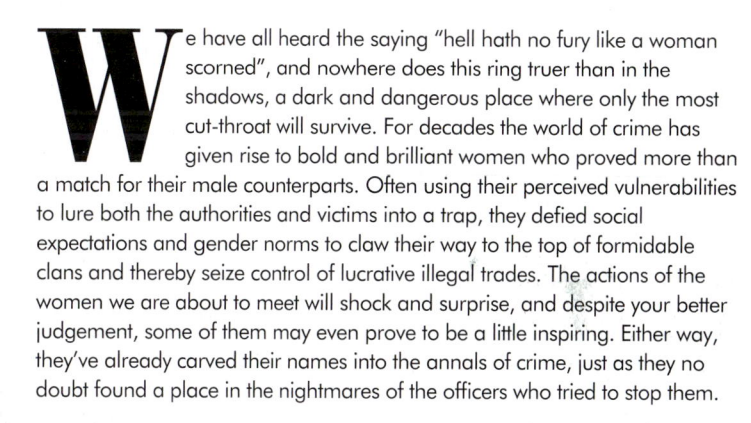

We have all heard the saying "hell hath no fury like a woman scorned", and nowhere does this ring truer than in the shadows, a dark and dangerous place where only the most cut-throat will survive. For decades the world of crime has given rise to bold and brilliant women who proved more than a match for their male counterparts. Often using their perceived vulnerabilities to lure both the authorities and victims into a trap, they defied social expectations and gender norms to claw their way to the top of formidable clans and thereby seize control of lucrative illegal trades. The actions of the women we are about to meet will shock and surprise, and despite your better judgement, some of them may even prove to be a little inspiring. Either way, they've already carved their names into the annals of crime, just as they no doubt found a place in the nightmares of the officers who tried to stop them.

Arizona Donnie Clark
UNITED STATES 1873–1935

You might know her as Ma Barker, or Kate Barker, and you may well have heard of her by reputation, for it was J. Edgar Hoover, the then director of the FBI, who named her "the most dangerous, resourceful, and vicious criminal mind of the last decade". This was an honest characterisation of a woman renowned for her ruthless ways in a time known as the "public enemy era". This spell of the 1930s was famous for many notorious gangsters coming to wider attention and a time when the FBI began to keep lists of wanted criminals charged with serious crimes.

A commanding presence blessed with impeccable organisational skills, Ma Barker utilised her repertoire to facilitate the criminal pursuits of her four sons. This gang of siblings and their allies (the Bloody Barkers) were responsible for countless bank, payroll and post office robberies and numerous kidnappings throughout the Midwest, spanning from Texas to Minnesota. The bond with her boys was strong, and as the head of the family Ma would often be called on to use her acting skills as a distraught mother to bail her brood out of jail.

It has been claimed that Ma never got blood on her hands herself and that Hoover used her as a scapegoat when instructing the FBI to shoot her. Thanks to the many stories and songs that recall Ma's colourful life, Hoover's orders could never fully erase the memory of this sly matriarch of the underworld.

Sara María Aldrete Villareal

TAMAULIPAS, MEXICO 1964–PRESENT

Once the leader of a group dubbed by the media as "the Narcosatanists", or "Los Narcosatánicos", Sara María Aldrete Villareal was looked on by her followers as somewhat of a matriarch, who named her "the Godmother". The cult was famed for human sacrifice, including numerous murders in Matamoros, Tamaulipas. The followers of this satanic cult were instructed – and coerced – to carry out heinous acts of violence, ritualistic killings and the theft of drugs, with the drug dealers pushing narcotics across the U.S. border targeted.

Aldrete herself was initiated into the cult in the 1980s by Adolfo Constanzo, a fortune-teller who insisted to Aldrete and the group that all sacrifices would grant them immunity from punishment and law enforcement. This was because of their tireless work in disrupting drug smuggling in the area. Due to the transient nature of border towns, with many people entering the U.S in search of a better life, or those crossing the border for more nefarious reasons, bodies for sacrifice were plentiful, and it is believed by investigators that Aldrete played a key role in the torture and slaughter of countless individuals. On one occasion she selected a sacrifice, cut off his nipples and boiled him alive at an old warehouse in Matamoros where scores of other victims had previously been taken, the only remains of their dismembered bodies left cooking in a large pot.

In May of 1989 detectives raided one of the cult's hideouts in Mexico City where Constanzo was lurking. At his behest another member of the group shot him in the head so he would avoid incarceration. Aldrete was less fortunate and was captured and sentenced to 62 years in prison. However, she was released in 2002 having served only 13 years. She has since been interviewed by the BBC and released a book titled *El Ángel de la Oscuridad* (*The Angel of Darkness*), but where she is today is a mystery.

Bonnie Elizabeth Parker

UNITED STATES 1910–1934

Born into a life of poverty in Texas, Bonnie Parker quickly got used to struggling to make the ends meet. She worked tirelessly as a seamstress and waitress before turning to a life of crime and becoming one of the early 1930's most notorious outlaws. Her criminal career commenced when she met and fell in love with Clyde Barrow, who had stolen her mother's car. Prison escapes and daring bank robberies ensued as the two embarked on a crime spree across the United States, a trail of destruction left wherever they went. The pair became not only a media sensation but the most infamous criminals in American history. Bonnie was held up by the public as a daring and glamorous figure despite her litany of crimes and almost celebrated by the media, often portrayed as a tragic heroine only following a life of crime for the man she loved.

Despite both spending time in prison the pair always reunited, each time resuming their illegal ways with the assistance of other gang operatives. By 1933 the gang was responsible for numerous murders, including those of law officials, and the hunt for the duo gained pace. The pair's reign of terror finally ended in 1934 in a hail of bullets as they were shot dead by law enforcement officers. Due to their notoriety a staggering 20,000 members of the public came to view Bonnie's body at the funeral home once it was returned to Dallas, Texas.

WOMEN OF THE UNDERWORLD

Kathleen Mary Josephine Leigh
📍 SYDNEY, AUSTRALIA **1881–1964**

Known also as Kathleen Ryan or Kathleen Barry, or just plain Kate to her closest friends, this was a lady you didn't cross. Not just a criminal mastermind in her homeland of Australia, the Queen of Surry Hills was a ruthless cocaine smuggler, bootlegger and notorious brothel owner. Her home served as a central hub for illegal betting and gambling syndicates as well as a storage facility for black market stolen goods. As a prominent figure in Sydney's infamous razor gangs, Leigh regularly crossed paths with the equally ambitious Tilly Devine, and to say the pair didn't get alone would be an understatement (they remained arch nemesis until a truce later on in life).

Leigh was one of the leading proprietors of sly grog, running more than 20 establishments in the area. Some were upmarket, where questionable politicians and dubious businessmen would be hosted. Others were more of a shop front for selling under-the-counter alcohol with a hefty price tag. During the razor wars of the 1920s and '30s the business was in the thick of the action, with sales flourishing not only in booze but also opium, cocaine, stolen property and of course the oldest trade in the book – prostitution.

Despite being handy with a bladed weapon, Leigh employed minders to watch out for rival gangs or the authorities, but the latter did manage to catch up with her on several occasions; Leigh served 13 jail terms and amassed some 107 convictions. Even so, she would later be remembered and lauded by many for her philanthropic work, her patriotism during World War II and as a matriarch and benevolent sly grog seller. Others chose to label her "the worst woman in Sydney". The jury is still out on this one.

Matilda Mary Devine (née Twiss)
📍 AUSTRALIA **1900–1970**

Matilda "Tilly" Devine became known to many as one of Australia's most notorious gangsters. Born in London, England, Tilly relocated to Sydney in 1920, and over the ensuing 40 years she established herself as not only a wealthy madam but one of the most underhand and formidable underworld women the country had ever witnessed. Tilly and her husband Jim were in good criminal company at the time as they worked alongside the likes of Norman Bruhn, Frank Green and Guido Calletti. Tilly sold her wares, charging top dollar due to her good looks, while Jim worked as her protector, pimp and "get-away man" alongside selling cocaine and opium. In addition to engaging in prostitution Tilly also facilitated it, being arrested on 79 separate occasions for prostitution offences. Police reports described her as "a prostitute of the worst type and an associate of the worst types of prostitute, vagrants and criminals".

Often charged and fined for consorting with known criminals and fighting rivals, multiple illicit activities were connected to Tilly throughout her life, including the formation of razor gangs and the sale of sly grog. Following a spell of bronchitis and later cancer, Tilly died on 24 November 1970.

Ron Saw wrote an obituary in *The Daily Telegraph* that encapsulated her character and eventual demise, and it can only be described as caustic yet accurate: "A vicious, grasping, high-priestess of savagery, venery, obscenity and whoredom … She died friendless and alone, and for that she must be pitied. But if they hold a wake for her the sorrow will be slobber and crocodile tears. She was a wretched woman."

María Dolores Estévez Zuleta
◉ MEXICO **1906–1959**

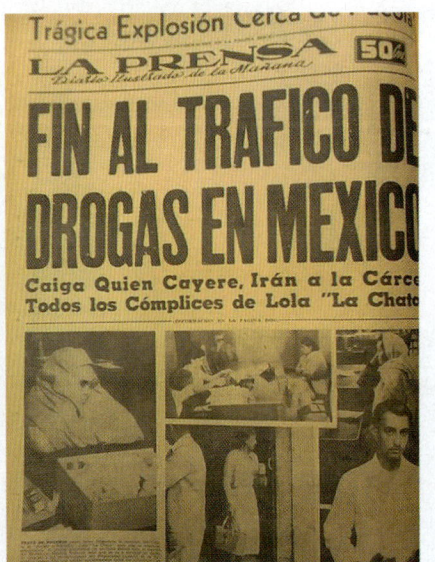

Another pioneering female drug lord and gangster of her time, María Dolores Estévez Zuleta, more commonly known as Lola la Chata, was a prominent figure in the Mexican drug trade from the 1930s to the '50s. Lola excelled in this murky world, establishing herself as a major player in the international drug and narcotics market, trafficking heroin, marijuana, morphine and many other illicit substances. With bold determination and a sharp business mind she gained notoriety and was even featured regularly in the newspapers, where she was sensationalised as a highly dangerous yet glamorous figure. This influence and her natural cunning helped Lola to expand her empire on a global scale. She was even able to sell drugs both in and outside of prison walls for almost 30 years at a time when the trade was becoming ever more sophisticated. Lola went on to evade a lifetime prison sentence and continued to trade in narcotics. Her illicit activities strained relations between the U.S. and Mexican governments, a tension that resulted in a presidential decree aimed at halting Lola's operations. It was unsuccessful, and she continued to operate until her death from a rumoured heroin overdose in 1959. Ironically, of the 500 attendees at her funeral, a third were believed to be former police officials.

❝ **WITH BOLD DETERMINATION AND A SHARP BUSINESS MIND SHE GAINED NOTORIETY AND WAS EVEN FEATURED REGULARLY IN THE NEWSPAPERS, WHERE SHE WAS SENSATIONALISED AS A HIGHLY DANGEROUS YET GLAMOROUS FIGURE** ❞

Bessie Starkman
◉ CANADA **1890–1930**

Bessie Starkman became known as the first high-profile female crime boss in Canada during the Prohibition era. Alongside her spouse, the well-known mobster Rocco Perri, Bessie ran a hugely impressive drug-smuggling and bootlegging enterprise. Primarily responsible for overseeing the financial aspects of the sales of forbidden alcohol, Bessie ensured that business remained profitable. She was a shrewd operator, keeping profits up and law enforcement and rival gangs at bay. Although her criminal career was brief she made an enormous impact on the people of Hamilton. Gunned down at her home as she got out of her car, her murderers were never caught. Her funeral took place in Hamilton and was one of the largest ever seen at that time.

Maria Licciardi
◉ NAPLES, ITALY **1951–PRESENT**

Word on the street is that Maria Licciardi was one of the most influential and powerful bosses of the Camorra crime syndicate in Naples from the early 1990s until her arrest in 2001. Following the death of her husband and arrest of her brothers, it was down to Maria to take over and front the Licciardi clan, which she did with aplomb. She went by many nicknames, including "the Godmother", "Princess" and "the little one" (owing to her diminutive stature), but what she lacked in height she made up for in determination, guile and cold business acumen.

With a prominent place not only on Italy's most wanted list but also as head of the clan, which was based in the suburb of Secondigliano in Naples, Maria became one of the founders of the larger criminal organisation the Secondigliano Alliance, famed in part for controlling a large portion of organised crime in the area. A day's work involved cigarette and drug smuggling, extortion, enforcing protection rackets and receiving stolen money. Maria even introduced the sex trade into the gang's bursting portfolio for the first time.

Her demise came in 2001 when a shipment of heroin came into Naples that proved to be too pure, thus killing numerous customers. Gang wars followed, resulting in the death of almost 120 people and the incarceration of Maria. Released in 2009, she served as the inspiration for the chain-smoking female boss in the popular television series *Gomorrah* (2014–2021), based on the book by author Roberto Saviano.

One of the many victims of the Camorra lies died in a car

Cheng Chui Ping
📍 UNITED STATES **1949–2014**

Some called her Sister Ping; the authorities chose "The Snake Head". The latter seems to be the more fitting epitaph for a merciless business woman and the leader of an underground criminal enterprise responsible for the trafficking of over 3,000 illegal immigrants from China into the United States. Cheng Chui Ping knew the ships were faulty and unlikely to survive the arduous journey from Hong Kong to New York via Guatemala, and yet she charged $35,000 per person for the promise of a better life. For those who could not pay, Ping would send gangs to abduct them and then rape, beat and torture them until they cleared their debts. Failing that, additional gangs would be dispatched to pay their families a visit.

Many died or drowned during the dangerous crossings that made Ping a millionaire, including ten people in 1993 when a rusty freighter carrying 300 terrified and starving immigrants ran aground. Then in 1998 another of her ships capsized (this time off the coast of Guatemala) in an incident that claimed the lives of 14 Chinese passengers.

In the two decades that Ping ran the smuggling ring she amassed a fortune of $40 million from money laundering, trafficking and putting desperate and scared people on boats that she knew were unsafe. Finally caught and convicted in 2000, she died in prison from cancer at the age of 65.

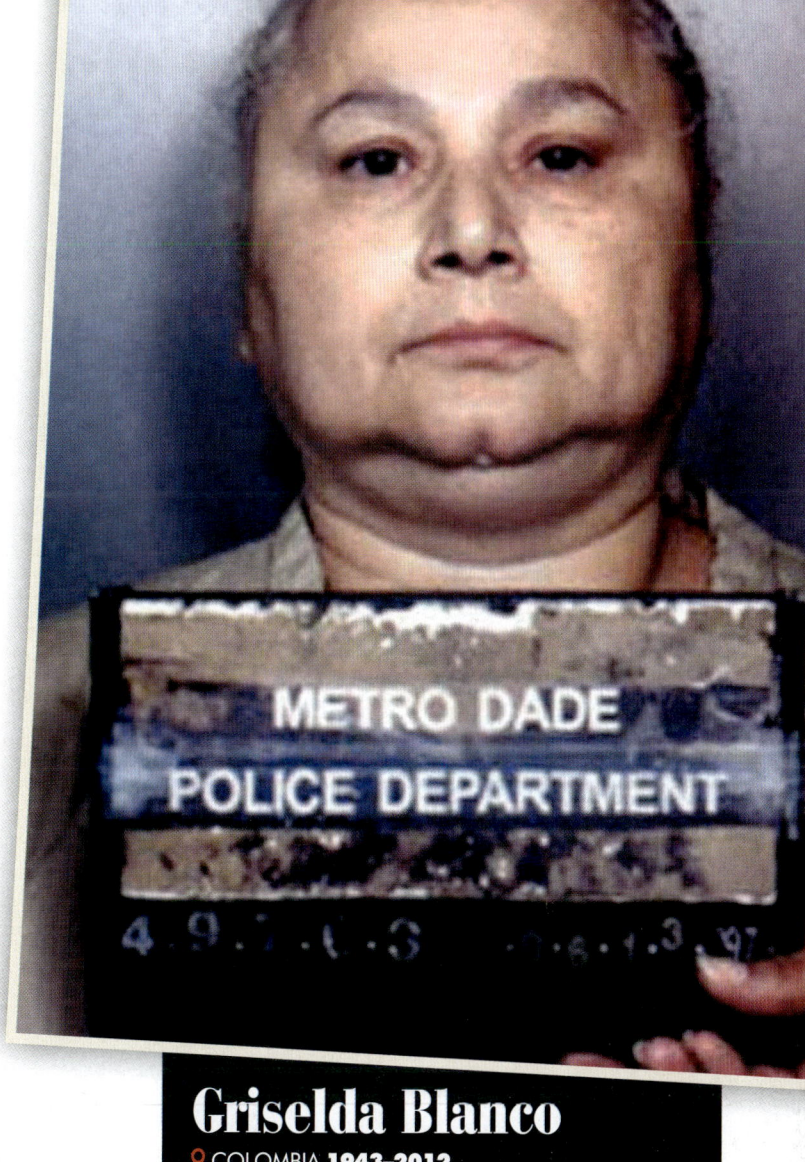

Griselda Blanco
📍 COLOMBIA **1943–2012**

Fittingly known as the "Black Widow", Griselda Blanco Restrepo cut a formidable figure in the drug world of 1970s Miami. Rumoured to have been part of the Medellín Cartel, the queen of narco-trafficking is reported to have been the first-ever billionaire criminal, amassing over $80 million per month at her peak, all through the proceeds from her lucrative business of smuggling cocaine into the United States from Colombia. In order to transport this white gold from the south of Florida up to New York, Griselda invented special underwear for her female smugglers to wear.

When she wasn't running her cocaine empire she enjoyed ordering killings and watching the torture of her victims – around 2,000 of them to be precise. This included her three husbands and, most tragically of all, a two-year-old boy, who was shot instead of his father, the intended target.

In order to eliminate her competition Griselda invented a practice whereby gunmen on motorbikes would shoot rivals down in the street, with a number of these assassinations taking place in broad daylight. This ruthless behaviour plunged Miami into a period of intense violence that came to be known as the Cocaine Cowboy Wars.

Rather poetically, the "Black Widow" was herself shot dead outside of a butchers in Medellín, Colombia, in 2012 by an assassin on a motorbike.

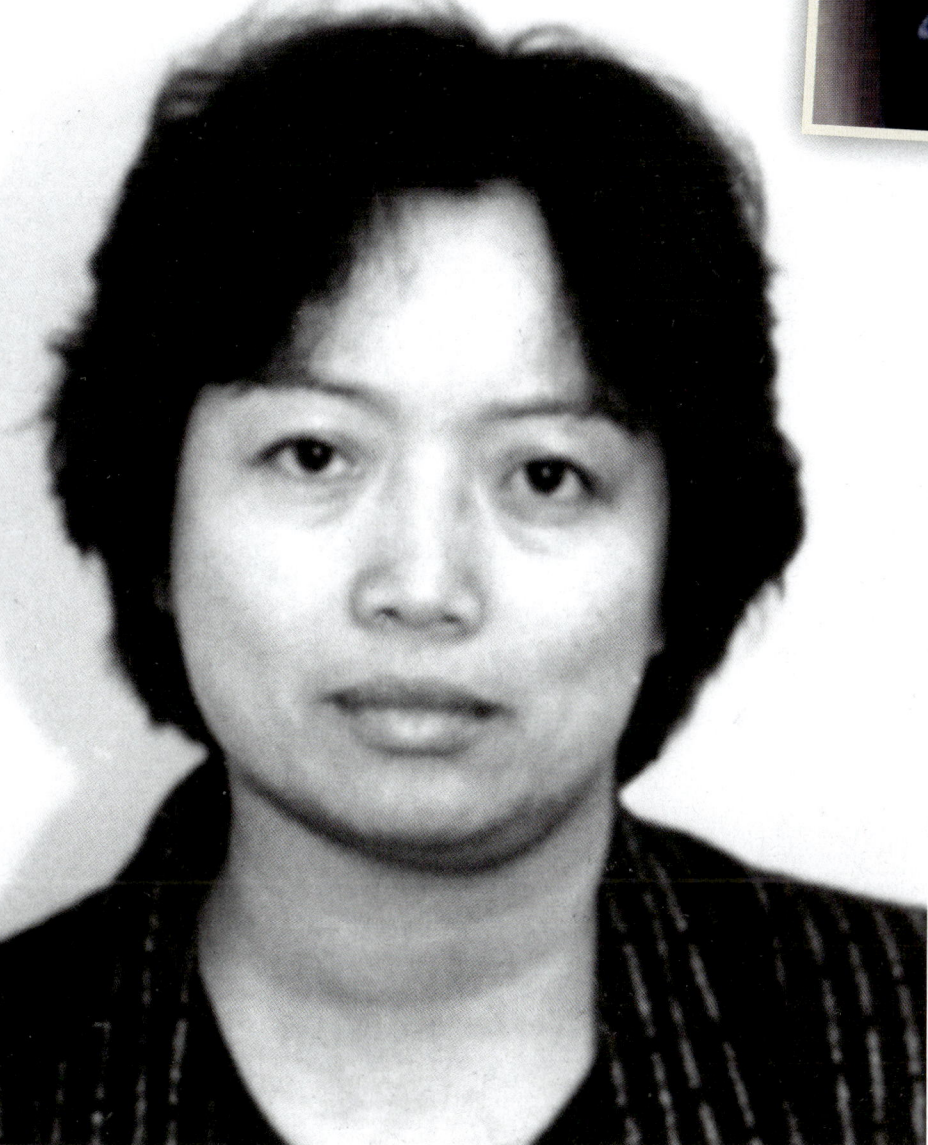

Eastern Promise

| 58 |
YAKUZA FAMILY

| 64 |
THE 14K TRIAD

| 70 |
THE RUSSIAN MAFIA

| 76 |
THE WORLD'S WEIRDEST GANGS

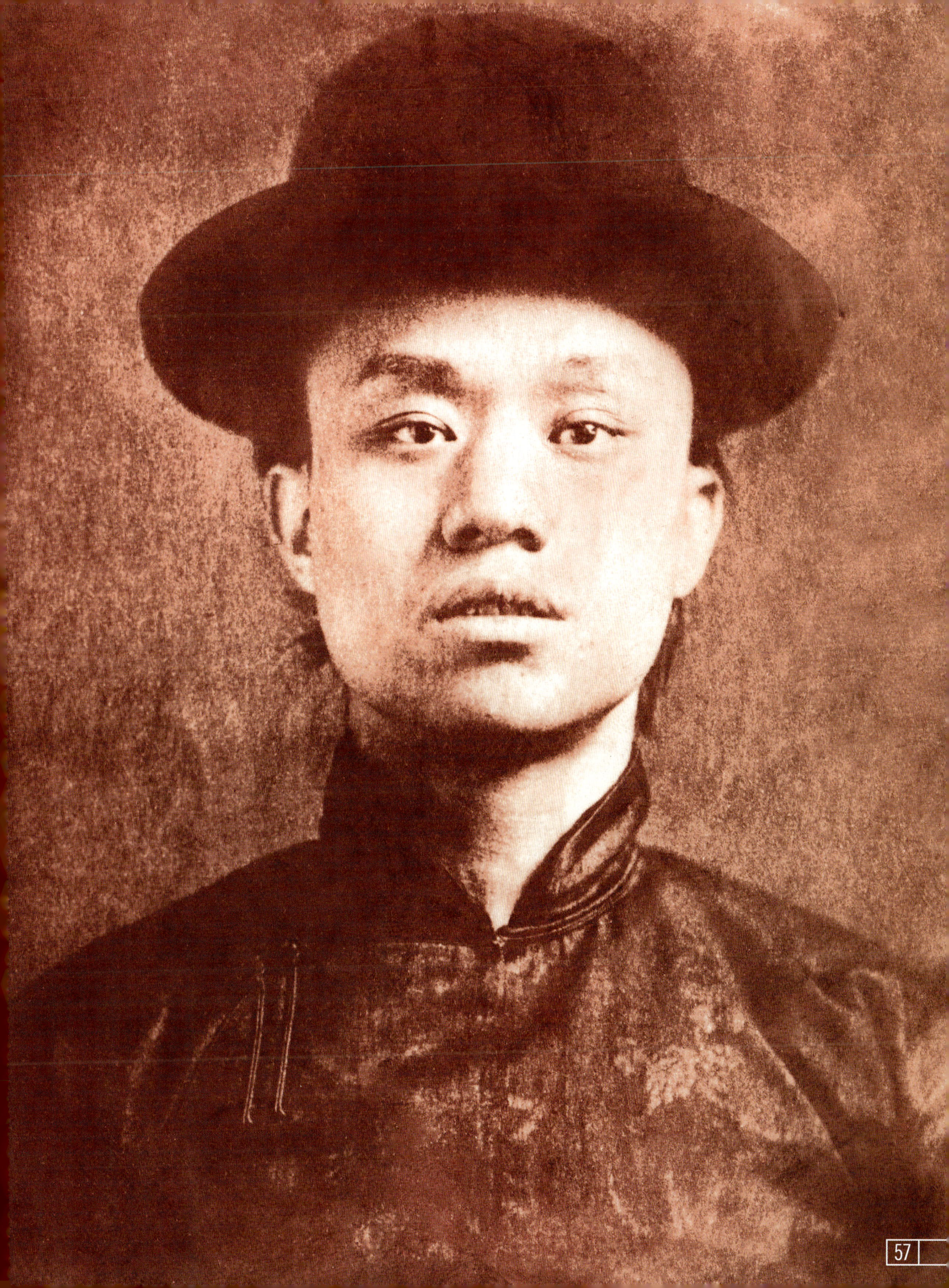

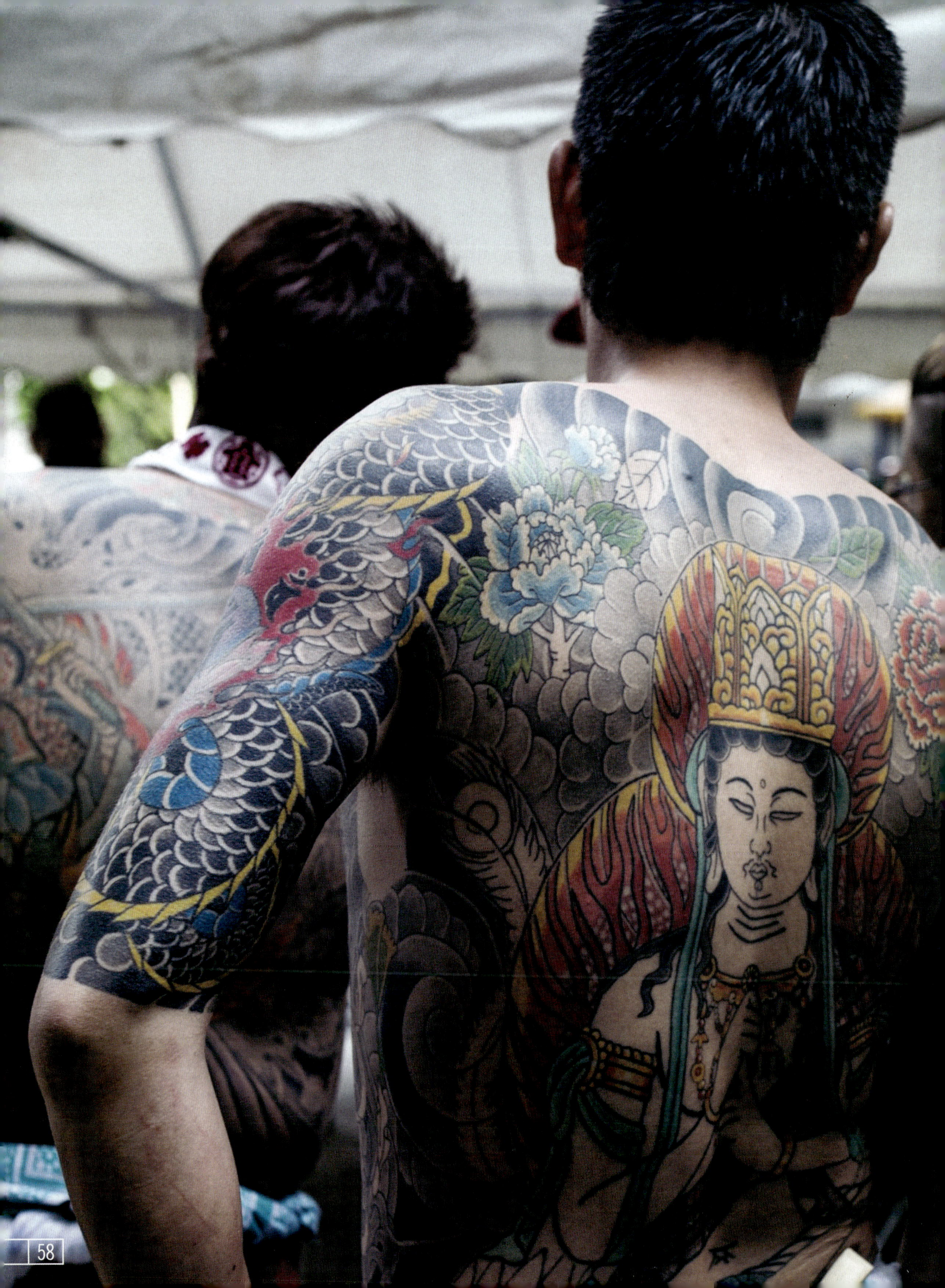

Japan's Infamous Yakuza Family

THE YAKUZA ARE FEARED THROUGHOUT THE WORLD, BUT IT IS THE GANG'S KNACK FOR FINANCE AND CORRUPTION, NOT VIOLENCE, THAT MAKES THEM SO SUCCESSFUL

WORDS DAVID HUTT

At the peak of the Italian Mafia's control of organised crime in the United States during the 1950s and '60s, there were an estimated 5,000 fully fledged members and a few thousand more associates. By comparison, today there are an estimated 86,000 members of the Japanese yakuza and the numbers are only growing. Their world has long been one of mystery and intrigue to outsiders. From the centuries-old tradition of full-body tattoos to the world of globalised, financial capitalism, the yakuza skirt both the old and the new, emblematic of a modern-day Japan that is deeply traditional yet outwardly ultramodern.

The word 'yakuza' roughly translates as 'hooligan' or 'worthless scamp'. In the 1960s, however, the police warned against using the term, since they feared it romanticised the noble outlaw, and implored people to instead use the term 'boryokudan', meaning 'violent group'. The yakuza often refer to themselves as 'ninkyo dantai', meaning 'chivalrous organisations', which isn't actually quite as outrageous as you might think.

The history of the yakuza dates back to the Edo period, between 1603 and 1868, which saw the rise of two groups of itinerant merchants. The first were the tekiya, often translated as 'peddlers', who travelled the country, typically selling low-cost and shoddy goods. Theirs was a reputation of deception. The other group was composed of the bakuto, roaming gamblers who made their money playing traditional Japanese dice games. Both groups were considered of low-class, almost outlaws, who did not conform to the norms of Edo society.

However, as the centuries progressed these two social groups began to take on more formal, hierarchical structures. The tekiya formed organisations, sometimes recognised by the government, with a system of leaders. The bakuto, meanwhile, consolidated their position by expanding into the loan shark racket in Japan's illegal gambling houses. The word 'yakuza' is believed to have derived from the world of bakuto gambling. In Oicho-Kabu, a Japanese card game similar to blackjack, the worst possible hand is an eight, a nine and a three, which, when expressed phonetically, is 'ya-ku-za'.

By the turn of the 20th century, with the rise of industrial Japan, these two groups had cemented their positions as structured organisations of outlaws and misfits. Then came World War II, which destabilised the traditions of Japanese social hierarchy and created a black market that the nascent criminal groups were only happy to partake in.

Many years earlier, in 1915, a man named Harukichi Yamaguchi formed an organisation that became known as the Yamaguchi-gumi. Starting with only 50 members, the group's main task revolved around the ports of Kobe, in southern Japan, where they provided dockworkers to different companies, effectively making it a loose labour union. However, it wasn't long until their business acumen grew.

The rise of the Yamaguchi-gumi to become today's most powerful yakuza group began in 1946 when Kazuo Taoka became the third kumicho (boss). Known as the 'godfather of all godfathers', Taoka reigned until 1981 and saw the expansion of the criminal organisation from a small, local family network into Japan's largest. The Yamaguchi-gumi's operations soon expanded to gambling, protection rackets and money lending. Members were advised to start legitimate businesses so that they could make and launder money. Soon they expanded into the construction and loan industries and found success in the entertainment industry, even managing some of Japan's top post-war stars. By doing so, the organisation branched out to ensnare prominent businessmen and politicians. With its power growing, the Yamaguchi-gumi soon ventured beyond the confines of Kobe, armed with the latest weapons available on the post-war black market. Fierce battles for control spread throughout western Japan, and as the Yamaguchi-gumi rolled over smaller, local outfits, they formed a network of groups affiliated with the organisation.

Importantly, Taoka also reorganised the structure of the organisation, creating a system where underbosses were elected and the hierarchy of power cemented. To ensure the security of the organisation, in 1962 he divided his underlings into two groups: directors of the legal enterprises and directors of the fighting groups. The former were forbidden from having soldiers, a smart move that not only prevented internal power struggles among the more wealthy and powerful members but also meant that violence would become a last resort, thereby preventing trouble from the authorities. The measures implemented by Taoka effectively changed the Yamaguchi-gumi into a capitalist organisation, one bent on making money first but always prepared to use the threat of violence as required.

At the same time, the two other most powerful yakuza groups were consolidating their power. Today the Sumiyoshi-kai is the second-largest yakuza group in Japan. It began operations in the late 19th century when members of the bakuto group in Tokyo formed the Sumiyoshi-ikka. In 1958, the third leader of the Sumiyoshi-ikka brought together 28 groups from a number of cities, including the capital, to form the Sumiyoshi-kai. Unlike the Yamaguchi-gumi, it operates on a conglomerate structure, with a looser chain of command, and its leader shares power with other godfathers. While both organisations have warred in past decades, in 1996 the head of the Yamaguchi-gumi sat down with his Sumiyoshi-kai counterpart for a glass of sake to mend relations.

The third most powerful yakuza organisation is the Inagawa-kai. Based in the Kanto region to the south, it was founded in 1949 as the Inagawa-gumi before changing its name in 1972. Though smaller than its two rivals, the Inagawa-kai was one of the first organisations to expand operations overseas.

It was only in 1992 that the Japanese Government passed the first openly anti-yakuza legislation, which attempted to limit their activities. Yet, remarkably, no law makes it illegal to be a member of a designated criminal organisation. The government recognises 22 yakuza outfits and 'regulates' them, though often this simply means legitimising them. The Yamaguchi-gumi's headquarters in Kobe, for example, takes up a two-block building. The organisation's corporate emblem is known to most Japanese people, and its newsletter, *Yamaguchi-gumi Shinpo*, includes haiku and advice on angling.

"The yakuza are not confined to the shadows. They have office buildings, business cards, even fan magazines. They are heavily involved in construction (including public works projects), bid-rigging, real estate, extortion, blackmail, stock manipulation, gambling, human trafficking and the sex trade," wrote Jake Adelstein, an American journalist and crime writer who lives in Japan. "They often use civilians to

ABOVE Top members of the Yamaguchi-gumi attend the funeral of their boss, Masahisa Takenaka. Taoka's short-lived successor was assassinated by the Ichiwa-kai in 1985 after less than a year at the head of the yakuza organisation

> **" THE YAKUZA ARE NOT CONFINED TO THE SHADOWS. THEY HAVE OFFICE BUILDINGS, BUSINESS CARDS, EVEN FAN MAGAZINES "**

JAPAN'S INFAMOUS YAKUZA FAMILY

The Big Four Families

YAMAGUCHI-GUMI
六代目山口組
Date established: 1915
HQ: Kobe
Members: 8,100

SUMIYOSHI-KAI
住吉会
Date established: 1958
HQ: Tokyo
Members: 3,800

INAGAWA-KAI
稲川会
Date established: 1949
HQ: Tokyo
Members: 3,100

AIZUKOTETSU-KAI
五代目会津小鉄会
Date established: 1868
HQ: Kyoto
Members: 2,000

Honour Among Thieves?

THE YAKUZA MIXES FEAR WITH CHARITY, REFLECTING THE SOCIAL DEPRIVATION MOST MEMBERS COME FROM

Like any good criminal organisation, the yakuza understands how to manipulate ordinary people. When the tsunami hit Japan in 2011, members of the yakuza were first on the scene, dispensing food, water and blankets. While this is sensible business, keeping communities on side, it is also a way to give back to the alienated societies most members hail from. It is thought a third of all yakuza members are of Korean descent, a group that still faces discrimination in Japanese society.

Another historically maligned group are the burakumin, who were originally members of the lowest social order in feudal Japan, outcast because their work was considered impure. Although the end of the feudal laws came in 1869, the discrimination surrounding this caste survives today, and as late as the 1980s it was estimated that more than 50 per cent of yakuza members were burakumin.

The yakuza might be engaged in the business of stocks and venture capitalism, but low-level crime, like operating dog fights, continues

61

front their operations, taking out small business loans offered by the Japanese Government and defaulting on payment. A financial analyst for a major investment bank in Japan estimates that 40 per cent of all small business loans made nationwide went to companies created by the yakuza."

The evocation of the 'common good' is often the justification of the Japanese government. The strength and hierarchy of the yakuza prevents open warfare from smaller operations, while the profit incentive of legitimate business, – and outright corruption – means that they do not have to engage in low-level crime. "The yakuza tend to be gentler than their Italian cousins. In general, they are not involved in theft, burglary, armed robbery, or other street crimes. Inter-yakuza gang wars do break out on a semi-regular basis, but rarely do they attack public figures," Adelstein wrote.

While stability might be guaranteed, the other side of the coin is that the yakuza has its tentacles in almost every area of Japanese society, particularly politics. At times this has resulted in violence. In 2007, the mayor of Nagasaki was assassinated after reportedly trying to prevent the Yamaguchi-gumi from winning public works contracts. Yet most of the time the relationship between the yakuza and the political class is cordial.

It is in finance where the yakuza dominates. In the early 1990s, the Yamaguchi-gumi's leader, Masaru Takumi, set about creating a new breed of 'economic yakuza', and he told his members that, "From now on, the first thing a yakuza needs to do when he gets up in the morning is read the business section of the newspaper." Soon, the organisation began investing in venture capital firms, buying up stocks and bonds, becoming well-heeled stock-traders who have the added benefit of engaging in market manipulation.

The yakuza's power might have been built on changing with the times, but many of its rituals remain distinctly traditional. One of the most well-known of these rituals is the yubitsume (literally 'finger shortening'). The tradition began among the bakuto in feudal Japan. When a person couldn't pay their debts, the cutting off of a finger, typically the small finger, was taken as a repayment. It is also believed to be deeply symbolic. Since the person missing his finger cannot grip traditional Japanese swords tightly, he thereby has to rely on the group for protection. The practice was continued into the 20th century by the yakuza as a form of punishment. The guilty person lays his hand on a cloth and then, using a sharp knife, cuts off a portion of his own finger, usually above the top knuckle. The sliced-off finger is then graciously offered to the superior as an act of penance. If that person commits more offences, more fingers must be offered up.

The other commonly known ritual of the yakuza is the full-body tattoo. While tattooing has a long history in Japan, dating as far back as 300 BCE, it was looked down upon during the Meiji period as a sign of criminality. Again, like the yubitsume, the yakuza's propensity for full-body tattoos originated with the bakuto, who similarly tattooed their bodies to show which clan they belonged to. Tradition was that when playing cards, members would play bare-chested, revealing their affiliation, a tradition that continues today.

In September 2015, something happened that few had expected: thousands of members of the Yamaguchi-gumi broke away from the organisation to form a new gang called the Kobe Yamaguchi-gumi after being expelled for disloyalty. An earlier split in 1984 led to years of assassinations, bombings and gun fights, and the Japanese tabloids predicted that there would be "a sea of blood" following this sudden division.

Sure enough, in November 2015, Tatsuyuki Hishida, leader of second-tier Yamaguchi-gumi affiliate group the Aio-kai, based in Yokkaichi, was found dead in his home. He had been bound and bludgeoned to death with an iron pipe. Then, as 2016 progressed, the violence intensified. Street brawls, shootings and arson attacks spread. At least one murder was linked to the conflict. In January and February, the Yamaguchi-gumi attacked the breakaway group on the latter's red-light turf, injuring dozens. "There's no denying that a gang war is taking place," said Taro Kono, Japan's chairman of the National Public Safety Commission, on 4 March of that year.

The following day, a truck was rammed into an office of the Kobe Yamaguchi-gumi, while shots were fired into an office in another city. What's more, the division sent shock waves through the rest of the major yakuza organisations, with many having to decide which of the new organisations to follow.

However, the feared sea of blood thankfully never washed over Japan. This is ultimately because the yakuza are not as willing to engage in open warfare as much as other mafias as it would risk the stable balance they enjoy in the political and business world. Indeed, the yakuza has survived when other criminal groups have failed because they are usually so adept at keeping a lid on the worst excesses of their most disruptive members and therefore avoid upsetting the authorities.

In fact, so enmeshed in Japanese society are the yakuza that they remain virtually untouchable by the government and inseparable from most avenues of daily life.

RIGHT An ex-yakuza shows his severed small finger, clutching a Bible. This mutilation marks his criminal background out to all

The busy red light district of Kabukicho near Shinjuku in the centre of Tokyo is controlled by the yakuza groups

JAPAN'S INFAMOUS YAKUZA FAMILY

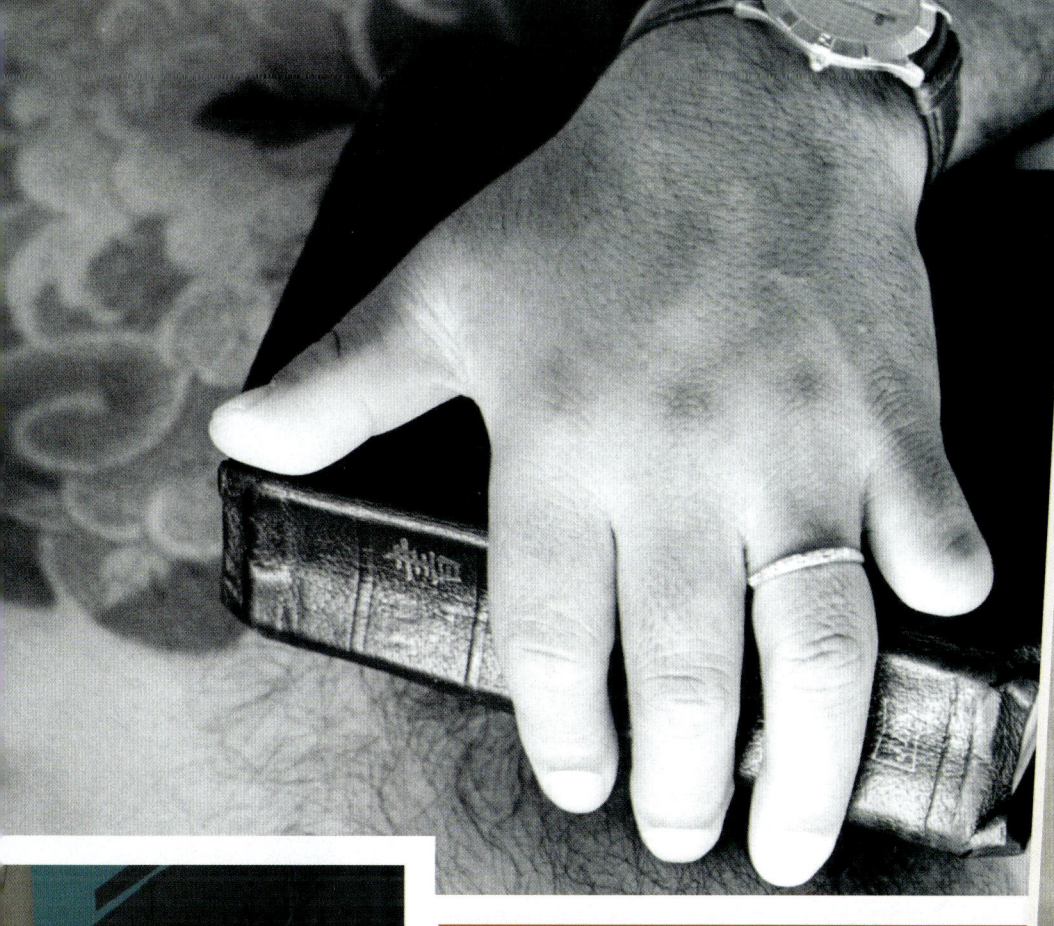

Kaoru Inoue shows off his tattoos in this photo taken in the early 1980s. Today he is a Christian pastor

Samurai Syndicate

OYABUN
The oyabun, or kumicho, is the head of the organisation and oversees the entire operation. They run it like a family, and the death of every oyabun leads to a renewal in the outfit.

SAIKOKOMON
Directly below the oyabun is the saikokomon (senior adviser), who is chiefly in charge of the administrative side of the organisation, typically business angles, and is rarely involved in violence.

WAKAGASHIRA
On the forceful side of the division, the waka gashira, or first lieutenant, is in charge of commanding the gangs loyal to the organisation. He is the main go-between for the organisation and the gangs' local bosses.

SHATEIGASHIRA
Next to the wakagashira are the second lieutenants, who are the local bosses of the different gangs affiliated with the organisation.

SHINGIIN
Every good business needs good counsel, and this law adviser is in charge of making sure the legitimate businesses remain legitimate and that the illegitimate businesses are not threatened.

KYODAI
The general hierarchy below the organisation's bosses and the local chiefs is composed of 'brothers'. The kyodai, or elder brothers, are in charge of the actions of the shatei.

KAIKEI
Below the law adviser are the accountants who are responsible for managing the flow of money. This is either from illegal means to areas where it can be laundered, or from legitimate means back into the mix.

SHATEI
The 'younger brothers' are overseen by the kyodai and are often the newer, less-experienced members of the gangs who do most of the legwork.

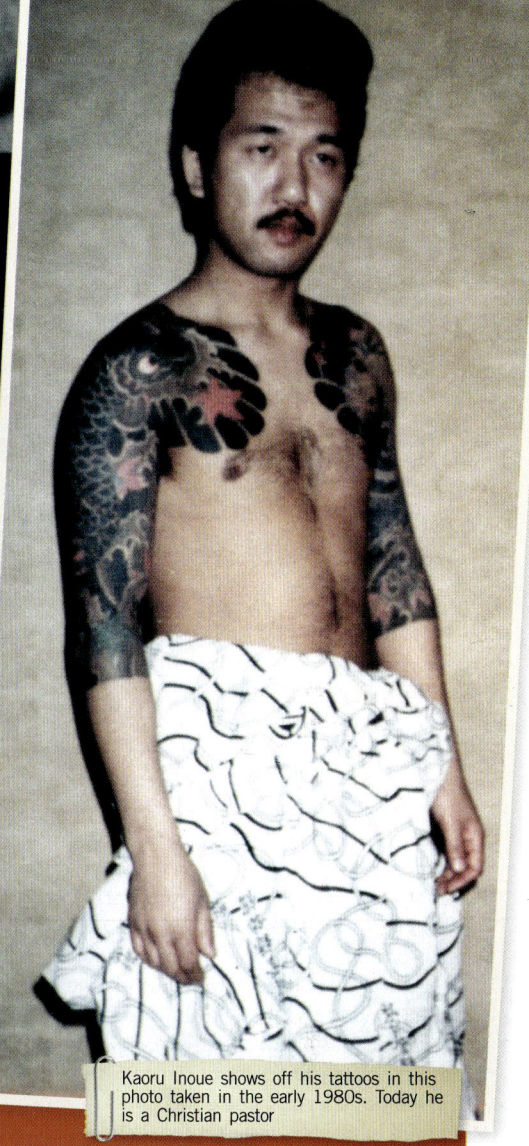

The 14k Triad

THE MOST INFAMOUS HEIR TO CHINA'S CENTURIES-OLD SECRET SOCIETIES, THE 14K TRIAD MIX AMBITIOUS OPPORTUNISM WITH SAVAGE VIOLENCE TO RULE HONG KONG'S UNDERWORLD

WORDS PAUL FRENCH

1997 – the eve of the Hong Kong handover. It was a historic moment. The Union flag was about to come down after 99 years of the city serving as a Crown colony. Hong Kong was about to become a Special Administrative Region of the People's Republic of China, answering to Beijing and no longer to London. British troops were packed up and moving out of the Prince of Wales Barracks overlooking Victoria Harbour; the APCs of the People's Liberation Army were massed on the border at Shenzhen. The city was nervous; the rain was pouring down – locals said it was a bad omen. The infamous Wan Chai red light district was partying late, all too aware that this could be the final all-night party for some time if the territory's new communist rulers clamped down.

I was in town to write about the handover. It was past midnight by the time I left the city's Foreign Correspondents' Club and made my way to a down-at-heel Wan Chai hotel. It was now officially the last day of the British Empire in the Far East. The talk in the FCC had been of Prince Charles arriving and 'last' governor Chris Patten leaving and whether Beijing would press its repressive hand on Hong Kong's jugular or leave the city to do what it did best – make money.

On a back street, light suddenly spilled out of a shuttered mahjong parlour, sandwiched between an all-night dumpling restaurant and a karaoke bar where drunk teenagers were warbling Cantopop ballads. Inside, you could assume, big money was being gambled on the exquisitely carved ivory tiles. Middle-aged men in shirtsleeves ran out covering their heads and screaming. Behind them came young men in black suits with machetes, slashing wildly. The pursued suffered nasty gashes to their arms and scalps. Several fell to the ground and lay motionless in the road while others writhed in agony, women now coming out of the parlour and crouching down by them, trying to staunch their wounds. Taxis screeched to a halt; passers-by screamed.

It was over in less than a minute. The slim-looking young men in black disappeared into the narrow alleys that ran between the shops along the back street. Blood ran into the gutters, mixing with the rainwater and the red neon shine off the pavement that characterises a rainy Hong Kong. Waiting for ambulances to cart away the injured, local residents smoked, looked grim and said it was the 14K taking care of last-minute business before the PLA arrived.

The rival Sun Yee On Triad might be older, but in 1997, the 14K was the largest and most ensconced Triad gang in Hong Kong. It was a movement born in 1945 out of hatred for the communists. Created by Kot Siu-wong, a lieutenant-general in the Kuomintang (Chinese Nationalist Party), a leader pitched in a death struggle for control of China with the communist Red Army. In 1949, the Kuomintang finally lost the struggle and its leaders fled to Taiwan. But Kot and his gang, based in the southern city of Guangzhou, crossed the border and set up shop in British-controlled Hong Kong. They became known as the 14K, and there are two theories as to why that are both plausible.

The first is that Kot founded the gang with just 14 members; the second is that 14 stands for the road number of their former HQ and 'K' for Kowloon, the cramped working-class area just across Victoria Harbour from the bright lights of Hong Kong's Central district. This is where the 14K first launched their various illegal operations, including loansharking, extortion, gambling, prostitution and the smuggling of both arms and people.

From Hong Kong, the 14K rapidly spread internationally – across South East Asia's myriad ethnic-Chinese communities, to the migrant Chinatowns of Europe and North America and down to Australia and into South Africa. While its stronghold remained the financial supercity of Hong Kong, it set about establishing itself in the PRC in order to take advantage of the one-party state's meteoric economic rise and the legion of criminal opportunities now available.

By 1999, just two years after the handover, the 14K had become the largest Triad organisation in the world, with an estimated membership of 25,000 foot soldiers. But they were about to be challenged again, this time in the Portuguese colonial enclave of Macao, a veritable Mecca for gambling, prostitution and money laundering, where law was lax and enforcement negligible.

Lisbon was about to hand Macao back to Beijing and the Triads were nervous once again of what communist rule

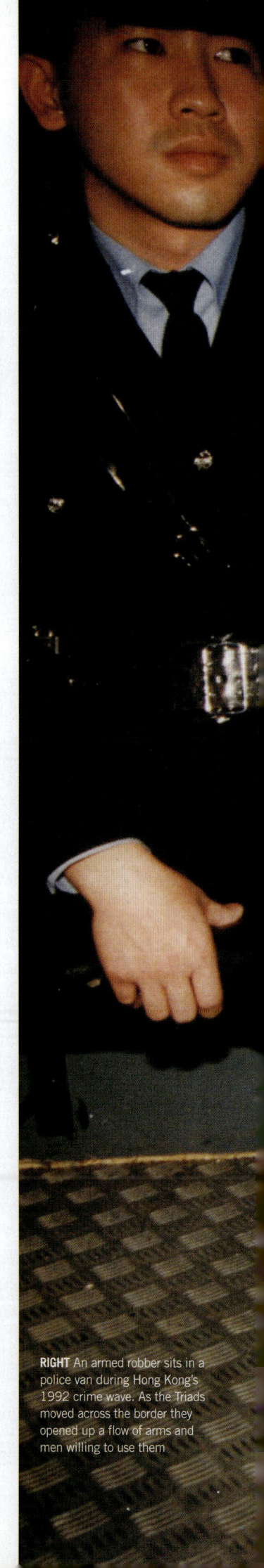

RIGHT An armed robber sits in a police van during Hong Kong's 1992 crime wave. As the Triads moved across the border they opened up a flow of arms and men willing to use them

65

ABOVE Hong Kong police launch a raid in 1992. They regularly found themselves outmatched by Triads, who often carried submachine guns

would mean. The Macao casinos were largely controlled by the Shui Fong Triad, a smaller group also based in Hong Kong. The 14K's leader, 45-year-old Wan Kuok-koi (nicknamed "Broken Tooth Koi") knew that new casino licenses were about to be issued and Macao was about to move from being a sleepy backwater of vice and gambling into a resort location open to a billion Chinese. Within a few years Macao's gaming revenues would exceed those of Las Vegas. It was a prize well worth killing for, and Broken Tooth Koi, who'd been born in the slums of Macao, declared war.

When I visited Macao in 1999 it was no longer a place to wander idly among the charming cobblestone squares and quaint street markets. It was a place to be nervous, and everyone was. When a car backfired, pedestrians involuntarily found themselves crouching in fear. That year the 14K went to war with the Shui Fong, and foot soldiers from both sides unleashed a wave of tit-for-tat assassinations – not just of each other but Portuguese gaming inspectors and local customs officers too. Their preferred modus operandi was firing machine pistols from the pillion seats of fast mopeds that could disappear quickly into the rat runs of Macao's old town. Innocent people got hit and killed; a spate of car bombings evaporated Triad leaders but also murdered tourists. The Portuguese police, just months from going home, were overwhelmed by the killing spree.

Then two things happened. One we can prove, one we can't, and probably never will. A Portuguese court convicted Broken Tooth Koi on various criminal charges, including trying to kill the police chief in Macao, and sentenced him to 15 years' imprisonment. The 14K got a lot of bad publicity and reportedly opted to downplay its Macao operations, retreating to Hong Kong to lick its wounds and re-establish a new command structure. Secondly, and this is purely a rumour, it's claimed that mainland Chinese security officials summoned the 14K and Shui Fong gang bosses and read them the riot act. Stop the killings or, after Beijing takes control on 20 December 1999, you'll face PLA hit squads.

It was just ten years since Tiananmen Square and this was a threat to be taken seriously.

Whatever the truth of events, by the time the PLA crossed the border at Zhuhai and their APCs rumbled into downtown Macao's historic Senado Square, the streets were quiet. The Triads had retreated. But it wasn't the end for the 14K. Rather it was time for a re-positioning. As China moved into Hong Kong and Macao, the 14K went in the opposite direction and started doing business in the People's Republic itself.

In 2012, Broken Tooth Koi was released from jail and returned to Macao. Police feared the worse, but nothing much happened. Things have generally been quiet in both Hong Kong and Macao over the last 25 years. Hong Kong has carried on with making money from international banking, while Macao became home to international casino operators such as Sands and MGM. Things seem orderly. Au Kam-san, a legislator in Macao, told the Hong Kong media that things would stay calm: "The only thing [the 14K] fear in the world is the Chinese Communist Party."

Looked at another way, things are far from calm, but they've changed. For most of the second half of the 20th century there was really no point in the 14K taking the risk of re-entering China. There was little to no opportunity to make money as the famines of the 1950s gave way to the prolonged political terror of the Cultural Revolution in the 1960s and '70s. With the death of Mao in 1976 change became possible, but it came slowly through the 1980s and '90s. The 14K had enough money from their old trades of extortion and prostitution, as well counterfeiting currency. They did move into new areas, ones that promised big financial

"BLOOD RAN INTO THE GUTTERS, MIXING WITH THE RAINWATER AND THE RED NEON SHINE OFF THE PAVEMENT"

THE 14K TRIAD

The Secret Language of the Triad
TRIADS TRADITIONALLY USED HAND SIGNALS TO COMMUNICATE. THESE ARE SOME OF THE MORE ELABORATE

TOP DOG
This symbol denotes the leader of a particular Triad society, such as the 14K. The Hong Kong government administration takes Triad hand signs very seriously – any movie featuring Triad hand signing is automatically classified as Category III (restricted to over-18s only).

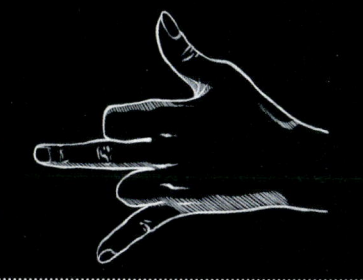

SECOND IN COMMAND
The next rung down. The use of hand signs is crucial to binding together members of the organisation and is also useful in establishing and indicating rank.

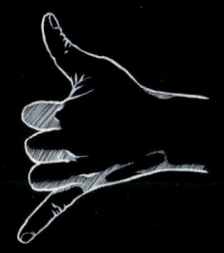

DOING TIME
A ranking official who has committed a serious crime – or is serving a prison sentence – in service of the Triad.

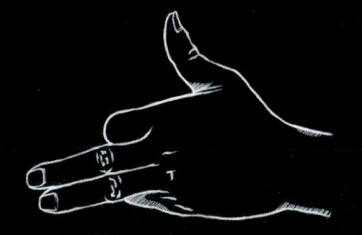

ORDINARY OFFICIAL
Another symbol meaning 'official', this time without the scars of a lengthy prison sentence.

KAI
Kai, Chi'ing, Sau and Chuk are universal and are used to communicate between Triad groups.

CHI'ING
Used together, Kai and Chi'ing indicate that an outstanding fee has been paid.

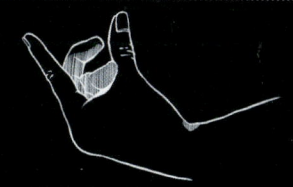

SAU & CHUK
These related gestures – Sau and Chuk – in turn indicate that the fee has been received.

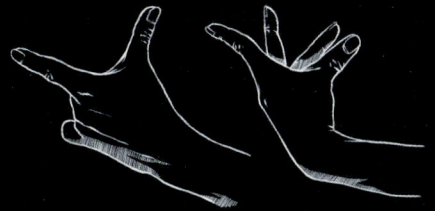

> **" ANY MOVIE FEATURING TRIAD HAND SIGNING IS AUTOMATICALLY RESTRICTED TO OVER-18S ONLY "**

rewards without massive prison sentences: pirated DVDs and fake luxury goods. Wiser to concentrate on international expansion while poverty and peasant-wracked southern China provided a steady flow of new foot soldiers to enforce the 14K's rackets and start up business in human trafficking. By the late 1990s and early 2000s, the 14K were deeply involved as 'snakeheads', with 14K operations in China as well as in key locations for people trafficking in Rotterdam, London and most major European cities. But as 21st-century China has boomed, the business opportunities have arguably become too good to miss out on.

Drugs remain a mainstay of 14K operations. After 1949, when the traditional opium and heroin routes out of China were shut down, they looked elsewhere. The collapse of the French Empire in Indo-China provided opportunities, but Ho Chi Minh's victory there eventually closed that channel. During most of the 1960s, '70s and '80s, Burma's Golden Triangle was the main supplier and processing centre for 14K heroin shipped on to Europe and North America. But now things have changed there too.

Most recently, evidence has surfaced that the 14K are concentrating on methamphetamine and ecstasy (and any

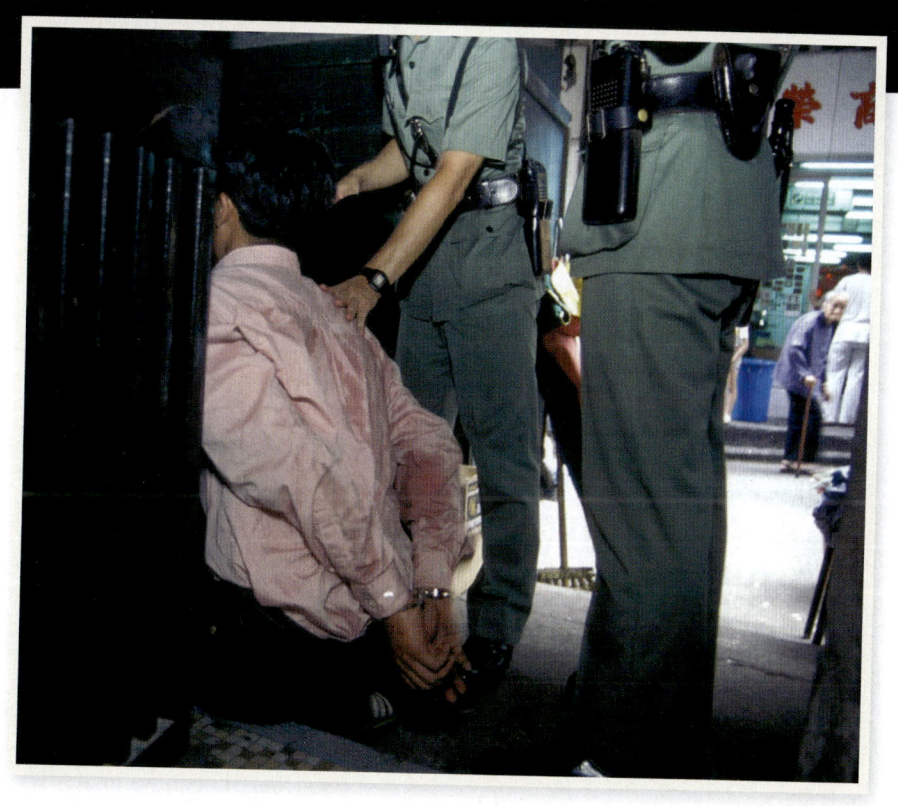

ABOVE The rougher neighbourhoods of Kowloon, across the bay from the city's prosperous Central District, is the traditional home of the 14K Triad – possibly providing them with the 'K' in their name

number of variants thereof). Where are they getting the bulk chemicals needed to mass-produce these narcotics? China, allegedly, where the 14K have bought up or opened major chemical factories to make exactly what they need to supply both the Western market and Chinese customers. China is now one of the world's biggest producers of methamphetamine, in large part thanks to the 14K.

Like all organised criminals today, it appears they are looking for low-risk scams, and the internet, especially in the form of pornography and online gambling, is the ideal hunting ground. But the 14K have also reportedly been deeply implicated in a range of health care frauds in Japan – essentially white-collar crime. Increasingly, the 14K are less obvious. Sharon Kwok, a City University of Hong Kong sociologist focusing on the Triads, says, "Many Triads have gone into more legitimate businesses." It's also true that the police have scored some major victories using 'ghosts' (undercover police that infiltrate the gangs). Lee King-wa, a Hong Kong-based author who writes about Triad issues, says the 14K now no longer have elaborate initiation rituals as they used to, as these can be used as evidence to prove membership. But they haven't gone away.

With the 14K now ensconced in mainland China and with its global network still strong, here is how a 14K deal looks these days:

The Chinese PSB raided and closed a massive chemical and methamphetamine production facility in city of Lufeng, a couple of hundred kilometres east of Hong Kong. The chemicals were en route, via Hong Kong and Manila, to supply Mexico's Sinaloa Cartel with the raw materials needed to produce crystal meth, as demand has skyrocketed in North America. Hong Kong Customs alerted American intelligence to other shipments traced back to Lufeng, and when U.S. agents raided a cockfight south of Manila, they found representatives of the Sinaloa Cartel taking possession of the chemicals. Tipped off by the Americans, the Philippines Drug Enforcement Agency raided a meth lab in Manila financed by the Mexicans and set up by the 14K. Product from the lab was being shipped to Mexico before being smuggled into the U.S.

However, the 14K don't always need partners. Shortly after the Lufeng bust, authorities in Belize intercepted a shipment of meth from China thought to be from a 14K-financed chemical factory worth an estimated $10 billion.

Things have reached a point where many analysts now believe that local Chinese Communist Party officials have entered into deals with the 14K and other Triad groups to enrich themselves. 14K-sponsored chemical works, like Lufeng, are reportedly legion in China today. Lufeng got busted on Beijing's orders because foreign intelligence and policing agencies got involved. China was embarrassed, but the manufacturing, processing and exporting of narcotics

> **"THEY ARE LOOKING FOR LOW-RISK SCAMS, AND THE INTERNET, ESPECIALLY IN THE FORM OF PORNOGRAPHY AND ONLINE GAMBLING, IS THE IDEAL HUNTING GROUND"**

THE 14K TRIAD

continues, which begs a crucial question: if the Communist Party is sometimes turning a blind eye to the 14K, what do they ask of the Triad in return?

It's likely that this disturbing question was one of many in the minds of the students who participated in the Umbrella Revolution in 2014, a series of sit-in protests across Hong Kong. Wary of the growing influence a corrupt Chinese Government was wielding over the city, protestors armed with umbrellas (their only defence against the pepper spray fired at them by the police) took to the streets to demand that Hong Kong retained a level of autonomy. Despite their peaceful methods the students soon found themselves in a troubling situation, especially those courageous enough to rebel in Mong Kok, a tough working-class district of Kowloon and long a Triad stronghold. Confronted by burly men wearing identical masks and chanting pro-Beijing slogans, the student protestors stood little chance, and many were literally pinned down by casually – perhaps professionally – violent masked assailants who warned them to 'go home'.

Most people that witnessed these attacks believe that the men were Triads, perhaps 14K, and often (to judge from their accents) from across the border in Guangdong province. They had been bussed in and specifically instructed to attack the protestors. This, many believe, was payback; part of the new deal struck between Beijing and the Triads. However, mainland China is a large country with many provinces who all have, or have had, their own organised crime syndicates. Thanks to China's relatively new freebooting capitalism there is no shortage of young men looking to emulate the success of the Triads they have seen mythologised in countless movies and comic books.

In the early 2000s, a successful chain of restaurants specialising in spicy Sichuan food appeared in Shanghai. The food was good, the prices reasonable, and it attracted the new Shanghai middle classes looking to spend their disposable income in smart places. Then one day I arrived at a local branch for lunch to meet a photographer friend. He was outside snapping pictures. The place was trashed, littered with smashed chairs and overturned tables, the long front plate-glass windows shattered. He'd arrived as it was all finishing. Just as the lunch-time rush started a dozen young men with country accents dressed in black suits with white gloves had turned up and demanded money from the owner. He had refused and they had promptly wrecked the place.

Nobody knew who they were. They weren't 14K or any other known Triad. They were just young guys coming to the city from their dirt-poor village and seeing phenomenal wealth. They wanted some and this was their way to get it. Seventy years after Kot Siu-wong formed the 14K Triad, a new generation of desperate young men were forming their own gang. Who's to say they won't be just as successful?

The Way of the Initiate
THE TRIADS ONCE HELD ELABORATE CEREMONIES TO WELCOME NEW MEMBERS

THE SUMMONING
The would-be Triad is summoned to the lodge by a notice on red paper or a strip of bamboo. The Triad lodge can be held in someone's home or the back room of a bar.

THE ENTRY
The initiate removes his shoes and socks and takes off his shirt to bare his chest before entry. He is met by three archways that he must transit en route to full membership.

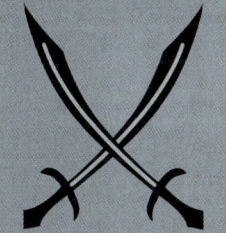

THE FIRST ARCH
The initiate must perform a ritual dance, some ritual call-and-response, and then pass through an arch of two swords. This is called 'Passing the Mountain of Knives'.

THE SECOND ARCH
On the other side of the 'Loyalty and Righteousness Hall' the initiate hands over his initiation fee in a little red envelope to a waiting official called the Vanguard.

THE THIRD ARCH
The bamboo hoop of the 'Heaven and Earth Circle' represents the initiate's rebirth into the world of the Triad.

JOURNEY TO HELL
The initiate enters the main hall and takes a symbolic journey through the underworld represented by 'The Stepping Stones', 'The Two Plank Bridge' and 'The Fiery Pit'.

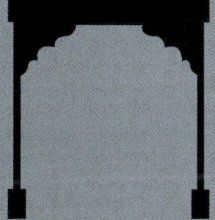

THE ALTAR
After a senior Triad reads poetry, the initiate then washes his face and dons white robes and straw sandals. The initiate recites the 36 Oaths and pledges his loyalty.

THE SACRIFICE
A chicken is slaughtered and its blood dripped into a bowl of wine. Yellow paper is burned and the ash added to the mixture. The initiate drinks it and the bowl is shattered.

The Russian Mafia

KNOWN IN THEIR MOTHERLAND AS VORY V ZAKONE OR BRATVA, THESE GANGLAND TSARS ARE NEITHER NEW KIDS ON THE BLOCK NOR CLONES OF THE FAMED COSA NOSTRA

WORDS ROBERT WALSH

What many call the Russian Mafia predates the fall of the Iron Curtain. It's existed since the time of the Tsars and survived and outlasted both the Russian Revolution and communism. Journalists and broadcasters call it the Russian Mafia in much the same way the yakuza are often called the Japanese Mafia; the term is simply more recognisable. Writers tend to use the simplest sound-bite available, but in fact Russian organised crime is very different from the original Mafia and has never been more powerful than it is today. Today's 'Mafiya' has links to the American and Sicilian mafias, the Chinese Triads, Colombian and Turkish drug traffickers and the Camorra, one of Italy's lesser-known gangs. Their rackets are many and varied: arms dealing, drug trafficking, people smuggling, extortion, gambling, loan-sharking, internet scams, fraud, murder for hire and stock market manipulation, to name a few. Anything that's profitable and illegal, Russian gangsters will do it.

Originating in the 18th century, wandering bandit gangs were opposed by both the Russian state and legitimate society. From there they evolved into a multinational criminal superpower with their own structure, secret language, history and traditions. Russia's gangland also took full advantage of communism's collapse. Originally a motley crew of bandits known as 'Vory V Zakone' (thieves-in-law) living in the 'Vorovsky Mir' (Thieves World), today they're the 'Russkaya Mafiya' (Russian Mafia) or 'Bratva' (Brotherhood).

The rules have always been simple: live entirely by crime, never do anything that helps legitimate society, the gang comes first and, above all, never inform. Recruitment was relatively simple, too. Under communism, thousands were imprisoned in the gulag, a penal network spread throughout the Soviet Union. Within the gulag prisons there evolved a criminal hierarchy with a constant supply of new recruits. A convict could enter alone and friendless but leave a fully fledged gangster with significant backing. New recruits brought with them many different skills, so everyone was able to add to their criminal repertoire. With corruption endemic among communist officials at all levels, bribery and intimidation ensured their continued survival and growth.

By communism's fall, the 'Redfellas' were already firmly entrenched. The resulting chaos gave them unlimited opportunities to become a multinational crime syndicate to rival the likes of the Triads, American and Sicilian mafias and yakuza. But using pre-existing networks, Russia's gangsters moved faster and further, developing new rackets while defending and expanding old ones. They've always been open to pursuing new forms of crime with complete disregard for the violence and bloodshed involved. What took the original Mafia centuries to achieve Russia's gangsters have established in mere decades – and they've not been fussy about how it's been achieved. They'll bribe, intimidate or kill anybody opposing them, including each other.

RIGHT With the fall of the Iron Curtain, organised crime boiled over in Russia as major players in the Vory V Zakone made moves on a weakened government

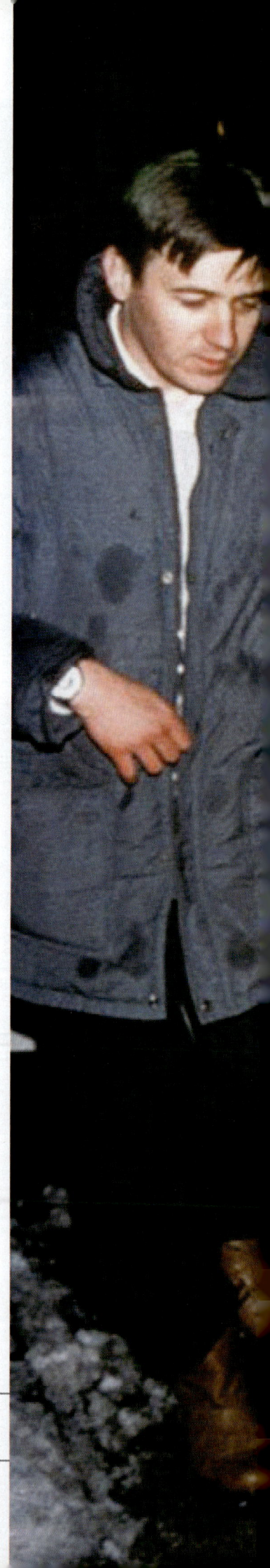

71

TOP Favourite weapons of the Russian mafia include sawn-off shotguns and, of course, the infamous AK-47

ABOVE (CIRCLE) Smuggling drugs and lucrative duty-free goods number among the Vory V Zakone's most popular rackets

The American Mafia usually avoid murdering politicians, journalists, judges, prosecutors and law enforcement officials, fearing potential consequences. The Russian gangs don't. American mobsters usually avoid especially spectacular murders, making 1929's St. Valentine's Day Massacre a part of their history, not their future. The Russian gangs don't. Murdering what American gangsters call 'civilians' (people who are not linked to organised crime) is also rare among American mafiosi, though not their arguably more brutal Sicilian counterparts.

In Western society, public hostility usually results in the authorities responding with crackdowns, which are bad for business. But what of the Russian mobsters? Believing their public image to be better served by extreme violence than discretion, they are unfazed by such acts. The more brutal and blatant their violence the better. Even families of opponents are fair game on the basis that fear generates obedience. The more people who fear them, the more obedient they become. Russian gangs deliberately choose spectacular and sadistic methods of murder, such as the Viking 'Blood Eagle', drive-by assassinations using anti-tank rockets, and even inserting a victim into a wood-chipper while they're still conscious.

On 10 November 1996, Yelena Likhodei, wife of assassinated Afghanistan veteran Mikhail Likhodei (himself murdered by a bomb exactly two years previously), died when a remote-controlled explosive was detonated during a memorial event held in honour of her slain husband. When her husband was murdered Yelena had been injured, but this time she was killed along with 12 other people. Dozens were injured by the bomb, which has been placed deliberately at Likhodei's graveside by mobsters. Crime is their stock-in-trade, extreme brutality their everyday hallmark.

Unlike the American or Sicilian mafias, Russia's gangs lack a clearly defined structure. A Mafia boss runs the family. Below him is his 'consigliere' (adviser). Below the consigliere ranks an underboss who commands 'caporegimes' (captains). Each 'capo' leads a 'borgata' (crew) of 'soldatos' (soldiers), the lowest-ranking full members of the organisation. At the very bottom of the heap are associates. The associates are either aspiring members or professional criminals who don't want full membership or can't have it because they lack Italian blood on both sides of their family. Henry Hill (of *Goodfellas* notoriety) was only ever an associate due to his mixed Sicilian-Irish parentage, meaning Hill could never have become a full member, or 'made man'.

Russian gangs work on a more fluid basis, making it harder to identify their members. The structure varies between gangs, with an estimated 6,000 gangs operating in Russia amid constantly changing alliances and feuds. It's extremely difficult to define a single gang's structure, let alone which gangs are allies and which are at war with each other. Broadly speaking, a Russian 'godfather' is a 'pakhan.' His chief advisor (similar to a consigliere) is a 'Sovietnik'. Below him is a 'kassir' or 'kaznachey', the gang's 'fixer' for bribing police, lawyers, judges, civil servants, legitimate businessmen and politicians. A brigadier is broadly similar to a capo. A 'boevik' is a senior enforcer controlling other enforcers, assassins and bodyguards known respectively as 'kryshas', 'torpedos' and 'byki'. The lowest rank is 'shestyorka', broadly similar to an associate. Shestyorka aren't full members, merely low-level crooks used for menial tasks.

This structure makes it much harder for law enforcement to fight them. America's RICO (Racketeer Influenced and Corrupt Organisations) laws were purpose built to combat conventional organised crime groups like the Mafia and outlaw biker gangs. They've proven less effective against Russian mobsters indicted in the U.S. Even convicted Russian mobsters have usually served relatively short sentences in American prisons (which they regard as kindergartens compared to gulag prisons) before being deported back to Russia. Russia lacks similar anti-gangster laws and, courtesy of endemic corruption, these gangsters are unlikely to face prosecution anyway.

You might also think that recruits to Russian organised crime come entirely from the underworld. They don't. Communism's collapse spelled redundancy for thousands among the Soviet armed forces and intelligence organisations like the GRU (Main Intelligence Directorate) and KGB (Committee for State Security). Facing such a stark reality, many former military and intelligence members joined Russia's underworld. Some bosses are even former KGB officers. They have transferable skills in corruption, bribery, blackmail, extortion and intelligence gathering and are willing to order assassinations. Former armed forces personnel also join, including members of Spetsnaz (special forces) who operate as both bodyguards and assassins. Even members of the KGB's feared Alpha Teams (responsible for what the KGB politely called 'direct action' or 'special tasks') have been known to hire themselves out.

Russian gangsters are often clearly identifiable by a selection of tattoos, whereas, in the American and Sicilian mafias, tattoos are strictly forbidden. Like the inkings favoured by the yakuza and Latin American gangs like MS-13 and the Mexican Mafia (also unrelated to their American and

> **"YOU MIGHT ALSO THINK THAT RECRUITS TO RUSSIAN ORGANISED CRIME COME ENTIRELY FROM THE UNDERWORLD. THEY DON'T"**

THE RUSSIAN MAFIA

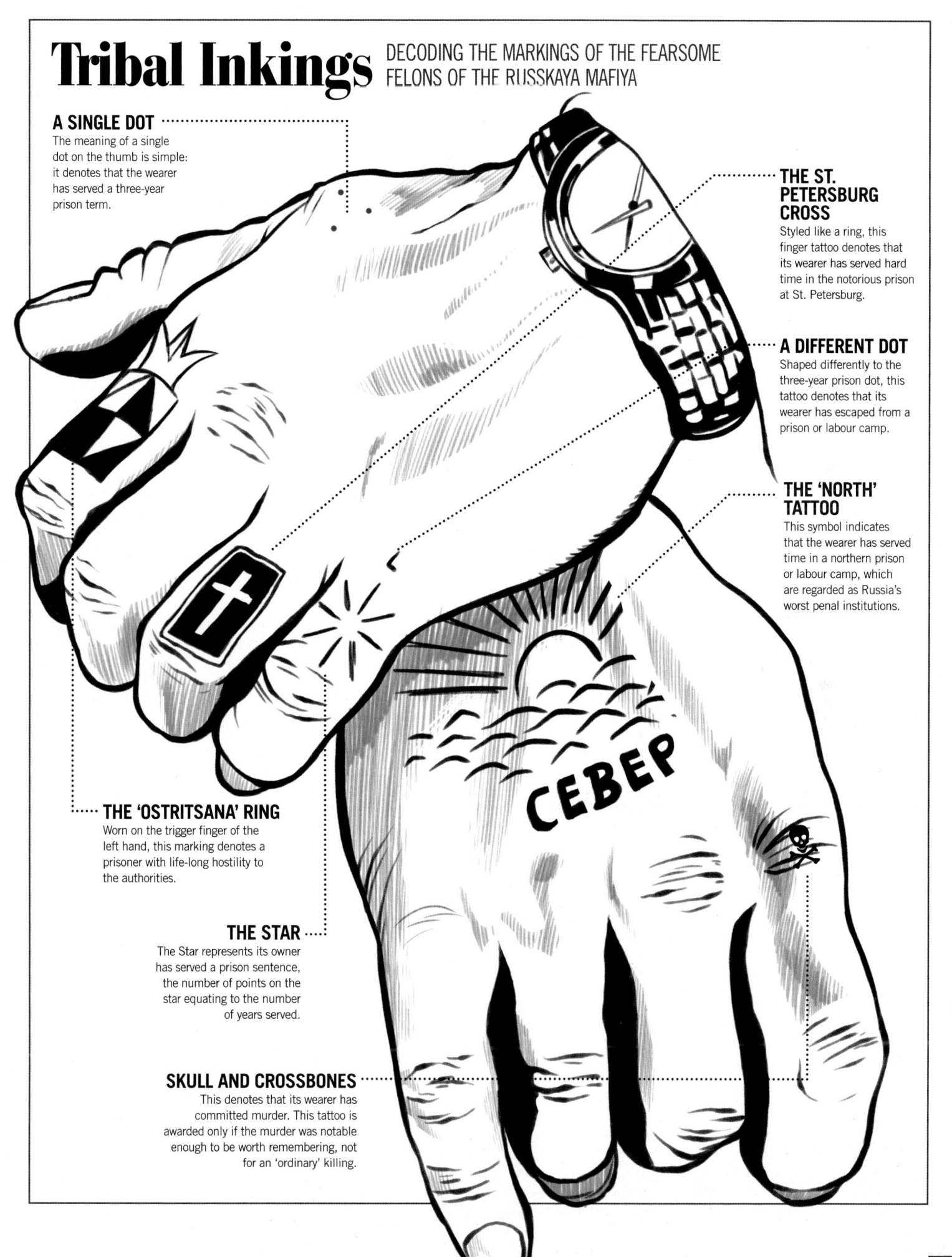

Tribal Inkings
DECODING THE MARKINGS OF THE FEARSOME FELONS OF THE RUSSKAYA MAFIYA

A SINGLE DOT
The meaning of a single dot on the thumb is simple: it denotes that the wearer has served a three-year prison term.

THE ST. PETERSBURG CROSS
Styled like a ring, this finger tattoo denotes that its wearer has served hard time in the notorious prison at St. Petersburg.

A DIFFERENT DOT
Shaped differently to the three-year prison dot, this tattoo denotes that its wearer has escaped from a prison or labour camp.

THE 'NORTH' TATTOO
This symbol indicates that the wearer has served time in a northern prison or labour camp, which are regarded as Russia's worst penal institutions.

THE 'OSTRITSANA' RING
Worn on the trigger finger of the left hand, this marking denotes a prisoner with life-long hostility to the authorities.

THE STAR
The Star represents its owner has served a prison sentence, the number of points on the star equating to the number of years served.

SKULL AND CROSSBONES
This denotes that its wearer has committed murder. This tattoo is awarded only if the murder was notable enough to be worth remembering, not for an 'ordinary' killing.

73

Sicilian counterparts), every tattoo has a meaning. A spider's web pointing upwards denotes an active member, while a downward-pointing web indicates a retired gangster. A strand of barbed wire on the forehead indicates its wearer has been in prison, with the number of barbs signifying the number of years served. A cat's head signifies good luck. A tattoo of the Waffen SS insignia shows the wearer may harbour fascist sympathies. A skull highlights that they have committed murder.

Despite their sense of tradition and heritage when it comes to inking themselves, Russian gangs have been quick to move with the times, recruiting computer experts and hackers to enable them to commit internet fraud and online extortion. Accountants and economists launder money and abuse the international banking system. Members of entirely legitimate businesses like drug companies, shipping companies, airlines and banks are recruited to further international and domestic rackets such as smuggling drugs, arms and people. Broader recruitment gives Russian gangs a reach that extends far beyond Russia's borders. Officials in every branch of public life are also employed secretly, often taking huge bribes to award government contracts to outwardly legitimate businesses secretly run by gangsters through squeaky-clean front men. Judges, politicians, civil servants, lawyers and law enforcement officers have been recruited to the point that one estimate suggests that nearly 40 per cent of Russia's wealth has been accumulated by the criminal underworld. Endemic corruption at all levels has made that possible.

The American and Sicilian mafias also lacked the collapse of communism, when the former Soviet Union suddenly became a gangster's paradise, allowing them unprecedented expansion at home and abroad. Under communism they developed and controlled the black market, taking advantage of communism's inability to provide many Russians with even basic essentials. Working with corrupt communist officials, they supplied food, medical equipment, fuel and anything else that Russians were willing and able to pay for. While the original mafias have always employed corrupt public officials, Russian gangsters have far greater access. Their reach extends from the top of Russian society right down to the officer on the beat. In Russia corruption is endemic and far greater than in the U.S. or Sicily.

Russian gangsters have proved expert at infiltrating legitimate businesses, bribing or threatening legitimate businessmen into co-operating and murdering those who refuse. Computer fraud, using hackers to rob banks and businesses, or extortion by threatening to destroy company websites unless ransoms are paid is a particular speciality. It's a highly lucrative racket that the original Mafias have been relatively slow to exploit. While Sicilian and American gangsters have largely stuck to committing traditional gangland crimes, Russians have quickly developed modern, hi-tech rackets that utilise the unique social and political conditions of today's Russia, which given the current state of global affairs sparked by the war in Ukraine is an ever-shifting landscape of opportunity.

Another major difference is the relative lack of ex-members becoming informants or giving evidence at trials. The Sicilian Mafia has seen some former members betray them, notably Tommaso Buscetta. They call reformed mafiosi 'pentiti' (repentant). The American Mafia, on the other hand, has seen increasing numbers of mafiosi become informants and witnesses. Usually, American mafiosi wanting to make deals sign a formal agreement with Federal or State law enforcement. Then they testify at trials of their former colleagues before vanishing into the Witness Protection Programme under false identities.

ABOVE The gangs of the Vory V Zakone were forged in Stalin's gulags, where prisoners got tough or died

Some familiar names include Joe Valachi, whose testimony before a U.S. Senate committee lifted the lid on the American Mafia, forcing FBI director J. Edgar Hoover to finally admit that it actually existed. Henry Hill, although only a Mafia associate and never a made man, testified against many fellow mobsters. Salvatore "Sammy the Bull" Gravano testified against legendary boss (and former friend) John Gotti (after Gotti betrayed him), among many others. Gravano then hugely embarrassed authorities when, while living in Arizona under a false identity, he earned a 20-year sentence for dealing drugs to school children.

Russian mobsters are far less likely to 'rat'. Not going through a wood-chipper or suffering the Viking 'blood eagle' ritual (also known as the 'Viking's revenge') doubtless proves persuasive, but there are other reasons. If convicted abroad, most other countries' prisons are far less unpleasant. Gulag veterans regard British or American prisons as akin to holiday camps compared to their Russian equivalents. If they're extradited to Russia, a big enough bribe or threat usually secures their release via 'legal technicalities' or suspiciously easy jailbreaks. In Russia, money and fear speak loudest.

All in all, the Russian Mafia doesn't exist in the same sense as its Italian or American predecessors. In fact, it doesn't exist in the same form at all. Between 'Goodfellas' and 'Redfellas' there are vast cultural, historic and social differences. They're similar only in their criminal occupation. With over 500,000 members spread across more than 50 nations, there's certainly no contest when it comes to which organisation has the biggest reach.

ABOVE Located in the Russian village of Kuchino, Perm-36 is the only museum in Russia to have been created on the site of a former gulag camp. It speaks to the conditions faced by Russian convicts

THE RUSSIAN MAFIA

"GULAG VETERANS REGARD BRITISH OR AMERICAN PRISONS AS AKIN TO HOLIDAY CAMPS COMPARED TO THEIR RUSSIAN EQUIVALENTS"

The Mafia's Wrath
METHODS ENLISTED TO PUNISH DISOBEDIENCE CAN ALMOST GUARANTEE NO COPY-CAT BETRAYALS

THE 'VIKING'S REVENGE'
Also called the Viking 'blood eagle', this is the most feared punishment for any gangster who informs. Victims are pinioned face-down. An imperial eagle is then cut into their back with a sword or machete. Their ribs are then removed, their lungs placed either side of their body and their entrails torn out. If possible, the victim is kept alive and conscious throughout this horrendous punishment.

ROCKET LAUNCHER DRIVE-BY
Anti-tank rockets are freely available to Russian mobsters – and they certainly make use of them. A vehicle simply drives slowly past the victim's home or business while a hitman stands up, takes aim and launches the rocket into the building through a door or window. It's not exactly a subtle method of assassination, but it certainly makes a powerful statement.

THE WOOD-CHIPPER
An industrial wood-chipper is useful if you're a tree surgeon or gardener (or if you're the Coen brothers looking for a cool plot device for your movie, i.e. *Fargo*). It's equally useful for punishing anybody who defies Russian gangsters or steals from them. The victim is abducted and fed through the wood-chipper. They're usually fed slowly, feet-first and still conscious in order to prolong their suffering.

The World's Weirdest Gangs

WORDS BEE GINGER

IT AIN'T ALL GUNS, DRUGS AND BANK ROBBERIES – SOME GANGS ARE OUT FOR FAR STRANGER THINGS

When we think of gangs, our minds tend to imagine smart-suited gangsters speaking in hushed tones, an air of intrigue about them as they enjoy an espresso outside a trattoria in Naples, lit cigarette in hand, hidden weapon in the inside pocket of a finely tailored jacket. There are some gangs, however, that are so unusual that fitting them into any mould would be a struggle.

These strange denizens of the underworld have a truly unique style of their own, bizarre methods and targets that we will explore here. To put it bluntly, these criminals found their niche and didn't hold back from wringing everything they could out of it.

THE WORLD'S WEIRDEST GANGS

Piranhas
◉ VENEZUELA

We live in an age where beauty has become not only an obsession but big business. The South America nation of Venezuela is a prime example of where society's hunger for beauty and products has gone too far. For it is in these crowded streets that the Piranhas roam in search of hair. Yes, you read that right. These street gangs will spot their prey and attack their victims from behind by cutting off their hair. The motive behind these aggressive assaults? The hair will be sold on the black market and to hair salons, where it will be fashioned into hair extensions that can be sold on for hundreds of dollars. Piranhas may look innocuous as they stroll along the street or hang around in shopping centres, but they are wielding concealed scissors and constantly on the lookout for a high quality product to innocently pass by. The problem has become so bad that many people have begun to take preventative measures by shaving their heads and donating their hair to children's cancer charities.

Sakawa Boys
◉ GHANA

In recent years Western Africa has become known for one thing, and unfortunately it's not its impressive landscape or awe-inspiring wildlife. It is fraud, which has become big business, particularly in Ghana, a nation of almost 33 million that boasts large gangs of internet fraudsters and highly lucrative criminal swindles. You might well have received a few emails yourself promising large sums of inherited money or found other similar phishing scams in your junk folder.

One of the biggest scams – and the most favoured of the Sakawa Boys – is pulled off inside online chat rooms, where they pose as attractive Westerners to lure their victims in the name of love. This is also known as catfishing, and these boys have dedicated their whole lives not to the pursuit of love but cold hard cash.

Business is so profitable that there are actually schools where Ghanaian teenagers attend classes to learn the trade from the 'experts'. Sakawa is a way of life for these youngsters, the name being a term for accumulating large amounts of money. They wear their ill-gotten gains as a badge of honour, dressing in flashy clothes and driving expensive cars. The situation has become an epidemic in the country, one that the government has so far been unable to combat.

77

Sukebans
📍 JAPAN

They might look like innocent school girls, but don't be fooled, for the Sukebans of Japan are just waiting to cause trouble. Originating in the 1960s, these girl gangs had a reputation for smoking, skipping school and generally behaving like delinquents. Over time, however, crimes like shoplifting overtook time in the classroom, and with it came drug offences and violence. School uniforms were covered in gang symbols and the members dyed their hair in vibrant colours. One of the largest groups in the 1970s, the Kanto Women's Delinquent Alliance, boasted an incredible 20,000 members, and although numbers began to decline in the 1980s and 90s, recent reports suggest they could once again be on the rise.

The Dinner Set Gang
📍 NEW YORK CITY, U.S.

From the music to the fashion, not to mention major societal reforms and global events, the 1960s and '70s were an exciting time to be alive. They were also decades in which lavish dinner parties were commonly laid on by New York's leading families, and it was these swanky soirees that piqued the interest of the aptly named Dinner Set Gang.

This trio, which comprised Dominick Latella and Pete Salerno (brothers not only in crime but married to two twin sisters) plus getaway driver Carmine Stanzione, targeted rich New Yorkers while they were hosting an evening meal with friends. These dinners could last all night, meaning the rest of the house would be unattended, leaving the gang plenty of time to break in and loot the joint. This brazen crime provided easy pickings, and with many of the properties being situated on the water, escape by boat was easy.

Known as the 'Fat Cats' by law enforcement, the gang identified their targets in the pages of *Town and Country*, *Architectural Digest* and *Forbes*, following the money from Palm Beach to New England coinciding with the social season and disposing of their shoes on the highway to avoid detection.

Rumoured to have stolen an estimated $150 million in cash and jewellery from some of the country's wealthiest families, including the Macys, Pillsburys, Du Ponts and even the entertainer Liberace, the Dinner Set Gang took some time out from burglaries during the 1980s but resumed their enterprise in the '90s, when they were finally arrested.

Chewing Gum Gangs
📍 BRITAIN AND EASTERN EUROPE

Granted, the name is a little difficult to take seriously, but for newsagents across Britain this was a crime wave no one saw coming. The year was 2012, and the country was witnessing a large influx of Romanian immigrants, a very small minority of whom had one thing in mind: gum – and lots of it. Soon large quantities of chewing gum were being stolen from supermarkets and shops countrywide. But why would these thieves snatch gum instead of a host of other goods? The reason is that in Romania chewing gum is used as a form of currency in certain situations. For example, when paying for a low-value item with a note, the seller may give you a stick or packet of gum in lieu of change.

Now this spell of sticky behaviour might not sound like something worth spitting your, well, gum out about, but in fact it became big business, with numerous criminal gangs smuggling the gum across the sea to Europe where it was used as a cash substitute on the Romanian streets. Gang members who were caught faced the full force of the law, with jail terms and fines (which couldn't be settled with gum) handed down.

THE WORLD'S WEIRDEST GANGS

The Notorious Nipple Gang
📍 THAILAND

Although the name might elicit a snigger, the grift of this gang is not only cunning but airs on the side of sinister. Made up from a group of sex workers selling their services across the country, the scheme is simple: entice a punter (usually a man and most often a tourist), take them back to their hotel room or lodging and take them to bed. So far, so simple you think. Well, here comes the part where the gang earns its name: prior to finding a target, the sex workers applied a liquid sedative to their breast called Rohypnol, more commonly known as a date rape drug. Once the punter has tasted this powerful sedative it doesn't take long until he is rendered unconscious, and the moment he's out cold the sex worker will rob him blind and then quickly flee the scene of the crime.

Outlaws on the Open Road

82
THE HIGHWAY TO HELL

88
MEET THE MONGOL HORDE OF AMERICA

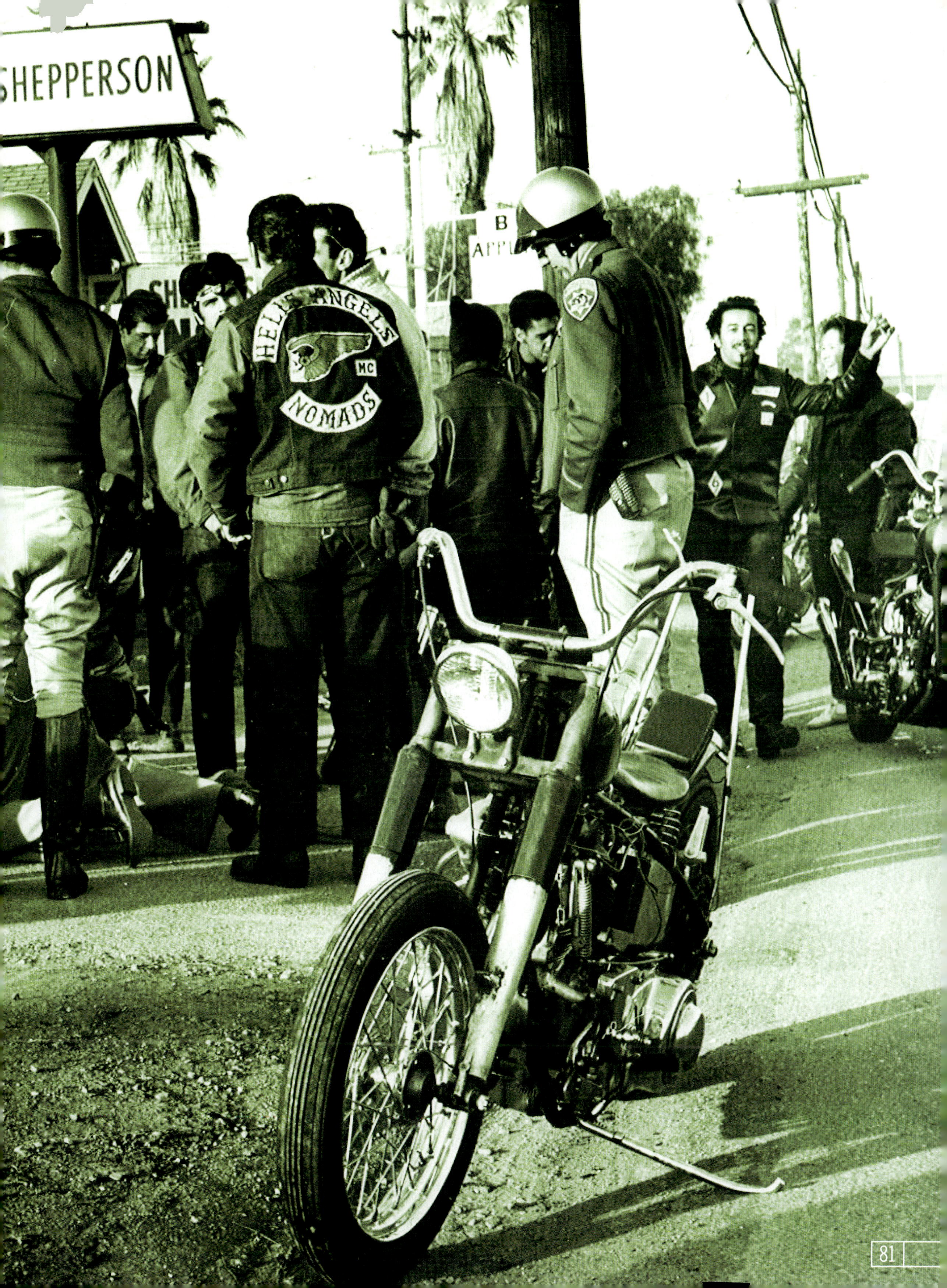
SHEPPERSON
HELLS ANGELS
MC
NOMADS

Christie (in the centre) founded the Ventura chapter of the Hells Angels and served as its president. His crew was a tough, tight bunch that was always ready to throw down – with their president's consent

The Highway to Hell

THE ROCK STARS OF THE MOTORCYCLE OUTLAW CLUB CIRCUIT ARE BOLD, BRASH AND IN EQUAL TERMS RECKLESS. FORMER HELLS ANGELS PRESIDENT GEORGE CHRISTIE TALKS ABOUT THE ORIGINAL 'ONE PERCENTERS'

WORDS SETH FERRANTI

Every year, tens of thousands of Harley-Davidson-riding, leather jacket-clad bikers storm into South Dakota, bombarding the state for the Sturgis Motorcycle Rally, the largest biker gathering in the world. The town's population explodes as groups of wild men on motorcycles boom down the highways and commence drinking, drugging and raising hell. The rally attracts its share of motorcycle enthusiasts and weekend warriors showing off their new Harley-Davidsons or latest biker accessories, but to thousands of Hells Angels – members of the United States' most notorious motorcycle club – it's not a once-a-year vacation, it's a way of life.

Ever since World War II, California has been strangely plagued by a gang of, in the words of Hunter S. Thompson, "…filthy, frenzied, boozed-up motorcycle hoodlums called the Hells Angels". They were formed in 1948 by the Bishop family and Otto Friedli, bikers who most likely ran amok at the Hollister biker riots that inspired Marlon Brando's 1954 film *The Wild One*. The Hells Angels took its name from a World War II bomber squadron that adopted the nom de guerre from Howard Hughes 1930 movie *Hell's Angels*, at the same time as the club embraced the "one percenter" label thrust on to them by the media after the Hollister riots. The American Motorcycle Association had declared that "99 per cent of motorcycle riders are law-abiding citizens and only one per cent are outlaws."

"I was introduced to the Hells Angels, who were at the top of the food chain in the outlaw bike culture. To hang out with them and to be recognised by them was everything if you were trying to live in that culture, so it was like being on top of the world for me," 30-year Hells Angels veteran George Christie, who was president of the Los Angeles and Ventura chapter and wrote a book about his time with the club, *Exile On Front Street*, tells us. "A young man hanging out with the most recognised and notorious outlaw bike club in the world – it was like living a dream, like running away and joining the circus. I ran away and I joined the Hells Angels."

The emblem for the club is the winged death head, an angry looking skull that wears a helmet with feathers streaming behind it. It screams, "Don't fuck with the Angels or we'll eat you alive." These patches are 'the colours' of the club, denote membership and are sewn on the back of denim or leather jackets. Another patch is adorned beneath the emblem with the local chapter name, which is usually the city or locale where the chapter has its home base in.

Law enforcement has long claimed that the most universal common denominator in identification of a Hells Angel is the way they appear – long hair, beards and lots of tattoos, denim and leather clad, like modern-day Viking warriors come to life riding mechanical steeds that thunder down the highway in a disciplined formation, carrying an impending sense of chaotic revelry before them like heavy metal knights. Brimming with brazen confidence and a total lack of regard for anyone or anything that has the audacity to get in their way, including law enforcement, a typical member rides on average 30,000 kilometres (18,641 miles) a year.

"People don't wake up every day and go, 'Gee, what kind of crimes can I commit today?' It doesn't work that way,"

ABOVE Rolling into cities 100 or more bikes at a time, the Hells Angels are an event to witness, but the residents of the places they visit often fear the worst

Christie explains. But the MC has lived up to its lawless image over the years with tons of fully patched members, prospects, associates and hangers-on being arrested and convicted for crimes like drug trafficking, weapons possession, assault, bombings, arson and even murder. Remarkably, in 1969, the Hells Angels allegedly planned to kill Rolling Stones singer Mick Jagger after he criticised members of the MC for stabbing a spectator to death at the infamous California Altamont Speedway show, where the Hells Angels were hired to provide security.

Due to their rapid growth in California, the Hells Angels became embroiled in a series of turf wars with different outlaw motorcycle groups, all of them competing to seize the crown as the most formidable gang. It battled the Mongols for years to control California. It's a running war that is still going on today and has claimed numerous lives through the bombings of enemy clubhouses, highway shootings and even attacks at biker funerals. Christie was in charge of the Los Angeles and Ventura chapters in Southern California when the beef erupted with the Mongols. This dispute originally started over a woman, quickly escalated into a blood feud and then made the news, most famously when three bikers were killed during a massive brawl at a Nevada casino in 2002 between the Hells Angels and Mongols.

> **"THIS DISPUTE ORIGINALLY STARTED OVER A WOMAN, QUICKLY ESCALATED INTO A BLOOD FEUD AND THEN MADE THE NEWS"**

"I realised in the early to mid-1980s that these guys were in it for the long haul and we tried to take the position that we were going to run them out of existence… there was no way that I ever thought that was going to happen after the first couple of battles," Christie says. "There was a sit down immediately after the first fight, which I thought as a leader was a bad idea. I told them let's let them stew on this a few days, let's just don't go sit down. The Mongols put the rocker on. They got machine guns on their bikes. I think it was kind of a wake-up call for them to see that they could challenge us. I think then and there the Mongols decided, 'Hey, you know what, we're going to dig in and we're not going anywhere,' and that's what they did. People got shot off their bikes. There were explosions. A 15-year-old kid got blown up."

For years the Hells Angels remained a California thing, but in 1961 the first international chapter was founded in Auckland, New Zealand. The Justice Department reports that the Hells Angels has around 2,500 patched members in over 250 chapters around the world. More than 100 of those chapters exist in the U.S., but internationally the Hells Angels chapters have been known to get very deadly very quickly. They handle their business as efficiently as Colombian sicarios backed by that big time cartel money.

"It's not like we were drug lords and we were fighting over control of this and control of that. It wasn't about that at all," says Christie.

"That's how a lot of the guys got themselves into trouble over the years, you know, they would become so intoxicated with the power they would make the rules up as they went along. And for an organisation that's supposed to be secret, all of a sudden our business was out on the street."

THE HIGHWAY TO HELL

Legions of the Damned

THEY'RE THE MOST WELL-KNOWN – AND MOST FEARED – MC IN THE WORLD, AND TODAY THE HELLS ANGELS HAVE CHAPTERS ON ALMOST EVERY CONTINENT

NORTH AMERICA – 117 CHAPTERS
The original motorcycle club chapter – Hells Angels MC Berdoo – is now over 75 years old and has spawned an iconic piece of Americana. George Christie formed California's Ventura chapter in 1978.

EUROPE – 251 CHAPTERS
Despite sharing a similar culture to the U.S., Britain took its time adopting the Hells Angels, the London chapter appearing in 1969. In 2008, the gang clashed with members of the Outlaws in an airport terminal in Birmingham.

ASIA – 13 CHAPTERS
The gang has translated its brand of anarchy less successfully to geographic Asia. The Night Wolves, Moscow's patriotic answer to the Hells Angels, is Russia's most popular MC and has strong support from President Putin.

SOUTH AMERICA – 25 CHAPTERS
The Hells Angels were exported to South America in 1993, with the Manaus chapter in Brazil. In terms of criminal enterprise, it made sense: the biker gang has had a long history of dealing with the drug cartels.

AFRICA – 11 CHAPTERS
In the same year the MC got a foothold in Latin America, the Hells Angels made the jump across the ocean to South Africa, proving that the brand was successfully transcending culture and language barriers.

AUSTRALASIA – 23 CHAPTERS
Arriving early in the MC's history, New Zealand's Auckland chapter popped up in 1961. It was the Hells Angels' fourth chapter and its first founded outside California, let alone the U.S.

Protecting the Patch
ONLY FOR THE GLORY OF THE CLUB

To a Hells Angel, their patch (their 'colours') is the most important thing in their possession. Wearing the patch on a jacket or saying that you are a Hells Angel carries a lot of weight, and some people take advantage of that for their own benefit, which is something the club won't tolerate.

"There was a guy in Los Angeles selling drugs with a Hells Angels patch," Christie says. "I waited for the guy in his car and I stuck a gun behind his ear. We took him out to the desert and he said he didn't have a patch, but we knew he did. When he saw that if he didn't take us back to get the patch he wasn't going to come back, he told us where it was. The cops put their own spin on it, the newspapers put their own spin on it and the district attorneys put their own spin on it."

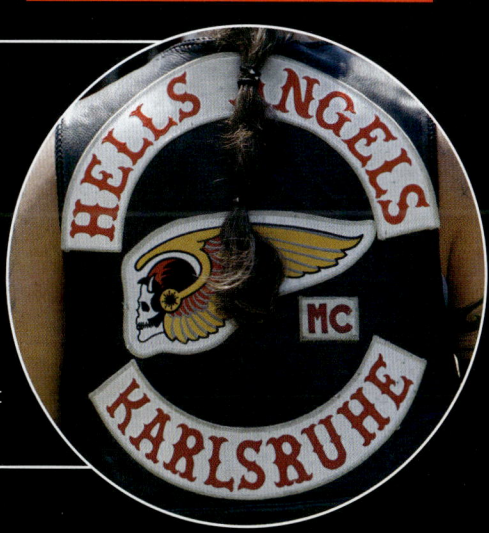

ABOVE The Hells Angels is the most notorious motorcycle club in the world. It has chapters and members in many countries outside the U.S.

BELOW George Christie in front of all his troops. His peers in the Hells Angels criticised him for bringing in younger members, but Christie thought the club needed new blood

The Quebec Biker War erupted in 1994 and lasted until 2002. The war saw multiple outlaw motorcycle gangs in Quebec and Montreal, Canada, battle for supremacy in the northern winterland. It pitted the Hells Angels against the Rock Machine and its allies. Law enforcement claims that 162 deaths can be attributed to this bloody battle royale waged for the right to be king of the Canadian biker scene. The most notorious Canadian Hells Angel was Maurice "Mom" Boucher, who served as president of the club and was found guilty in 1997 of murdering prison guards in his mad attempt to control the drug trade inside Canada's prison system and destabilise the justice system as a whole.

The Hells Angels has officially become a brand in the U.S., a trend that is spreading to its international chapters. The MC has cornered the market on being bad-asses, and if someone misrepresents the winged death-head emblem, the organisation isn't above taking legal action. In the U.S., the Hells Angels has 18 trademark registrations covering different variations of the death-head icon and additional trademark registrations in over a dozen more countries. Despite their free-spirited and even criminal legacy, the Hells Angels is now technically a business, and a legal one at that.

The Hells Angels sued the makers of the Hollywood movie *Wild Hogs* for copyright infringement. Other defendants have included Amazon, Toys 'R' Us, Walt Disney and Marvel Comics. Over the years the MC has translated its pop-culture image of heavily muscled and tattooed men in leather vests on motorcycles into a brand that is emblazoned across T-shirts, sunglasses, liquor, coffee mugs, and more. With plenty of legitimate interests to protect, the former biker outlaws must now call upon the same system that they've profoundly distrusted since their inception.

With the club being a staple of pop culture today, it's a big target for law enforcement, who are attempting to rebrand the Hells Angels from a biker club to a biker mafia. Federal agents are always trying to infiltrate the organisation. The MC has been infiltrated numerous times, leading to more in-depth background checks on prospects. References from prison are a plus. Private investigators are hired to fact check a new recruit's background claims. Christie dealt with many undercovers trying to sneak in.

"The cops that come, and their goal is to infiltrate, you know, become part of the situation," Christie says. "To me that's part of the game and you have to be aware of that. I was always really cautious about the people that came around the club and how I interacted with them. The thing is if I couldn't trace somebody back to their childhood, I really didn't want to make a close acquaintance with them. One of the things in Ventura, we pretty much could follow everybody back through a childhood friend and kind of know where they've been and what they've done."

Running investigations on the Hells Angels and other MCs has largely been the ATF's domain. An agent said the Hells Angels "…operate like a criminal organisation with a global infrastructure and a lot of money they can generate from members worldwide. If you go up against the Hells Angels to prove they are a racketeering enterprise, they do have the resources to fight tooth and nail and all the way to the end. You do not usually see those dynamics in street gangs like the Crips and Bloods."

Christie added, "A lot of these federal agents move to a town and they make an effort to come around an outlaw bike club. The next thing you know, they're riding with them, and I think it really falls back on the club members that they probably should have been more cautious and more prudent in what they were doing.

"I have much more disrespect for someone who betrays his friends by testifying against them than a cop that tried to infiltrate. I just kind of see that as their job, and it may sound odd to a lot of people, but I have more problems with a club member that flips because he got himself in a jam than a police officer that infiltrated an organisation. If you really stop and think about it – I'm not saying respect them or I want to be like them – I'm just saying it's a pretty ballsy move."

> **OVER THE YEARS THE MC HAS TRANSLATED ITS POP CULTURE IMAGE OF HEAVILY MUSCLED AND TATTOOED MEN IN LEATHER VESTS ON MOTORCYCLES INTO A BRAND**

Five years ago the State Department and the Department of Homeland Security placed the Hells Angels and other MCs on its criminal hot list, which included criminal organisations like the American Mafia, Triads and yakuza of Japan. This move made it more difficult for foreign members to enter the States for bike rallies and MC events.

Today's Hells Angels range from 70-year-old career criminals to 30-year-old professionals. But the loyalty that brought the MC together in the first place is still there, despite the infiltrations and targets on their backs.

"The way the system is set up nowadays, if you're making ends meet, you're lucky and you're satisfied in your daily routine and regimen just to make ends meet," Christie sighs. "I don't know, maybe I'm paranoid, but to me that's part of the system and the way it is set up. You know, you're so focused on making ends meet and feeding your family and putting a roof over their head that you don't have time to question people or raise your voice about things you don't believe or don't feel is right.

"I'm the same guy I always was. If it got right down to it and I had to take the law into my own hands, I probably would. I still don't feel comfortable calling 911, and I haven't yet and I don't think I ever will."

Old habits truly die hard, but in an ever-changing world you can't blame some for trying to keep them alive.

Meet the Mongol Horde of America

TAKING ITS NAME FROM GENGHIS KHAN, THE MONGOL MOTORCYCLE CLUB HAS LIVED UP TO ITS MONIKER WITH A BRUTALITY REMINISCENT OF THE LEGENDARY MONGOLIAN WARLORD

WORDS SETH FERRANTI

Anti-social and violent, the Mongols motto is "Respect Few, Fear None". Originally formed in Montebello, California, on 5 December 1969 after being refused membership into the Hells Angels due their Hispanic heritage, the 15 original Mongols were military veterans who loved to ride their Harley Davidsons. The soldiers coming home from Vietnam were looking for a niche, and they found it with the formation of the club.

The club's colours are black and white. Their patch is a member of the Mongol horde of ancient times riding a Harley Davidson. With a heavy presence in Southern California, the Mongols have grown exponentially over the years and now have chapters all over the United States and even in several foreign countries. With about 1,500 club members world wide, the majority – about 800 – reside in the club's Southern California stomping grounds. What they lack in numbers they make up for with continual doses of ultra-violence.

"A majority of the Mongols membership consists of Hispanic males who live in the Los Angeles area, and many are former street gang members with a long history of using violence to settle grievances," a Bureau of Alcohol, Tobacco and Firearms (ATF) report said about them. The ATF considers the Mongols the most violent motorcycle club in the United States of America. The Mongols have allied themselves with the Bandidos, Outlaws, Sons of Silence and the Pagans to compete for territory and members with the Hells Angels, the report stated.

The one-percenter outlaw motorcycle club that law enforcement accuses of being a criminal syndicate exists in an alpha-male-dominated culture where brotherhood, family and community is valued and cherished. Members claim that while it is a secret society it is not necessarily a criminal one, despite being targeted by the federal government. Clashes with police and other biker gangs, like the Hells Angels, have cemented the Mongols' reputation.

Major players in the drug trade within the club have been accused of running meth, cocaine and heroin and are suspected of having connections to the Mexican cartels. Gun-running, grand theft motorcycle and other crimes like robbery, extortion, money laundering, murder, assault and firearms violations have been the club's M.O. the feds claim.

The current president says the club is not a criminal enterprise and that they've changed their code of conduct, even kicking out drug abusers and criminals.

But that goes against one of the main patches they sport on their colours: "Mongols Forever, Forever Mongols". With a presence in 14 states and international chapters in 18 countries, the club gives out patches like the Boy Scouts give out merit badges. The skull patch represents criminal violence performed as a service to the club. They even have a catch-all emergency signal they send out to members when law

RIGHT To an outlaw motorcycle club member like those in the Mongols MC, their "colours" (memberships patches) are considered near to sacred

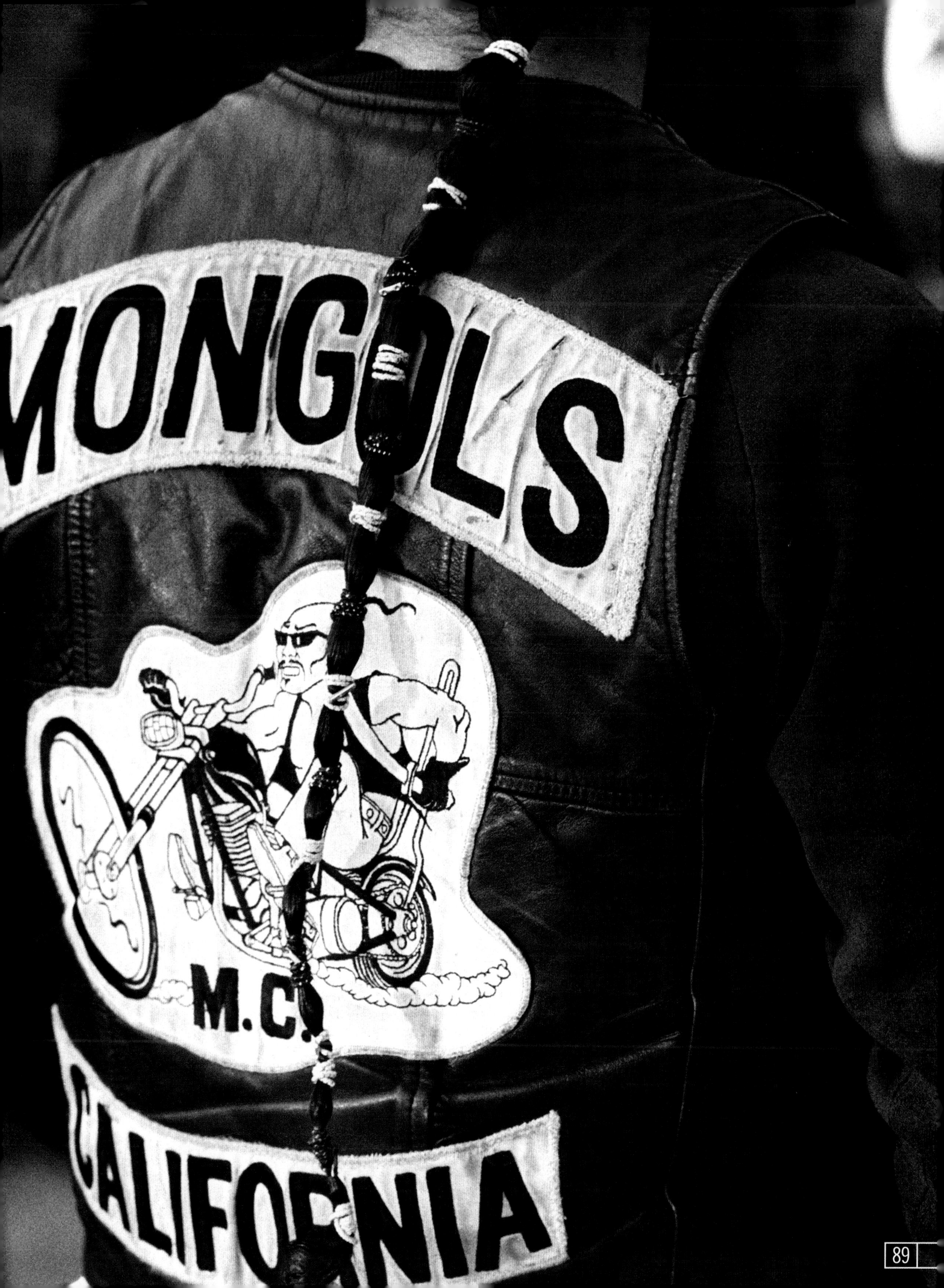
MONGOLS
M.C.
CALIFORNIA

enforcement is on the prowl – Code 55, which means hide all gang affiliation and lay low because the cops are out hunting Mongols. The club has gone from party-heavy disaffected Vietnam veterans to full-time criminals.

Undercover ATF agent William Queen infiltrated the Mongols in 1998. Going by the name Billy St John, the agent prospected, got patched up and attained a position as chapter vice president. The ATF, through Queen, conducted more than two years of investigation, which led to 54 Mongols being arrested and convicted of drug trafficking, motorcycle theft and conspiracy to commit murder in 2000.

"Prospecting inside the Mongols was a dangerous game," Queen wrote in his book titled Under and Alone: The True Story of the Undercover Agent Who Infiltrated America's Most Violent Outlaw Motorcycle Gang. "According to intel developed by the ATF, the Mongols Motorcycle Club had assumed the mantel of the most violent motorcycle gang in America, a close-knit collective of crazies, unpredictable and unrepentant bad-asses."

At the time, the Mongols only had about 350 full members, a small number of bikers in comparison to the more notorious Hells Angels. But the Mongols were known to bring it. They'd been clashing with the Hells Angels since the 1970s in a struggle to decide who was the preeminent outlaw motorcycle club in California. As the bodies dropped, law enforcement ramped up its focus on the motorcycle clubs.

"Their most significant violent acts in the '70s and '80s were committed against the Hells Angels, with who they fought and ultimately won a seventeen-year war," Queen wrote in Under and Alone. "But by the mid-90s, infused by the ruthless Latino gang mentality of East Los Angeles, the Mongols' indiscriminate violence spread outside the biker underworld and began to terrorize the general populace of Southern California."

The war with the Hells Angels put the Mongols on the map and defined who and what they were. Here was this little upstart outlaw motorcycle gang running rampant in Southern California, the home state of the bigger and more infamous club. The Angles didn't like that the Mongols wore a patch on their colours that said California. They told the Mongols to take it off, but the Mongols refused. What started off as fights, drunken brawls and stabbings turned into shootings and bombings. Seemingly nothing was off limits.

The two clubs were engaged in a vicious back-and-forth beef where bars and hangouts were blown up, members were executed and there was bad blood on both sides. Finally, the two sides got together and called a truce. It was agreed that the Mongols would hold sway over Southern California and the Angels would stick to their northern roots. The Mongols had vanquished the bigger and badder club. They had won the war but lost many members, so they opened the books again and started recruiting.

ABOVE Members of the Long Beach chapter of the Mongols Motorcycle Club in San Pedro, California, January 1991

ABOVE RIGHT The ATF proudly displays seized motorcycles and colours from members of the Mongols at a press conference after a successful undercover operation

MEET THE MONGOL HORDE OF AMERICA

In 2002, the much-publicised confrontation between the Mongols and Hells Angels kicked off again at Harrah's Laughlin (a casino in Laughlin, Nevada) in the form of the River Run riot. It heralded a new era of warfare between the two bitter rivals that had been sparked by the Mongols starting a chapter in San Jose. According to the pact, Northern California was Hells Angels territory, and the Mongols had violated the agreement.

Three men were left dead in Laughlin. Two Hells Angels, 27-year-old Jeramie Bell and 50-year-old Robert Tumelty, were shot and killed during the violent outbreak. One Mongol, 43-year-old Anthony "Bronson" Barrera, was stabbed to death. Six Mongols and six Hells Angels were convicted and sent to prison for being involved in the incident, but 36 others saw their charges dropped. More than 50 knives and multiple guns were taken into evidence by police. A video replay of the incident showed that the Hells Angels had thrown the first punch.

Ruben "Doc" Cavazos seized control of the Mongols MC after Laughlin and became its national president. Old-school members would later lay the blame at his feet for transforming the Mongols into a criminal organisation, one of the largest on the West Coast. His brother, Al "the Suit" Cavazos, and his son, Ruben "Lil Rubes" Cavazos, Jr., were instrumental in helping Doc to take over. Before he rose to power every member had to own and ride a Harley-Davidson, but Doc ignored that prerequisite in order to recruit Hispanic street gang members. These new members bypassed the prospect ritual and joined as part-time Mongols.

Doc had a tumultuous and high-profile run as the Mongols MC national president. He oversaw and participated in the filming of 'Mongol Nation', an episode of the History Channel's second season of *Gangland*, while he was also being investigated by the ATF in Operation Black Rain, which eventually led to 110 arrest warrants being issued in October 2008 for Mongol members in California, Colorado, Nevada, Washington and Oregon. The feds had managed to infiltrate the Mongols for a second time, with undercover ATF agents once more becoming patched members. *America's Most Wanted* were granted unrestricted access to the operation and filmed many of the arrests.

Doc and others pled guilty to racketeering charges, the president admitting to the authorities that he "...led a murdering, drug-dealing criminal conspiracy called the Mongols Motorcycle Club" and that "the Mongols' Registered Trademarks afforded a source of influence over the RICO enterprise that the defendant admits he established, operated, controlled, conducted and participated in."

In June 2004, Ray Nolan Waldron, a Mongol member, was accused of shooting to death David "LJ" Florentine, thought to be a member of the Hells Angels

Police raided his 256-square-metre (2,755-square-foot) home in South Hills, West Covina, and seized an arsenal of guns and a bulletproof vest. Doc was handed a 14-year sentence by the feds after becoming a government informant.

The Mongols' website summarised Doc's betrayal succinctly: "Ruben 'Doc' Cavazos flipped on January 23. He seems to have gone quickly and easily. He was the very first Mongol to plead guilty to count one of the indictment. As part of his guilty plea Cavazos agreed to the forfeiture of all right, title and interest in certain assets acquired or maintained by him as a result of his violation of the RICO statute including the Mongols' Registered Trademarks."

The site was admitting that the trademarks were subject to forfeiture to the United States. During a meeting in Vernon, California, on 30 August 2008, Doc was voted out of the club due to the majority of the membership believing that he was stealing from the club and provoking the Mexican Mafia.

"We are what everybody fears," Doc's son Lil Rubes said on the *Gangland* episode, but super gang La Eme, better known as the Mexican Mafia, didn't fear the Mongols at all.

In March 2004, the outlaw motorcycle gang and the prison gang were ready to go to war over pride and respect after a series of meetings set up to keep the peace fell apart. The beef started over the discovery of a meth lab by police that La Eme blamed the Mongols for. They told the Mongols they had to pay the tab for the discovered lab. Production was halted, equipment was confiscated and La Eme shot callers lost a viable income stream. On top of having the Mongols paying for the lab, the Mexicans decided the Mongols had to pay a cut of their drug proceeds as a tax to the prison gang. La Eme brought their demands to Doc, and he brought them to the club. Everyone said, 'Fuck it, we'll go to war.' But they didn't know what they were getting into.

La Eme controls the Sureños and boasts tens of thousands of soldiers in the streets ready to do their bidding. The Mongols became targets and gun battles erupted all over east Los Angeles. Vans full of Sureño gunmen would open fire on Mongols on the highway. On top of this, the beef with the Hells Angels was still an ongoing issue.

Doc was fighting a battle on two fronts at the time, forcing him to dodge several assassination attempts. His fellow MC members would search his car before starting it because they thought he was going to be blown up. It got so bad that Mongols stopped wearing their colours, but this didn't stop more than 20 members being killed. Finally, a payment was made to end the bloodshed. But the writing was on the wall. Many old-school Mongols blamed Doc for the carnage, and these issues lingered until he was kicked out of the MC.

U.S. District Court judge Florence-Marie Cooper issued an injunction from the court that prohibited club members, family members and associates from wearing, licensing, selling, or distributing the Mongol logo because, according to law enforcement, the logo and name were used to identify the club and as a form of intimidation to fulfil their goals. This was an extension of the ATF's 2008 Operation Black Rain. With Doc openly admitting that the logo was used to further the criminal enterprise, the feds were making an unprecedented move.

The government cited the guilty pleas to count one of the indictment by numerous defendants besides Cavazos as proof that the Mongols Motorcycle Club was a criminal conspiracy and the name and patch were subject to forfeiture. The government argued that the pleas demonstrated "a nexus between the violation of which the defendant has been convicted (or to which he has pled) and the property sought."

INSET "Big Al" Aceves (right) was one of the founding members of the Mongols in the 1960s, but he has since put his motorcycle club ways behind him to help those who want to get away from a life of violence and drugs

The Mongols started holding rallies to bring awareness to the federal lawsuit targeting the club logo. After much back and forth, the case was finally settled on 16 September 2015, when Federal District judge David O. Carter ruled against the forfeiture of all rights that the club had in regards to emblems and patches. He dismissed the case and the injunction. However, that wasn't the end of the Mongols' legal woes.

In 2018, a jury found the club itself to be guilty of charges of racketeering, drug dealing and murder. The Mongols demanded a retrial in 2022, claiming that David Santillan, who replaced Ruben "Doc" Cavazos as president in 2008, was in fact a government informant. While conceding that there was indeed a "stench" to the allegations against Santillan, Judge Carter dismissed the idea of a retrial.

The Mongols MC has continued to be in the news as recently as October 2023, when two members, Vincent Romanino and Joshualee Garcia, were arrested in Florida on suspicion of participating in the April 2022 murder of fellow Mongol rider Dominick Paternoster, who was shot to death in his Tampa home. Two of his suspected killers, Dylan Pascale and Paul Mogilevsky, had already been charged with first-degree murder.

It's alleged that the four men believed Paternoster, a father of three, was a snitch. "They shot him a whole bunch of times," said Pinellas County Sheriff Bob Gualtieri, who described the victim as "about as dead as you can get."

Yet despite all the negative press surrounding the club it keeps on growing, especially internationally. It's safe to say that these marauding motorbikers are going nowhere.

MEET THE MONGOL HORDE OF AMERICA

Mongol MC Worldwide Chapters

FROM ITS INCEPTION IN 1969, THE MONGOLS MC HAS GROWN OUTWARD FROM ITS CALIFORNIA ROOTS. THEY NOW HAVE CHAPTERS ALL OVER THE WORLD

- CANADA CHAPTERS: 1
- U.S. CHAPTERS: 84
- MEXICO CHAPTERS: 1
- BELGIUM CHAPTERS: 1
- SWEDEN CHAPTERS: 1
- ENGLAND CHAPTERS: 1
- GERMANY CHAPTERS: 5
- FRANCE CHAPTERS: 1
- ISRAEL CHAPTERS: 1
- SWITZERLAND CHAPTERS: 1
- ITALY CHAPTERS: 1
- THAILAND CHAPTERS: 6
- MALAYSIA CHAPTERS: 1
- SINGAPORE CHAPTERS: 1
- INDONESIA CHAPTERS: 1
- BRAZIL CHAPTERS: 1
- AUSTRALIA CHAPTERS: 12

LEFT William Queen managed to infiltrate the Mongols as an undercover ATF agent and later went on to write a book about his experiences

> "THE ANGELS DIDN'T LIKE THAT THE MONGOLS WORE A PATCH THAT SAID CALIFORNIA. THEY TOLD THE MONGOLS TO TAKE IT OFF, BUT THE MONGOLS REFUSED"

The sprawling city of Los Angeles is just one of the territories in California that the Mongols and Hells Angels have fought over

The Mongol Horde

THEY WERE NAMED AFTER THE INFAMOUS MONGOLIAN CONQUEROR, AND LIKE GENGHIS, THIS MC RULES OVER A VAST TERRITORY

The Mongols took their name from Mongolia's 13th-century empire, a nation of fearless horseback warriors who conquered vast swathes of Asia and Eastern Europe. Genghis Khan led a disciplined and vicious army that dominated their enemies, even though they were often outnumbered. The Mongols MC has carried on the Mongol tradition, except they ride motorcycles.

"Quality, not quantity!" boasts the Mongols MC website. "Brotherhood and Biking for over 40 years. We are the Mongols MC, the Best of the Best! The baddest 1%er Motorcycle Club known worldwide. The Mongols MC would like to thank you for visiting our official website. We appreciate all the love and support. The Club has taken some big hits recently, and has persevered through these hard times. We are back bigger, better and stronger. When we do right nobody remembers, when we do wrong nobody forgets. Live Mongol, die Mongol!"

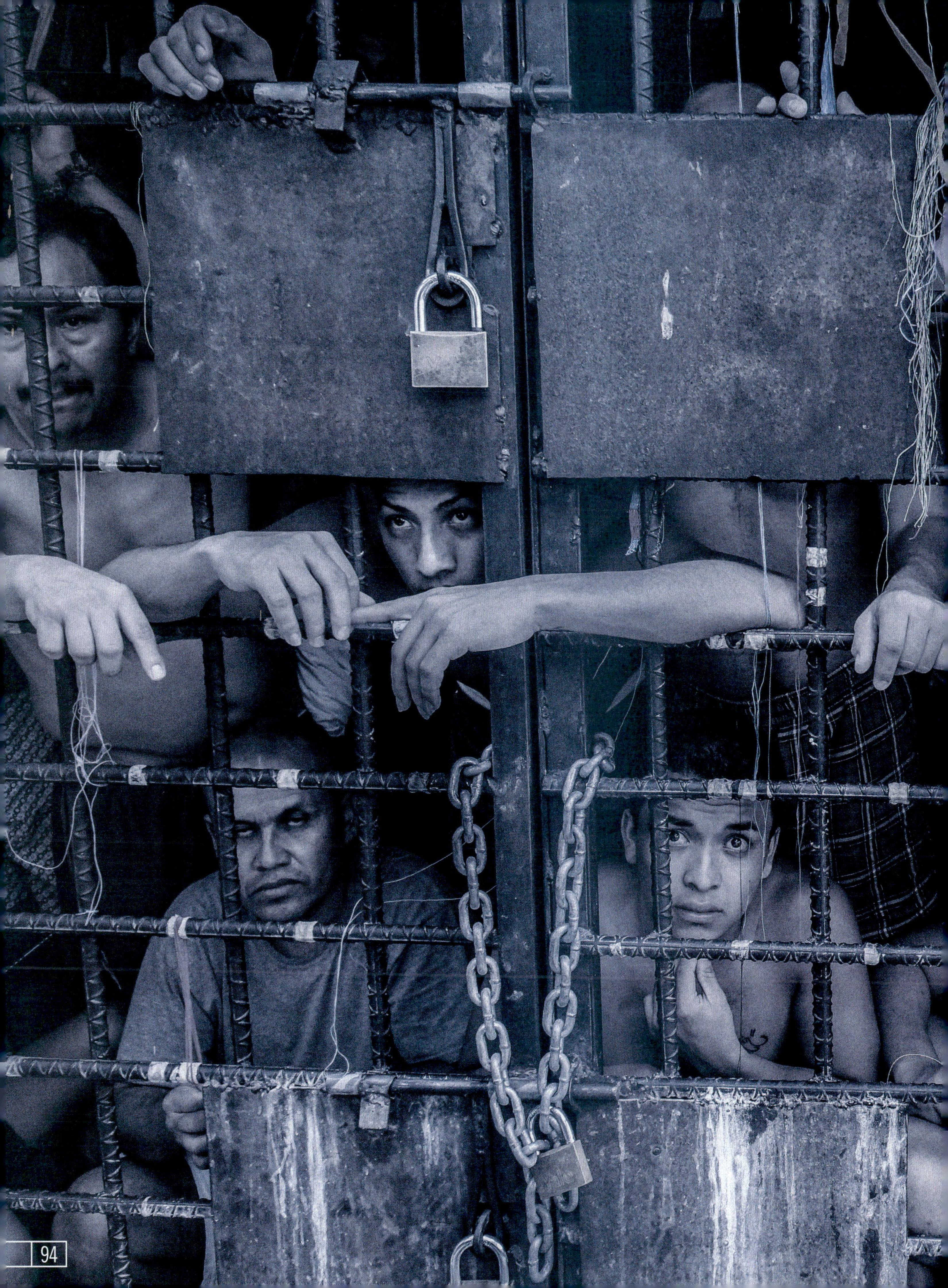

Cell Block Kingpins

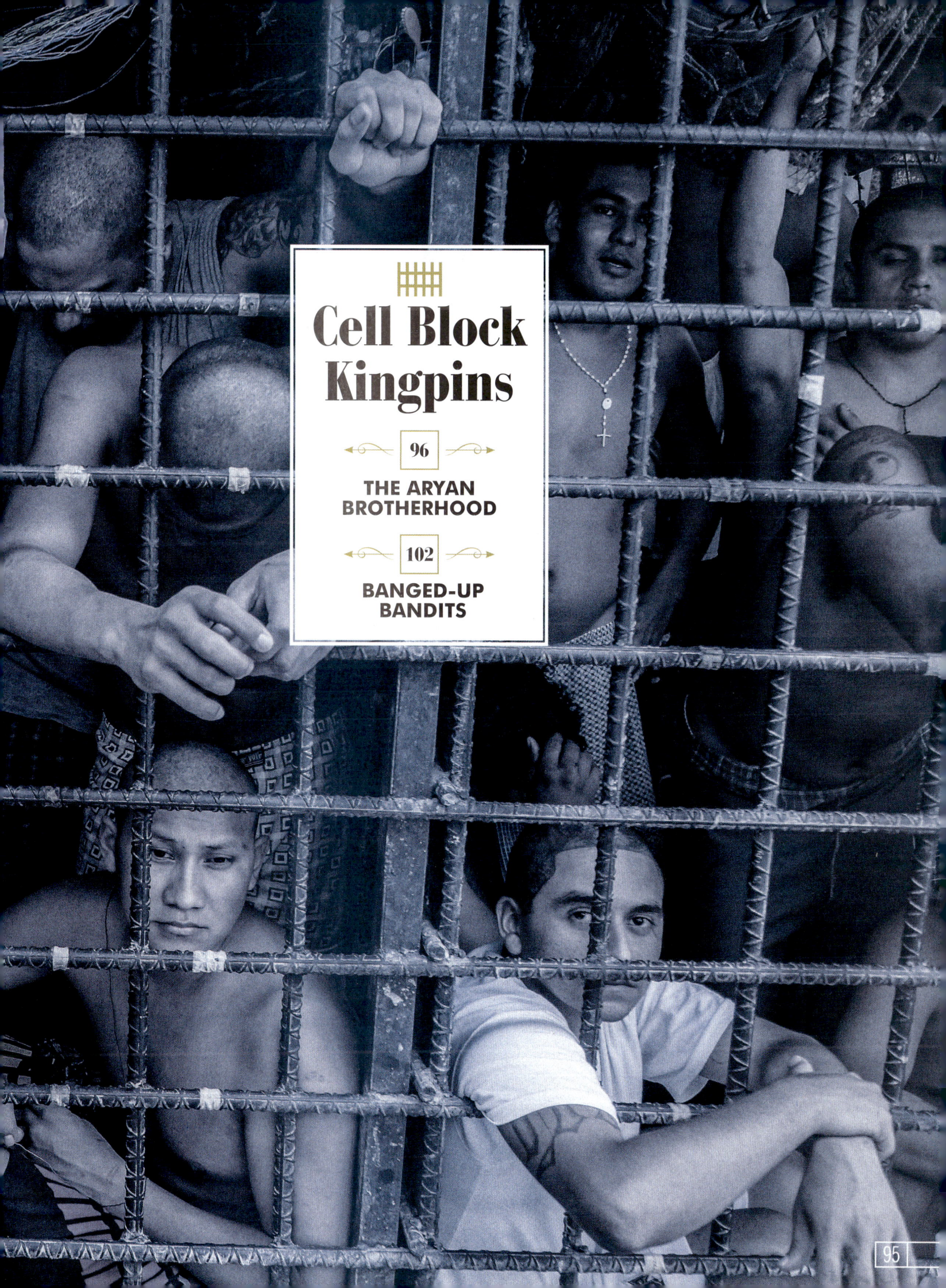

96
THE ARYAN BROTHERHOOD

102
BANGED-UP BANDITS

The Aryan Brotherhood

THEY MAKE UP 0.1 PER CENT OF INMATES, BUT THIS GANG ACCOUNTS FOR 20 PER CENT OF ALL MURDERS IN A PRISON SYSTEM STILL DIVIDED ALONG ETHNIC LINES

WORDS SETH FERRANTI

The Aryan Brotherhood formed in San Quentin prison in the California Department of Corrections in 1967 to protect white convicts from the predatory gangs that were taking root in the system. It was a volatile time in the United States, and this explosivity was amplified a hundred times over in the man-made netherworld of chaos and violence. It was go hard or check into the hole like a punk.

"What really got them originated was the white boys had to come together for protection purposes. The Blacks were acting like they ran shit, so the white boys got together to say you can run it, but you ain't running us," says Dog, a penitentiary veteran and long time AB associate. "They formed to take care of the whites in the California system because of the Black prison gangs. It was a way for them to make money – a protection racket."

The white supremacist group, which later adopted the moniker 'The Brand' due to the shamrock tattoo they used to signify membership, was made up mostly of prisoners with Irish, Scandinavian and German backgrounds. Convicts from 1950s biker gangs like the Diamond Tooth and Bluebirds formed the crux of the newly formed organisation. The Caucasian inmates consolidated under a neo-Nazi banner to watch each other's backs, show unity and handle their business in the yard. They were representing for the white race and making sure that no white inmates were exploited on their watch. By 1975, the gang was prospering inside the fences of the CDC, making power moves, calling shots and protecting their own.

"In the beginning, the AB had one true purpose, to stop Blacks and Mexicans from abusing whites. If you weren't picked up by the AB, you were dead," says an old-timer who has done stints in both California and federal prison. "The mentality back then was 'kill whitey.'"

The 1960s were a radical time in America, with the black power movement in full swing and minorities marching for civil rights. Behind the walls of the CDC, where Blacks, whites and Mexicans were crammed together like sardines, racial tensions were gravely exacerbated.

George Jackson, who formed the Black Guerrilla Family, wrote the celebrated prison memoir *Soledad Brother*. In his book he describes instances where Black inmates would attack whites on the tier just because of the colour of their skin. The former Black Panther had an unhealthy hatred of the system and all things white. In the depths of America's gulags, black prison gangs were making a power move.

With the Black Panthers holding iconic status in the urban centres in the radical 1960s, that mentality spilled over into the prisons, where race wars raged on unabated. The cauldron of hate created an atmosphere of tension in San Quentin, evolving into an all out war that erupted across the whole Californian system. The end result was the rise of the big four prison gangs, divided along strict racial lines, which provided a measure of safety for their members. Another author, Edward Bunker, a con who went to Hollywood when he got out (both as an actor and screenwriter, famously appearing as Mr Blue in *Reservoir Dogs*), wrote about life in the CDC in his book, *Education of a Felon*, which documented how whites came together to hold their own.

Along with the other race-based gangs, the AB took their place in prison lore as one of the fiercest and most violent to ever grace a California mainline. But the Aryan Brotherhood wasn't for everyone; exclusivity was the rule. They were very selective in who they let join, choosing prospective members with a great deal of scrutiny. "You can't sign up for The Brand," Dog says. "They have to pick you."

The Brand's motto is 'Blood in, blood out', meaning once you spill blood in order to join, the only way you are leaving is in a body bag. And, as now, if you wanted to join back then, you had to kill, or attempt to kill, a Black or Mexican inmate. The AB offered an exclusive membership to only the most violent, cunning and loyal convicts: the elite of the white race, as they saw it.

RIGHT A former member of the Aryan Brotherhood in Calipatria State Prison, California. Around half a century on from its foundation, The Brand is still a force within the prison system

ARYAN BROTHERHOOD

ABOVE AB members show off their tattoos. The organisation's long history has led to it adopting a variety of motifs, including the Viking warrior depicted on the upper body of the inmate first from the right

ABOVE San Quentin prison is the birthplace of the Aryan Brotherhood

ABOVE Con turned author Edward Bunker detailed the early days of The Brand in his prison memoir *Education of a Felon*

"You have to kill a Black to get in. Blood in, blood out. There's nothing wrong with that in my mind. We believe in being separatists," Dog says. "We got freedom of speech, freedom of religion. Being a separatist is a form of religion. It's like them old bylaws – Blacks can't eat here. ABs do time the way we want. We get high when we want to get high. We drink when we want to drink. And we fight and kill when we want to fight and kill."

The Aryan Brotherhood believed themselves to be a brotherhood of soldiers on the front lines of the prison race wars. They conditioned their bodies, minds and souls to go full blast at a moment's notice. A law enforcement official likened them to special forces, saying, "The AB is the most lethal killer this country has produced outside of Delta Force. With their thick bull necks, massive forearms, knit caps pulled low over their eyes and walrus-like moustaches they resemble Viking warriors or Old West outlaws." A fearsome sight indeed, an image cultivated to instil fear in the environment they found themselves in.

"A riot could happen over the smallest thing between races in the California prison system. A misunderstanding that became disrespect could get inmates seriously injured and even killed," says Bumperjack, a long-time Aryan Brotherhood member.

"I got involved with The Brand in 1985. Thirty years ago at Deuel Vocational Institution in Tracy, California. I had to get a green light on a guy who had jumped me in the county jail with two Northern Mexicans and he was the shot caller. They put me in the hospital after I beat him in a hand-to-hand altercation over me not paying rent on a pack of Camel smokes. This hit I made was my indoctrination into The Brand and I was credited with the initial part of making my bones."

"The system in California back 30 years ago when I entered was no joke. If you came into the system and had a problem with another inmate you had to get permission from The Brand if you were a white inmate. The prison gangs had control of all the prisons. There were a lot of stabbings and some fistfights," Bumperjack says. "In the California prison system as a white guy you didn't have too many options of who to run with. If you became a race traitor you were a target when the first riot jumped off. If you were white, let's say, in a Black gang."

The Aryan Brotherhood has been responsible for organised violence against Black inmates in federal penitentiaries at USP Marion in Illinois and USP Lewisburg in Pennsylvania. But despite their racial leanings the AB has become more of a racketeering enterprise over the years. "It's a criminal organisation first and foremost," the law enforcement official said.

"The AB has used murder as discipline. They used murder to keep their members in line and to spread fear and terror amongst the prison population." And in the process they became prison celebrities.

A chance to see a real AB put in 'real work' was bigger than watching the Super Bowl for those inside the belly of the beast. And the AB didn't disappoint. They killed by garrote and bludgeon and prison-made knives. They killed Black inmates, white inmates who didn't do what they said and even their own members who got out of line. They were violent, disciplined and fearless – a prison officials' absolute worst nightmare.

"They wouldn't sneak up and stab you," Dog says. "They'd do it right in the open. If a brother told you he was coming to kill you he was coming to kill you. They were not scared of nothing that I ever saw. Lots of killings. Putting hits on baby rapers and snitches. They don't hide from the police – they're doing life sentences. Even if their guy was wrong they ride with him. They don't fight fair. They'll all jump on you. Shit, they're like the Musketeers, all for one and one for all. They got shanks all over the yard. Easy access."

> **"WE GET HIGH WHEN WE WANT TO GET HIGH. WE DRINK WHEN WE WANT TO DRINK. AND WE FIGHT AND KILL WHEN WE WANT TO FIGHT AND KILL"**

ARYAN BROTHERHOOD

Tattoos Decoded

THE ARYAN BROTHERHOOD WEAR THEIR INK WITH PRIDE, AND EVERY IMAGE TELLS A STORY

THE SHAMROCK
The shamrock is the brand that gives them the name they go by in the pen – The Brand. It's said that when Michael "Big Mac" McElhiney, who had a big shamrock in the middle of his chest, arrived at USP Leavenworth in the winter of 1994, all he had to do was flash his shamrock and he was handed the keys to the white boy car on the compound. And if an AB member finds someone fronting with the shamrock tattoo, they will make them cover up the tattoo, burn it off, or even cut it off if that is what it takes. They are very touchy about who wears that tattoo or any other AB insignia, like lightning bolts on the underside of the forearms, which is another old-school indicator of AB membership.

IRON CROSS
A German military honour discontinued after World War II, the Iron Cross is often used by biker gangs and isn't inherently racist.

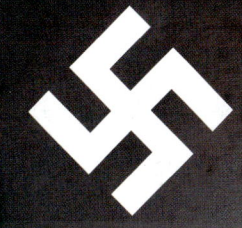

SWASTIKA
The symbol of the German Nazi Party since 1920, the Swastika has been the most potent standard of the far right since 1945.

88
The eighth letter of the alphabet in duplicate is code for the Nazi greeting 'Heil Hitler'. It's often coupled with other significant numbers such as "88/14"

14
A reference to the '14 Words' slogan coined by the nationalist leader Daniel Lane: "We must secure the existence of our people and a future for White Children."

Depictions of Adolf Hitler, as well as other infamous symbols of the Third Reich, are commonplace within The Brand

VALKNUT
Like Thor's hammer, the Valknut symbol – or 'Knot of the Slain Warriors' - is a Norse pagan icon that is also used by some white supremacist groups.

THOR'S HAMMER
Depictions of Thor's hammer are common in neo-paganism, but it's also a call back to the Nordic mythology favoured by the Nazi Party's inner circle.

> "IF YOU BECAME A RACE TRAITOR YOU WERE A TARGET WHEN THE FIRST RIOT JUMPED OFF"

CRUCIFIED SKINHEAD
Also used by non-racist skinheads, this symbolises sacrifice and can mean prison time served in support of the AB's cause.

SPIDERWEBS
Spiderweb tattoos on the elbows are a common feature throughout the prison system and represent incarceration – often for murder.

CELTIC CROSS
A neo-Nazi version of the Celtic cross, this symbol is associated with assorted far right groups, including the white supremacists the Ku Klux Klan.

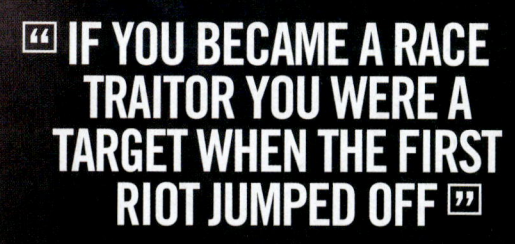

12
A tattoo of the number 12 represents the first and second letters of the English alphabet, 'AB', which stands for the 'Aryan Brotherhood'.

TRISKELE
The three-legged Triskele entered white nationalist lore as the emblem of South Africa's Afrikaner Weerstandsbeweging (AWB).

As the gang expanded into the federal system and other prisons across the nation in the 1980s and 90s their reputation preceded them.

The AB's leaders read works by Machiavelli, Nietzsche, Sun Tzu, Tolkien and the old standby, *Mein Kampf*. But the AB long ago subordinated its racist ideology to the acquisition of money. "The leadership became much more interested in power than race and started muscling in on the gambling, extortion and dope rackets," the old-timer says. As part of its bid to exert control over these prison industries, the AB adopted a structure in the 1980s similar to the Mafia, with a three-man council and a formal hierarchy that sent orders down the chain of command.

The Brand's leaders wielded so much control that they effectively served as powerbrokers in the California system and Federal Bureau of Prisons, maintaining order and dictating who could walk the mainline and the yard.

"Prison is where these guys live. We only punch the clock," a correctional officer says. "If you are going to spend your life in prison, why not be an AB member? They live like kings."

The Brand eventually ran much of the drug trafficking, gambling and prostitution behind the walls, and plenty more on the outside. The gang operates as a fully fledged criminal enterprise, using murder or the threat of it to enforce their authority. This power is maintained largely by controlling the drug trade. "Selling heroin to fellow convicts generates a lot of money for The Brand," says the correctional officer. "Several hundred thousand a year from a single prison. And how many yards do they control? You do the math."

In the federal system they established ties with jailed Mob bosses like Oreste "Ernie Boy" Abbamonte, Nicodemo "Little Nicky" Scarfo and the late John Gotti, the "Teflon Don". Associates from other gangs like the Dirty White Boys, Nazi Low Riders and Mexican Mafia do their bidding. They flood every compound they're on with heroin, shipping the proceeds back to California to be disbursed between other jailed members and leaders of the gang. The two commissions, one in California and the other in the feds, call the shots. Though never vast in numbers, the AB make up for it with violent acts that have helped to garner a fearsome reputation. Their far-flung associates, who number in the hundreds, exert power in whatever prison compound they are in to further the influence of the gang.

"The state of The Brand in the California system has been letting others do their bidding," Bumperjack says. "Because they are locked away in Security Housing Units, you can only have control to a certain degree as I see it. In 1989, they built Pelican Bay, and in 1988 they built Corcoran to take back control of the California prison system from all the prison gangs. And they didn't really succeed because The Brand uses others do their bidding on the mainlines. In the feds, they have all the power of The Brand locked up in ADX Florence, Colorado and prison officials think that if they take the head then the body will die.

"The Brand has been around a long time so they have a lot of influence, but overall they have slowly been losing control in both the state and federal prison system due to new cases, infighting and age. A lot of the leaders are dinosaurs."

On 28 August 2002, Assistant United States Attorney Greg Jessner indicted virtually the entire leadership of the gang. The indictment reached back more than 20 years, spanning three decades and 32 murders. Forty members were indicted of federal racketeering charges. The majority of the gang members were already doing life sentences, so 23 of them were eligible for the death penalty.

"This is a homicidal organisation," Jessner announced. "That's what they do. They kill people. I suspect they kill more people than the Mafia. They may be the most murderous criminal organisation in the United States."

The indictment was the largest capital case in the history of the U.S., with the AUSA using laws originally passed to target Mob leaders. "Inmates and others who do not follow the

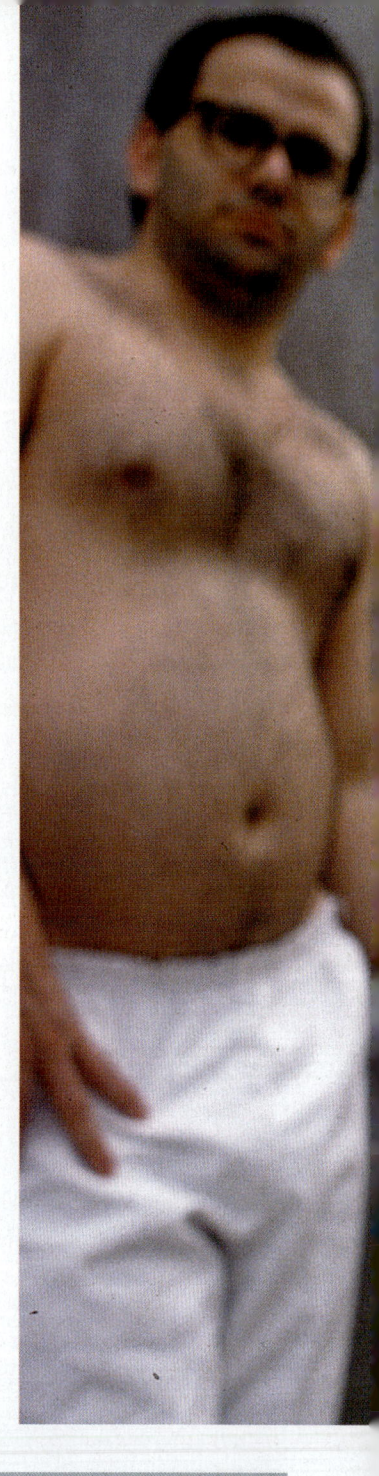

"THEY WOULDN'T SNEAK UP AND STAB YOU. THEY'D DO IT RIGHT IN THE OPEN"

Notorious Members
RINGLEADERS AND COLD-BLOODED KILLERS, THESE AB VETERANS' REPUTATIONS TRANSCEND PRISON BARS

BARRY "THE BARON" MILLS
The Baron was known as the brain of the Aryan Brotherhood. Until his death in 2018, he was responsible for much of their organisational structure and the formation of the three-man commissions in the California and federal prison systems. He became involved with the AB in San Quentin prison in the late 1960s after growing up in Northern California and quickly rose through the ranks as he returned to prison frequently.

A tactical and innovative gang leader whose word was law, he wasn't afraid to get busy himself when necessary but was equally adept at delegating and passing orders down the line. Credited with the longevity of the gang's criminal enterprises, the Baron was responsible for 14 murders and was convicted of nearly decapitating a man at USP Atlanta in 1979, for which he received a life sentence.

THOMAS "TERRIBLE TOM" SILVERSTEIN
Terrible Tom was sent to San Quentin at the tender age of 19. Soon after being paroled from that short bid he was sentenced to 15 years for an armed robbery charge and sent to USP Leavenworth, an AB stronghold, in 1977. He got involved with The Brand and murdered an inmate to make his bones.

Terrible Tom started the AB-DC Blacks race war by killing Raymond "Cadillac" Smith, the leader of the D.C. Blacks, in the USP Marion Control Unit, where the worst of the worst inmates were housed at the time. Still, Terrible Tom wasn't finished. In 1983 he killed Correctional Officer Merle Clutts at USP Marion with a prison-fashioned shank for disrespecting him. The Bureau of Prisons had something in store for him. They developed a special isolation cell, cutting him off from the outside world and human contact.

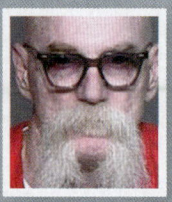

T. D. "SUPER HONKY" BINGHAM
Also known as "The Hulk", Bingham is a massive specimen of a man who benches 500 pounds (227 kilograms) and was known as Mill's chief enforcer. He was part of the three-man commission that controls activity in the federal prison system.

Up until the massive 2006 racketeering indictment against the Aryan Brotherhood, Bingham was actually scheduled to get out of prison after multiple decades inside. But with his conviction in that case he remained alongside his general at ADX Florence doing natural life in total isolation, with hardly any recreation time and limited correspondence. Another long-time AB member, he made his bones in the California Department of Corrections in the late 1960s and early '70s before being released, committing more crimes and graduating to the federal prison system.

ARYAN BROTHERHOOD

"PRISON IS WHERE THESE GUYS LIVE. WE ONLY PUNCH THE CLOCK"

ABOVE Three members of an unidentified white power prison gang. There are numerous derivatives of The Brand currently active in the U.S., including the infamous Aryan Brotherhood of Texas

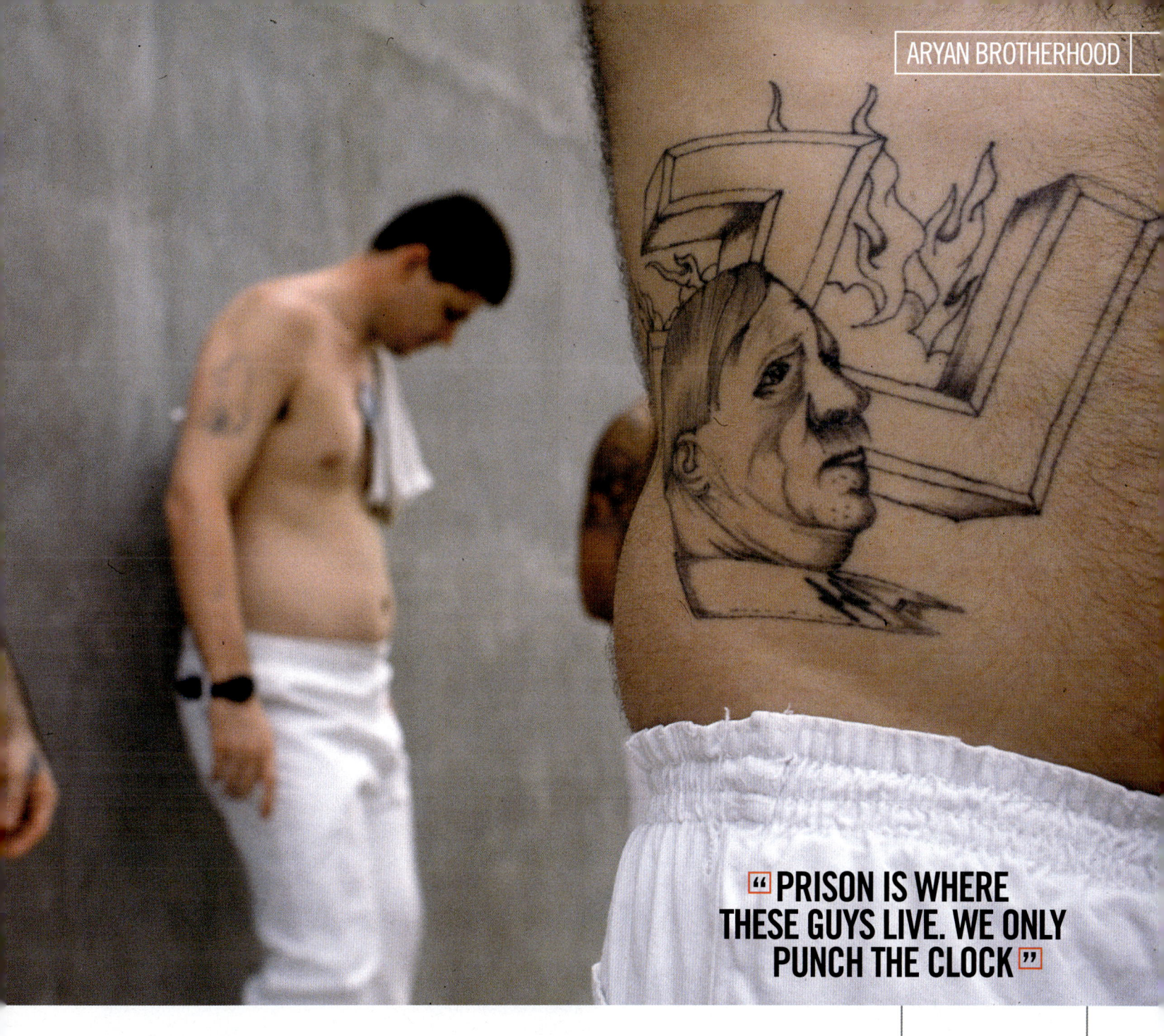

orders of the AB are subject to being murdered as is anyone who uses violence against an AB member or anyone who co-operates with law enforcement," the indictment read.

A main component of the case was the ongoing race war with the D.C. Blacks prison gang. The race wars in the federal system started on 22 November 1981 when the body of Robert M. Chappelle, a member of the D.C. Blacks, was found in his cell at USP Marion. He'd been killed by Thomas "Terrible Tom" Silverstein. Chappelle's death worried Bureau of Prisons officials, who thought it might spark a war, which it certainly did.

Raymond "Cadillac" Smith, the alleged national leader of the D.C. Blacks, was the next person to be slain. In the Marion control unit on 27 September 1982, Terrible Tom stabbed Cadillac 67 times, dragging his body up and down the tier so that those locked in their cells could see.

The race wars against the D.C. Blacks raged across the feds in the early 1980s and again in the '90s when two D.C. Blacks were killed at USP Lewisburg by AB members who stabbed them 35 and 34 times respectively. Barry "The Baron" Mills and the inventively named T. D. "Super Honky" Bingham were accused of ordering the killings at USP Lewisburg from their cells at ADX.

The subsequent case against them reached back 40 years to include stabbings, strangulations, poisonings, contract hits, conspiracy to commit murder, robbery and narcotics trafficking. Mills, Bingham, Silverstein and 39 other members of the AB received life sentences on top of the life sentences they were already serving. The prosecutors had won the case, but the jury refused to sentence the leaders to death.

Today the Aryan Brotherhood is not as powerful as it once was, but it has spawned imitators, and there are still members and associates in prison systems across the nation, with an estimated membership of approximately 20,000.

"The legacy of The Brand is the most dangerous white prison gang in the world," Bumperjack says, and long time members like him have come to see what it's really about. "If you join a prison gang in California it's 'blood in, blood out' so in reality you just sold your soul to the devil and should plan on living the rest of your existence incarcerated or getting killed by the gang," he says, succinctly summing up the story of The Brand, the most infamous prison gang in America.

Banged-up Bandits

THERE'S NOTHING LIKE HARD TIME TO MAKE A REAL CAREER OUT OF CRIMINALITY

WORDS BEN BIGGS

"Danbury wasn't a prison, it was a crime school," said legendary drug trafficker George Jung – or rather, the character played by Johnny Depp in the movie biopic *Blow*. Maybe that's not anything like a direct quote from the real "El Americano" but there's a hard truth to that statement: if you put hundreds of criminals behind steel bars and four walls of reinforced concrete, then take away the liberties they've taken for granted, it's going to toughen them up. Keep them there for years and they'll soon sort themselves into feral packs bound by their own laws and for whom non-members are fair game. The gangs found in prisons around the world are a breed unto themselves, each with their own ethics and a culture that sets them apart from the street gangs and criminal organisations on the outside. These six gangs are some of the most ruthless networks of inmates on Earth.

Barrio Azteca

TEXAS, U.S. **1986–PRESENT**

Today, this Mexican-American gang is 8,000 strong, with influence on the streets both sides of the Rio Grande. But Barrio Azteca formed nearly 40 years ago in the notorious jails, detention centres and Federal Correctional Institutions on the U.S. borderlands. It's in these festering swamps of pent-up violence and impotent criminality that "Los Aztecas" was born. In 1986, El Paso prison inmates banded together out of a dire need for protection, forming a loose constitution that has a golden rule: once you're in, the only way you're leaving Los Aztecas is in a body bag. For ten years Barrio Azteca was 'just' a prison gang, before the U.S. Government started handing Mexican inmates over to the Mexican authorities. If that was intended to break the power of this gang, it had the opposite effect. Barrio Azteca began to spread like a virus across Mexico's correctional facilities, and by the turn of the millennium the gang's considerable influence on both sides of the border had been recognised by the powerful Juárez Cartel, who recruited them into their drug-trafficking operations and their war against the Sinaloa Cartel.

In 2018, Barrio Azteca captain Eduardo "El Tablas" Ravelo Rodríguez was arrested in Uruapan, on the Mexican Pacific coast. Ravelo was on the FBI's top ten most wanted list after he had been indicted on charges of racketeering, drug trafficking and multiple counts of murder – including planning the execution of a pregnant U.S. consulate worker, her husband and the husband of another consulate worker. Sadly, cutting the serpent's head off only led to a power vacuum that quickly saw another take his place.

BANGED-UP BANDITS

Mexican Mafia
CALIFORNIA, U.S. 1950S–PRESENT

Neither founded in Mexico or by Mexican gangsters, the Mexican Mafia was born on the streets of Los Angeles in the late 1950s. "La Eme" was ostensibly formed to protect Hispanic criminals from other prison gangs, although as the power of the gang grew, its illicit activities expanded to encompass black market prison trading and provide home comforts for its members incarcerated in Deuel Vocational Institution.

From the very beginning, Luis "Huero Buff" Flores, one of the Mexican Mafia's founding members, sought to wrest control of Deuel through a campaign of fear and intimidation – via bloody violence and murder, of course. It soon became the prison gang to be reckoned with in Deuel. The Californian prison system responded by moving some of the Mexican Mafia members to one of the most notorious prisons around – San Quentin – in a bid to quell the rising violence. It did not have the desired effect: Rodolfo Alvarado "Cheyenne" Cadena, a 16-year-old member who would later rise through the ranks to become boss, stabbed another inmate to death in the recreation yard within hours of stepping off the prison bus. Rather than diluting the power of the gang, the authorities had simply seeded "La Eme" to another prison.

With around 500 members inside the prison system today and tens of thousands more in California's many Hispanic street gangs, the Mexican Mafia enjoys considerable power statewide and is involved in a number of criminal enterprises such as trafficking drugs, arms dealing, extortion and robbery.

103

The Ñeta Association
PUERTO RICO, U.S. **1979–PRESENT**

In 1979, Puerto Rico's ageing (and now demolished) Río Piedras State Penitentiary was a hotbed of corruption and violence. Carlos Torres Irriarte, who was also known by his Spanish moniker "La Sombra" ("The Shadow"), formed a protective group with a handful of fellow inmates who, like him, had been singled out for 'special' treatment. The Ñeta Association was made up of political prisoners who were unlike the prison's criminal majority and, before they found safety and power in numbers, many of their kind had already been robbed, raped, murdered and generally abused. But after just a year of violent clashes against Group 27, a prison gang Irriarte referred to as "insects", the Ñetas became a vigilante force to be reckoned with within the walls of Río Piedras. But they didn't keep this moral high ground for long.

The story goes that in the spring of 1981, Group 27 leaders paid off guards to turn a blind eye as Irriarte was stabbed and then shot on his daily exercise regime, although the prison authorities said that Irriarte's own lieutenants had him killed, so the Ñetas could move into the business of drug trafficking that Irriarte vehemently opposed. Regardless, with Irriarte out of the way, they were free deal drugs and expand – but not before extracting a particularly brutal revenge on Group 27's leader, Raymond "Manota" Ayala Ortiz. After days of digging with spoons through the prison walls to Manota's cell, the Ñetas broke in and stabbed him to death, cut his body into dozens of pieces and send parts to his mother, as well as Group 27 members and the prison warden. It was a statement that the bloodiest of drug cartels couldn't have made better themselves, and it put the Ñetas at the top of the pecking order. They can be found all over Puerto Rico's prisons today and have even infiltrated East Coast U.S. prisons.

The Numbers Gang
SOUTH AFRICA **LATE 1800S–PRESENT**

South Africa has some of the toughest prisons in the world, breeding a particular variety of institution-hardened hoodlums like no other. Arguably the most infamous are the Numbers Gang, whose members are spread across the country's prison system and whose heritage dates to the late 19th century. It has a unique and intricate hierarchy, split three ways into factions that can be recognised in successful criminal organisations worldwide.

The 26's take care of earning money for the gang by whatever means, including smuggling and illegal gambling. The 28s are the enforcer arm, the gang's muscle, who shake down anyone that owes money and ferociously defend other members. The 27s are the most respected, defending the code of the Numbers Gang as well as being arbitrators between the factions. This digit-oriented system originates – or so the story goes – from the 1880s, when two gangs formed out of a single faction of highway robbers, the "2" denoting the two leaders followed by the number of members in each faction. Following violent disagreements over whether homosexual relations were allowed between members of the 28s, the 26s were formed and the Numbers Gang was born.

Around 150 years later, the 26s and 28s have to communicate through the 27s and sodomy is still used to bring unruly members to heel: for breaking rules, a Numbers Gang member may be raped by another inmate who is infected with HIV.

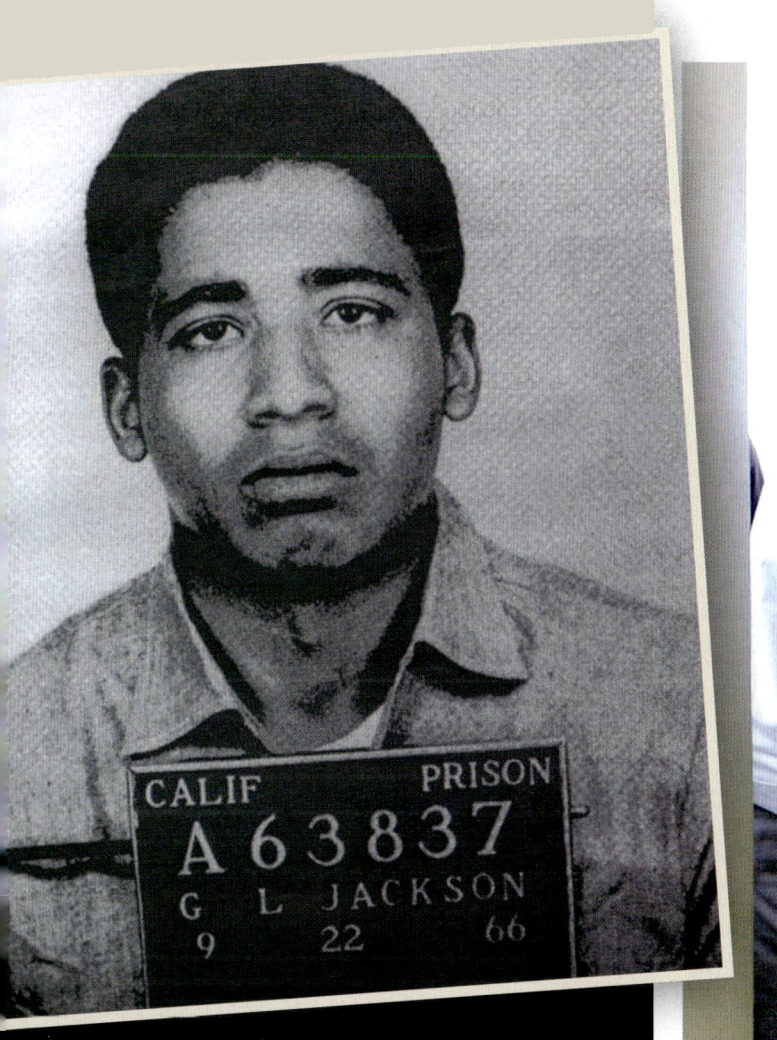

Black Guerilla Family
CALIFORNIA, U.S. **1966–PRESENT**

Unlike many prisons gangs, the Black Guerilla Family was founded by inmates with a strong political bent that was reflected in the burgeoning Black liberation movement outside San Quentin prison walls. On the surface, the Civil Rights Act of 1964 had set in motion the righting of many wrongs perpetrated against African-Americans, although non-whites and particularly African-Americans were still strongly discriminated against by the police, the courts and the prison system. Against this pervasive injustice inmates George Jackson and W. L. Nolen brought the weight of their Marxist ideology and street smarts to bear, and the BGF was formed in 1966. By the early 1970s, both founders had been killed by corrections officers in separate incidents, though that was anything but the death knell for the BGF.

For many years the gang had a wary alliance with the Black Panthers and its underground faction, the Black Liberation Army, before drug dealing and other criminal activities infiltrated the ranks. Since the 1980s the gang has strayed away from its politics to focus on the accumulation of wealth. With just 300 members in Californian and Maryland prisons, the BGF doesn't have quite the clout that it did 50 years ago. To ensure its survival, in recent years the gang has aligned itself with more powerful criminal groups such as the Bloods and the Crips, and it's firmly in the business of extortion, distributing illegal drugs and stealing cars.

Primeiro Comando da Capital
SÃO PAULO, BRAZIL **1993–PRESENT**

Brazil's broken and corrupt prison system has allowed inmates to organise in large numbers over the decades, forming some notable groups that include Primeiro Comando da Capital, or First Capital Command. Like many other prison gangs, PCC arose out of a need to protect its members – although at first the protection it sought was of a legal kind, from the Brazilian authorities rather than other criminals.

After a riot in 1992 that threatened the very existence of São Paulo's Carandiru prison, Brazilian security was sent in to seize control with extreme prejudice, killing 100 inmates in the process. Eight of the surviving inmates banded together with a prison gang known as the Red Command to fight for justice for the dead prisoners and to petition for better conditions for everyone else. Both noble causes, though dyed-in-the-wool gangsters and criminals being true to their nature, this was effectively a cover story. This suited the government at the time, for whom the rise of another powerful prison gang was bad publicity: the São Paulo governor called the gang "a fiction" and denied the existence of PCC right up until he couldn't.

In 1999, having spread to the streets of São Paulo, PCC gangsters executed the biggest and most devastating bank robbery in the city's history, stealing the equivalent of $32 million and leaving part of the building in rubble. Since then, PCC has orchestrated several heists, including a plot to steal an estimated $331 million from São Paulo's Banco do Brasil that involved excavating a 500-metre (1,640-foot) tunnel fitted with electricity and a ventilation system. It would have been the world's biggest bank robbery had investigators not swooped in and arrested the suspects. Bank robbing is still a regular source of income for PCC, which boasts over 20,000 members.

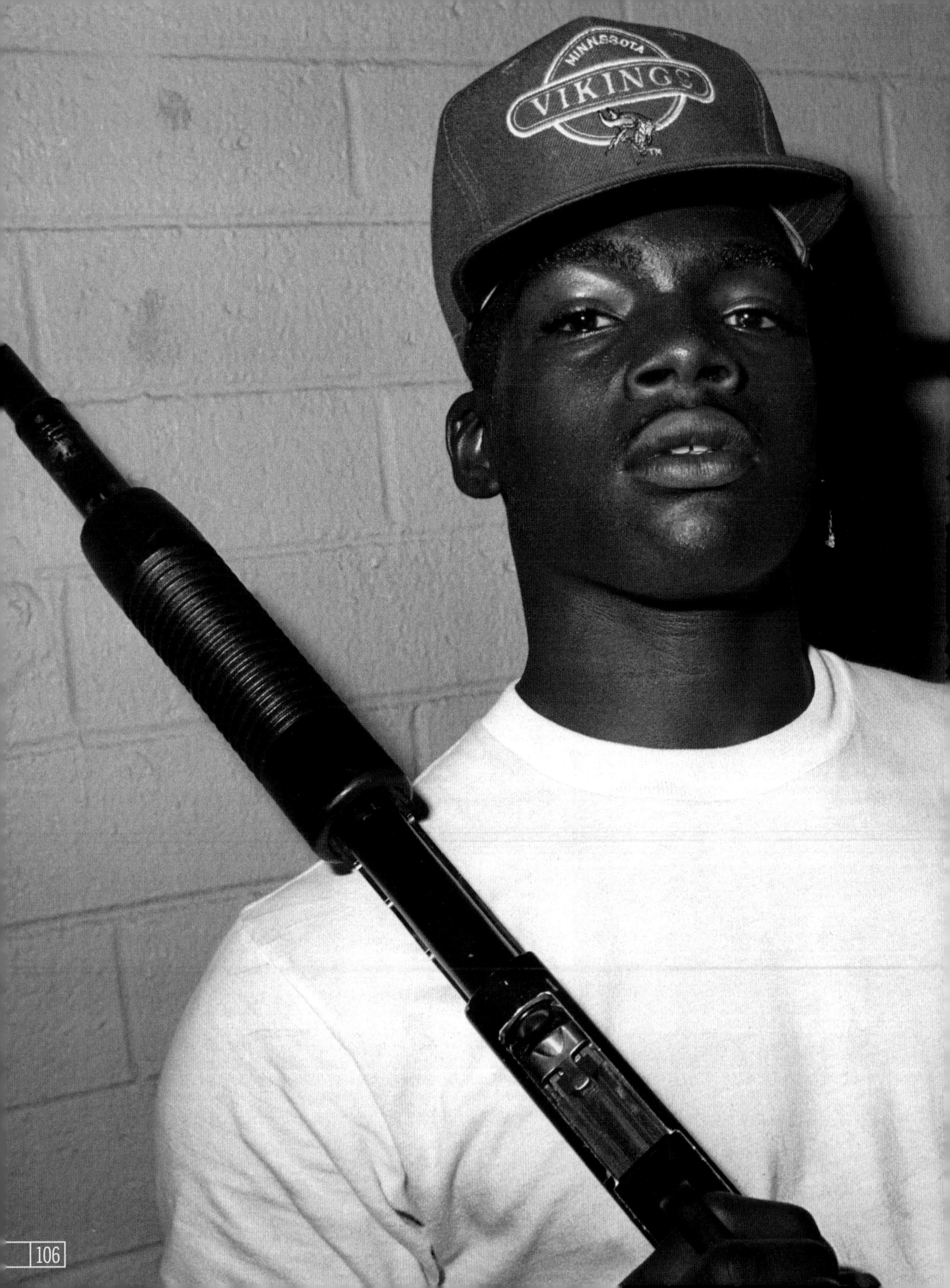
MINNESOTA
VIKINGS

Blood in the Streets

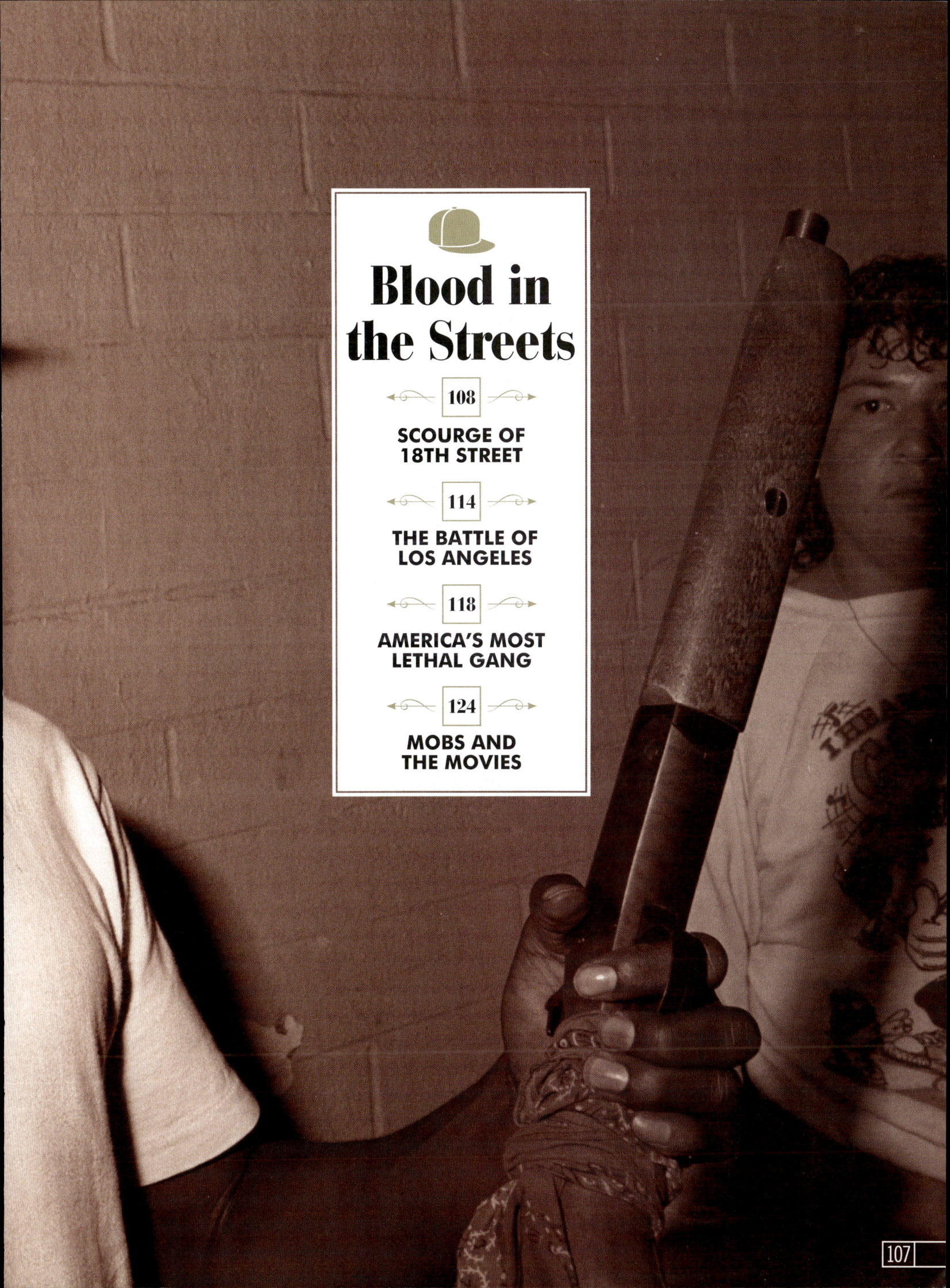

108
SCOURGE OF 18TH STREET

114
THE BATTLE OF LOS ANGELES

118
AMERICA'S MOST LETHAL GANG

124
MOBS AND THE MOVIES

108

Scourge of 18th Street

NEMESIS OF MS-13, THIS BRUTAL GANG HAS EXPLODED ACROSS SOUTH AMERICA, BUT ITS ROOTS ARE BURIED DEEP IN LOS ANGELES

WORDS SETH FERRANTI

In the chronicles of California street lore, the 18th Street gang – also known as M18, Calle 18, Barrio 18, LA18 or Mara-18 in Central America – reigns supreme as one of the behemoths of Los Angeles' gangster culture. It is an iconic underworld brand that has spanned countries and even continents, becoming a mainstay of the American Dream, gangster version.

Estimated to have close to 15,000 members in Los Angeles county alone, the various 'clickas' that operate in the greater metropolitan area form the nucleus of the multi-ethnic transnational criminal organisation steeped in 'vato loco' history, 'eme' edicts and 'cholo' culture. The gang originated and came to power in the Pico-Union area just east of what is today the Crypto.com Arena (formerly the Staples Center) in downtown LA (home to the scandalous Rampart Division) as an act of defiance in about 1965.

"Barrio 18 grew out of the Clanton Street gang, which was formed back in the 1920s in Los Angeles," Ioan Grillo, a Mexico City-based journalist and author of *Gangster Warlords: Drug Dollars, Killing Fields, and the New Politics of Latin America*, tells us. "Barrio 18 stood out from other Chicano street gangs by letting non-Mexicans in. Others – including Filipinos and even Indians – joined. Later, many Salvadorans, who arrived as refugees from the civil war, got in the mix."

Situated between the Santa Monica Freeway to the south and the Harbor Freeway to the east, original members were part of the Clanton 14th Street neighbourhood, but when that gang started kicking out anybody who wasn't Mexican-American, former members broke off and started a new gang, Clanton 18th Street, which eventually morphed into Barrio 18th Street.

"One of the reasons why original Clanton members began to reject the 18th click was because it was being led by a non Mexican-American named Rocky Lee Glover," Alex Alonso, editor at **Streetgangs.com**, says. "The new click members had to make a decision between falling in line with Clanton 14 and the strict rule of Mexican-Americans only, or take a defiant position to start their own gang and create Barrio 18th Street."

INSET During a gang member's initiation the new recruit is beaten by several members while they count to 18

ABOVE Salvadoran gang members show off their tattoos from behind bars. Members are always adorned with the number '18', which can be seen written out on both of the prisoners' left arms

Barrio legend holds that Rocky Glover and his supporters dropped the Clanton off their name and became rivals against their former cohorts. Over the years, 18th Street grew and came to dominate numerous Los Angeles county barrios – from Pico-Union to West Adams, to South Los Angeles to Inglewood and on into the San Gabriel Valley and East LA. Their policy of jumping in members, even those not of Mexican descent, fuelled their growth in numbers rapidly.

"Because of its aggressive recruiting techniques, the name of this gang has caught on and has been copied and mimicked in several other cities and countries around the world," Alonso says. "Contrary to popular belief, not all of the 18th Street neighbourhoods operate in unison, know each other, or even get along."

It's the biggest and deadliest street gang to originate in Los Angeles' criminal underbelly, a city that is infamous for its street gangs. 18th Street is more than 20 times the size of the notorious Bloods and Crips – noted LA gangs.

The FBI has reported that the gang currently has 30,000–50,000 members spread throughout North and Central America. In California, upwards of 80 per cent of the gang's membership are illegal aliens from Mexico and Central America, and 18th Street's primary recruitment targets have remained immigrant youngsters.

These disenfranchised criminals pour in over the border from their destitute home countries to transport drugs and invariably end up committing serious offences such as rape and murder, which are all sanctioned crimes in the millennial gangster handbook.

"Loyalty is gained by spilling blood," Grillo says. "If you want to join in Honduras or El Salvador, you have to kill people to get in. And it might not be one person, it might be three or even five. That level of violence is not commonplace in the United States, but south of the border it's anything goes and that makes a world of difference."

In Central and South America, gang tactics differ from those in the U.S. With more room to get away with crime, the criminals are bolder. The police are more corrupt too, willing to murder a gang member rather than arrest him. With the stakes that much higher, a new gangster's loyalty is put to the test in the ultimate fashion.

"In the U.S., they don't do that," Grillo says. "When they recruit people in the U.S., they will say 'go do this job', like take this kilo of cocaine over there. Do this job with risk, but not murder because they can't get away with that level of murder in the U.S. They can't kill people in the U.S. like they do in Honduras or El Salvador because the police will come down on them too hard. There is so much more they can get away with down there, which makes a world of difference."

The gang concentrates its efforts on the street-level distribution of cocaine, heroin and methamphetamine. Gang members also engage in crimes such as gun trafficking, assault, auto theft, carjacking, drive-by shooting, extortion, homicide, identification fraud and robbery. Someone in Los Angeles County is assaulted or robbed by an 18th Street gang member every day. The gang has left a bloody trail of victims, the body count rising each year.

In the mid-1990s, the Los Angeles Attorney's Office filed a complaint that said 18th Street gang members were a public nuisance. Prosecutors asked the court to grant an injunction that would prohibit gang members from congregating. They "terrorise and intimidate" law-abiding residents in their neighbourhood "by engaging in murder, attempted murder, drug sales, residential and car burglary, robbery, attempted kidnapping, and assaults with deadly weapons," the complaint said.

SCOURGE OF 18TH STREET

18th Street Spotting

COMMONLY FOUND ON THE UNITED STATES' WEST COAST AS WELL AS IN SOUTH AMERICA, 18TH STREETERS ARE EASY TO DISTINGUISH FROM LESSER GANG MEMBERS

According to the FBI, some factions of the 18th Street gang have developed a high level of sophistication and organisation. 18th Street gang members often identify themselves with the number 18 on their clothing and wear sports clothing from teams such as the Los Angeles Dodgers, Los Angeles Lakers and Oakland Raiders. 18th Street colours are blue and black; blue is to represent and pay tribute to the Mexican Mafia, and black is to represent the original colour for the gang.

18th Street members will use the symbols XV3, XVIII, X8, 666, 99 (9+9=18), and three dots in their graffiti and tattoos. Members are covered in tattoos all over their body, even their face. A big 18 is often sketched somewhere on their person, representing their set and letting rival gangs know who they are, sometimes in multiple places.

The gang's wide-ranging activities even put the FBI and Immigration and Customs Enforcement on alert. In the early 2000s up until the present day, the authorities have initiated wide-scale raids against known and suspected gang members, resulting in hundreds of arrests across the country.

"Defendants fire guns at members of rival gangs and members of the public at large… to show their 'bravado' and mastery over their 'turf'," the Superior Court complaint stated. "18th Street is a well-established gang that is involved in all areas of street-crime."

The gang's stronghold remains Los Angeles, but countless gangs outside the city have appropriated the moniker. "With that brand name," Alonso says, "they get instant recognition."

Law enforcement says that 18th Street has strong ties to the Mexican Mafia prison gang and deals directly with the Mexican and Colombian cartels. They've also pioneered the renting of street corners to non-gang dope peddlers, who are forced to pay 'taxes', sometimes at an hourly rate.

In 18th Street, there's no Godfather or Don Dada. Instead, the gang's older member 'veteranos' oversee a chaotic network of cliques, whose members share an intense loyalty to the gang's values and ambitions, which include abiding by a strict set of rules. Failure to obey the word of a superior or to show proper respect to a fellow gang member can result in an 18-second ass whooping, or even an execution for more serious offenses.

Through its affiliation with the Mexican Mafia, 18th Street has asserted control over the state prisons' narcotics trade. A lot of money is generated from the prisons through drugs. The 'big homies' from 18th Street who graduated to the Mexican Mafia in prison act as the 'shot callers' while the 'soldados' in the street 'put in work', following all the edicts sent out via 'kites' from the career prison gangsters.

"YOU HAVE TO KILL PEOPLE TO GET IN. AND IT MIGHT NOT BE ONE PERSON, IT MIGHT BE THREE OR EVEN FIVE"

On the street, the gang resembles a kind of children's army, with many juveniles involved in operations. While the veteranos remain in the shadows (often in prison), the youngsters bolster the gang's numbers and carry out its criminal activity. In secret meetings, the veteranos exchange plans, plot strategies, 'greenlight' enemies and share information on snitches and investigations.

The gang's structure and layers of soldados has insulated it from racketeering prosecutions but also kept 18th Street from becoming a traditional criminal syndicate. They regularly turn to children from elementary and middle school, looking for kids between the ages of 11 and 13 who are on the fringes of gang life. By offering protection, brotherhood and friendship they recruit fresh blood their ongoing gang wars.

When 18th Street surfaces, the quality of life suffers, causing despair for locals and problems for law enforcement. Cars are stolen, homes burgled, drugs sold and murders committed. Drug dealers are robbed and denizens of the street killed. It's a violent, ruthless world.

Since the 1990s, 18th Street has been one of the largest street gangs in Los Angeles with cells across a number of neighbourhoods. Gang leaders deported in the 1990s also helped spread the gang across Central America and into Mexico. Transplanted 18th Streeters also have exported their criminal ways to other states and countries.

"When gang members were deported back to Central America, they took the gang with them," Grillo says. "But in

Beat on the Street

18TH STREET GANG MEMBERS COME FROM A VARIETY OF CULTURES, SO GANG TERMINOLOGY HAS FOLLOWED SUIT

Clickas
The clique, set or subset of the gang that various 18th Street members belong to.

Vato loco
A respected OG or veterano who is not afraid to bust his gun or get his hands dirty.

Eme
The Mexican Mafia prison gang, which unofficially controls every Southern California gang because they run the prisons, and every criminal knows there's a high probability they will end up inside.

Veteranos
OGs or gang members who have been around a while and know the score on the street and in the prisons.

Greenlight
When 18th Street put a green light on someone that means it is open season to kill them.

Cholo
A Mexican-American barrio lifestyle. Cholos are suave, debonair gangsters who have a distinctive dressing style and way that they move.

Shot callers
The veterans that control the block or prison yard that gang members call home. Shot callers call the shots and make the decisions for the gang.

Soldados
The foot soldiers in the 18th Street gang, which uses a lot of underage kids to do their bidding, hold their guns and drugs or even take the rap for a murder.

An alleged gang member is subdued during a raid in San Salvador by a special anti-gang unit

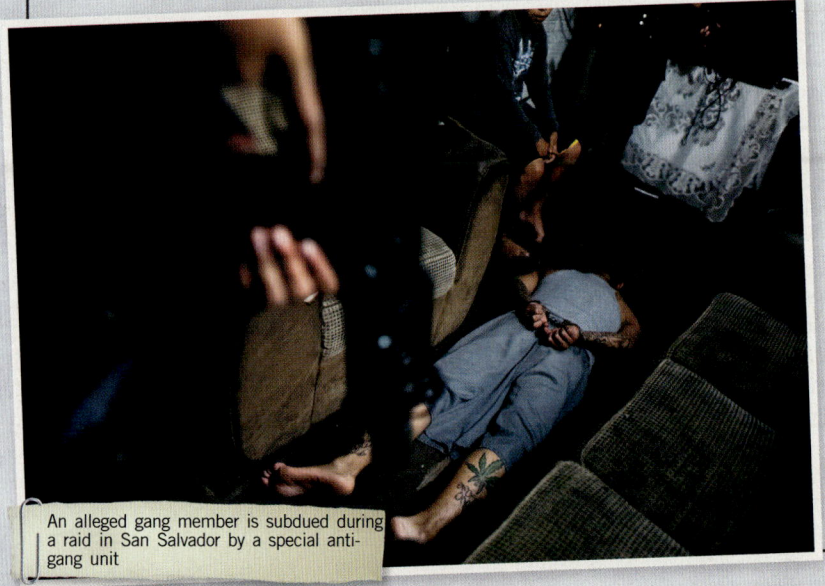

RIGHT Most members of the 18th Street gang are under 20, with some being recruited as young as 12 and not expected to live into their 30s

SCOURGE OF 18TH STREET

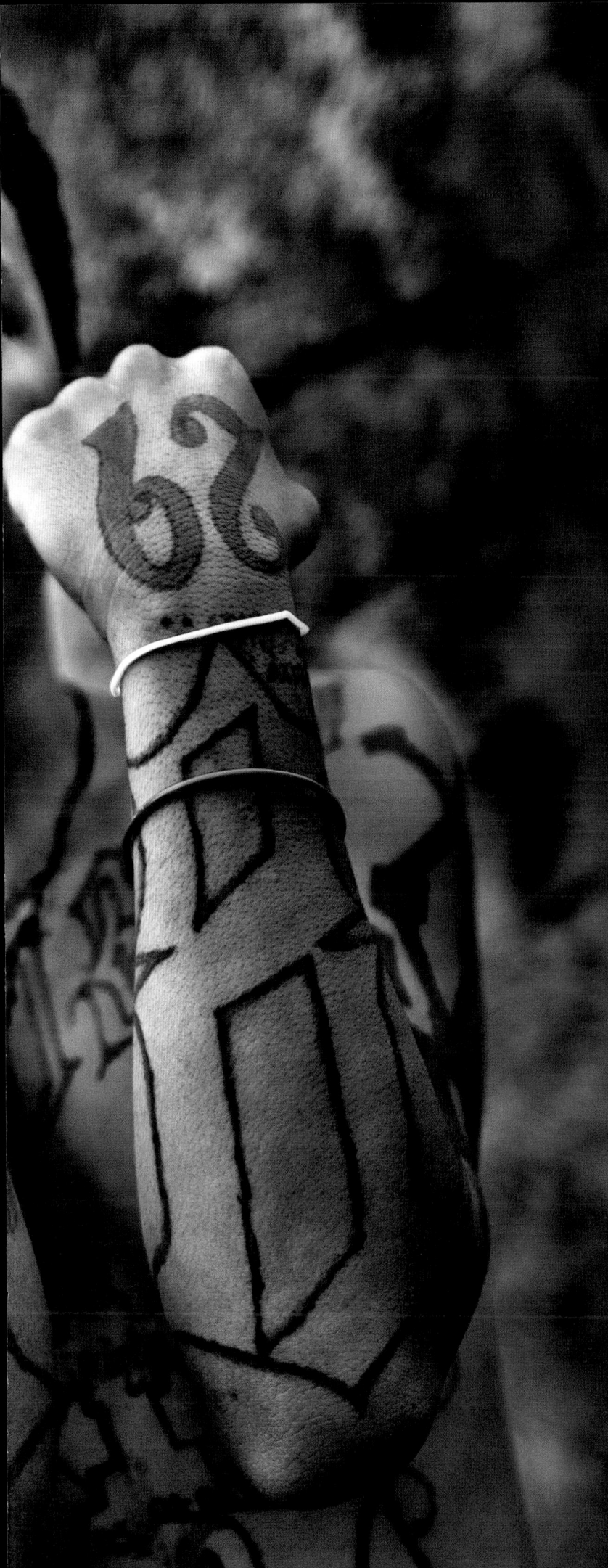

El Salvador and Honduras and Guatemala, they found they could get away with more than in the United States, as the police forces were much weaker. So they mutated, becoming much more violent. They got heavier guns and they recruited more people, and this new generation of gang members, they don't know the United States, they know the gang was originally brought there. They might have an American gang name, but they've never been to Los Angeles, and the level of violence is crazy."

The major gangs operating in Central America with ties to the United States are the 18th Street gang and their main rival the Mara Salvatrucha, also known as MS-13. As membership of the rival MS-13 also grew in Central America, they fought a bloody turf war with 18th Street that cut right across the region. Barrio 18 and MS-13 have helped turn El Salvador and Honduras into two of the most violent countries in the world.

"In Honduras, I asked when these guys got so violent," Grillo says. "Someone told me it was after they saw the movie *Blood In, Blood Out* dubbed into Spanish. The young gangsters all know that movie by heart."

As part of Los Angeles' storied gang culture, 18th Street stayed true to the tenets of gang membership: greenlighting enemies, disciplining their own members severely and taxing their own territories ruthlessly. The gang of now mostly second-generation and third-generation Hispanics has seemingly achieved the notoriety of a brand, a recognised force in gang and drug politics.

"18th Street is like a many-headed hydra," Assistant U.S. Attorney Gregory W. Jessner, who oversaw a prosecutorial task force targeting the gang, said. The LA gang has become one of the largest youth gangs in the Western Hemisphere. It's size and ability to recruit across ethnic lines make the LA-based network one of the most prolific gangs in the nation, and even the world.

However, it's not all bad news. Where once 18th Street and MS-13 had El Salvador gripped in fear as they killed each other and innocent civilians (the gangs have been known to light buses full of people on fire) and engaged in guerrilla urban warfare against the police, since 2022 the murder capital of the world has seen a dramatic drop in homicides. This is thanks to the government declaring a state of emergency, enabling it to use harsher measures against gangs. In 2021, there were over 1,100 murders. By contrast, in 2022 that figure dropped to 495.

Even so, crime still wreaks havoc across the region. El Salvador continues to lead the world when it comes to bloodshed, and Honduras, Belize and Guatemala are not too far behind. Latin America as a whole is seeing a spike in murders, ironically in part due to measures that have destroyed larger, dominant organisations, thereby enabling smaller factions to fight over the spoils of crime.

The Covid-19 pandemic didn't help either. "Everything shut down in Latin America during Covid-19 except organized crime," says Will Freeman, a fellow for Latin America studies at the Council on Foreign Relations, a New York-based think tank founded in 1921. "Organized crime groups… became more entrepreneurial. They diversified into new markets, new types of drug production and drug trafficking."

You can bet your last dollar that the likes of 18th Street will continue to fight for a share of the market for many years to come. After all, there's a killing to be made.

The Battle of Los Angeles

SINCE THE 1970S, BLOODS HAVE FOUGHT CRIPS IN SOME OF AMERICA'S MOST VIOLENT GANG WARS – BUT WHY?

WORDS DAVE SMITH

Search for the roots of one of the longest, most brutal gang-related conflicts of modern times and you quickly find yourself enmeshed in the defining geopolitical event of the 20th century – World War II. How war in Europe and Asia led to war on the streets of California is a sobering tale.

After the U.S. entered the war in 1941 the working male population of America's urban centres reduced in numbers, as many of those workers were drafted to fight and sent abroad. This created a manpower deficit that, coupled with government legislation that made racial discrimination illegal, led to an influx of African-American workers into industrial centres such as Los Angeles.

Legislation or no legislation, racism was as deeply entrenched in California as it was in the rest of the Western world, and many of these inbound workers found themselves unable to buy or even rent homes in many parts of LA. Pockets of Black populations grew in areas such as South Central, then a town outside the city centre. The situation was made worse by the prejudices of the legal establishment, one of whom was William H. Parker, LA's chief of police from 1950 to 1966. Parker, who is reported to have complained bitterly about the newly-arrived African-American workers and to have adopted bullying tactics towards them and to Latino residents, engineered a conflict between those communities and the police that has lasted decades.

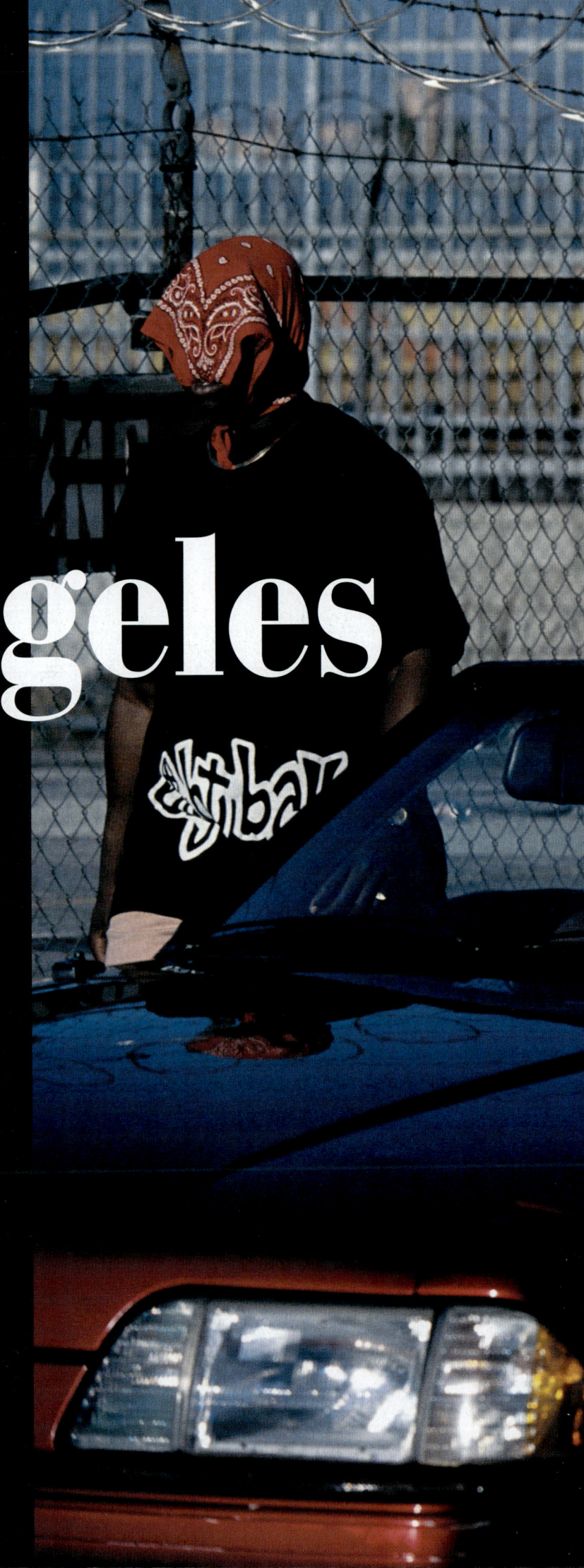

THE BATTLE OF LOS ANGELES

How were the residents of South Central Los Angeles to defend themselves against their supposed protectors? By banding together. When police officers meted out violent treatment to a Black resident who had failed a drink-driving test in August 1965, full-scale battles ensued with the local community, dubbed the Watts riots after the LA neighbourhood in which they took place. The Black Panthers party, formed of African-Americans who wanted to fight for racial equality, was founded in the wake of this upheaval.

Eight years after the Watts riots, a 20-year-old youth named Raymond Washington decided to form his own gang, the Crips, supposedly named after a 'crippling' limp acquired by his older brother when he twisted his ankle. Although Washington admired the ethos and practice of the Black Panthers, and his associates wore leather jackets in tribute to the party, the Crips were less focused on social justice and more on elevating themselves out of urban poverty by any means possible – violent if necessary and illegal by default. Within a couple of years of the gang's formation they began to identify themselves with the colour blue, after a blue bandana worn by a member called Curtis 'Buddha' Morrow, who was murdered in 1973.

A fellow gang leader named Stanley 'Tookie' Williams could have been a serious rival to Washington, but the two men decided to become allies and merged their gangs to form a large and powerful unit. Together they ran both the east and west sides of LA, gaining power when the Black Panthers started to wane around 1971. Their decline was largely due to COINTELPRO, a programme of subversive activities – later investigated and declared illegal – by the FBI, whose aim was to neutralise and disband any group that they regarded as a threat.

As the commentator Noam Chomsky explained it, "COINTELPRO was a program of subversion carried out not by a couple of petty crooks but by the national political police, the FBI, under four administrations... it was aimed at the entire new left, at the women's movement, at the whole black movement... Its actions went as far as political assassination."

One irony here is that the FBI, whose goal was supposedly to protect the American populace, enabled the rise of a much more destructive force through COINTELPRO than the Black Panthers. Once the Panthers were reduced in strength, the Crips flooded into the ensuing power vacuum, but they didn't occupy it alone.

In 1972, Crips members murdered a civilian called Robert Ballou, Jr., after he refused to hand over his leather jacket. In response, a group of unaffiliated neighbouring gangs united to defend themselves against the Crips, calling themselves by a slang word for comrades – 'Bloods'. Their chosen colour, red, reflected their name – and their approach.

Violence between the two gangs was sporadic at first, but over the next two decades the streets and prisons witnessed a steady rise in murderous clashes, especially after Washington and Williams lost control in 1979. The former was murdered by still-unidentified killers in a drive-by shooting, while the latter was arrested on four counts of murder and spent no less than 24 years on death row. Williams, who always maintained his innocence, became the subject of an international protest as his execution approached, as he had called for an end to gang warfare and become an acclaimed author. Unmoved by the public protest, the then Governor of California Arnold Schwarzenegger denied clemency and Williams died by lethal injection on 13 December 2005.

The gang rivalry was exacerbated in the 1980s when economic hardship befell Los Angeles, with the auto industry replaced by overseas imports. A new drug, crack cocaine, offered a way to make easy money and the Bloods and Crips took full advantage. As the gang members fought for supremacy over the drug's distribution, the murder rate spiralled and the gangs themselves threw out offshoots to other American cities: by 1990 both Bloods and Crips could be found in every large and midsized U.S. city.

Thanks to the rise of hip-hop and rap acts from South Central such as N.W.A, who pioneered the then new gangsta rap subgenre, rhymes about gang life entered a wider public awareness via MTV. N.W.A's songs 'Straight Outta

BOTTOM LEFT Graffiti pictured during the LA riots in 1992. Not coincidentally, this phrase is also the title of a well-known hit single by the rappers N.W.A

MIDDLE These guns were seized after FBI agents and LAPD officers arrested 50 people associated with the Five Deuce Gangster Crips, a South Los Angeles street gang

BOTTOM RIGHT Los Angeles burns in 1992. The riots were sparked by the beating of Rodney King after decades of tension caused by economic deprivation and police brutality finally erupted

THE BATTLE OF LOS ANGELES

Compton' and 'Fuck Tha Police' found a willing audience in white suburban households in and out of America, and rappers Schoolly D, Ice-T and N.W.A's own Ice Cube took the message even further. Hip-hop with violent, misogynistic overtones and explicit language soon became the norm into the 1990s and became a billion-dollar business by the middle of the decade thanks to artists such as Snoop Dogg, Eminem and another N.W.A alumnus, Dr Dre.

Hollywood jumped on board as soon it possibly could, releasing a slew of 'hood movies' of varying quality in cinemas throughout the Nineties: it didn't take long for Ice Cube and Ice-T to become bona fide film stars thanks to the 1991 movies *Boys n the Hood* and *New Jack City*. A perfect storm blew up in 1992, when riots erupted in LA after four white police officers were filmed beating an African-American motorist named Rodney King. Gangsta rap and the hood movies had established that such a disturbance could happen, and when it did it seemed that history and art had meshed to become a single, apocalyptic whole.

The Bloods and the Crips both orbited and populated this cultural narrative, rarely appearing by name in the songs and movies but continuing to perpetuate a cycle of violence as the years passed. Immersed in the LA riots, the two gangs agreed a ceasefire (the Watts truce) afterwards that lasted for some time. The murder rate between them dropped significantly, although the desire among young, directionless men who lacked guidance to be part of either gang was unfortunately as strong as ever.

Indeed, since 2000, Bloods and Crips activity has been uncovered in places where it had not previously been seen: in America's armed forces and online. It has been reported that YouTube videos have been used to intimidate and that the internet has enabled both gangs to commit crimes such as identity theft and fraud. Although incidents involving physical violence are said to have reduced in number overall, it seems that other gang activities continue to plague the streets.

Murders still grab the headlines from time to time, though. The killing in March 2019 of the rapper Nipsey Hussle (aka Ermias Asghedom) was one recent example, even though Hussle – a former member of the Rollin' 60s Crips offshoot – had invested time and money in making improvements to his community. A Rollin' 60s member named Lil AD told the *Los Angeles Times*, "We're going to carry what Nipsey wanted, what he was trying to preach in his songs. It don't make no sense that you're fighting over a block that you don't own." Indeed, gang violence was said to drop in the wake of the murder.

There's a long way to go though, and life in the poorer districts of Los Angeles is no easier than it ever was. Until those neighbourhoods' problems are solved, it seems that the Bloods and the Crips – whose numbers were estimated in 2008 to be as high as 20,000 and 35,000 respectively – won't be going anywhere just yet. While they continue to operate there will no doubt be more blood spilt.

BELOW Rolling 20's Bloods pose at a gang-member's gravesite (members of the gang's junior and senior hierarchy are present)

"IT DON'T MAKE NO SENSE THAT YOU'RE FIGHTING OVER A BLOCK THAT YOU DON'T OWN"

America's Most Lethal Gang

RISING FROM THE SLUMS OF EL SALVADOR THROUGH THE STREETS OF LA, MS-13 HAS BECOME ONE OF THE WORLD'S MOST FEARED INTERNATIONAL CRIMINAL ORGANISATIONS

WORDS PAUL FRENCH

The gang known as MS-13 was born out of the Central American civil wars of the 1980s, in particular the Salvadoran Civil War. After a decade of simmering tensions, the military-led government of El Salvador and the Farabundo Martí National Liberation Front (FMLN) – a coalition, or umbrella organisation, of five left-wing militias – became engaged in a bloody conflict. The United States of America became involved when it backed the government and supplied its firepower. By the time the conflict ended in the 1990s perhaps as many as 100,000 Salvadorans had been killed, legions more had been exposed to bloody fratricidal violence and the country was left in an impoverished state. Over that period thousands of Salvadorans migrated north to the U.S., primarily the city of Los Angeles. As with so many gangs the world over, the Mara Salvatrucha gang – which would quickly come to be known internationally as MS-13 – was formed in LA to protect Salvadoran immigrants from those that would prey upon them as newcomers to the city's often-violent melting pot.

MS-13 quickly became a force to be reckoned with. Organised into a collection of affiliate gangs referred to as 'cliques', it became an organisation known for its shockingly high levels of violence – violence that reached back into El Salvador as well as into Honduras, Guatemala, Nicaragua and Mexico. In the U.S., the gang rapidly expanded into other enclaves of Salvadoran and Hispanic immigration, including San Francisco, Washington, D.C., Texas, Boston, New York and even up into Canada.

In 2004, the FBI created the MS-13 National Gang Task Force. U.S. Immigration and Customs Enforcement targeted suspected MS-13 members. By 2011, more than 3,000 alleged members of MS-13 had been arrested and many deported back to El Salvador. With reports of MS-13 affiliates and cliques active as far afield as Spain, in October 2012 the U.S. Department of the Treasury labelled the group a "transnational criminal organisation," the first such designation for a U.S. street gang.

Despite the crackdown by government agencies, MS-13 grew in both the U.S. and Central America. It became a key international players in the fields of drug trafficking, robbery, human trafficking, extortion, illegal immigration, murder, prostitution, kidnapping and arms trafficking. However, the success of MS-13 in the U.S., the flow of cash back to El Salvador and the mass deportations of gang members to San Salvador meant that an LA street gang became an almost shadow state in El Salvador.

San Salvador is a city of over a million people, with many hundreds of thousands more in the city's overflowing suburbs of slums and favelas. It is the capital of El Salvador, a country of 6.3 million, the most densely populated nation in Central America. Since the FBI's deportations of gang members back to El Salvador in 2004, the city's crime rate has skyrocketed.

MS-13 has been at constant war with its largest rival, Barrio-18, which is an equally violent gang that also operates in the U.S. The municipal government and the local police have, until quite recently, been largely unable to contain the ever-worsening tit-for-tat violence raging across San Salvador, particularly its notorious Districts 5 and 6, where the gangs are deeply embedded in communities. The Salvadoran Army has been enlisted to fight the gangs, with some success. However, with 52 murders per 100,000 residents, the per capita homicide rate is almost ten times that of major cities such as New York (six per 100,000).

AMERICA'S MOST LETHAL GANG

A local leader of MS-13, in prison in San Salvador, shows a hand sign that represents his gang

119

ABOVE TOP MS-13's activities are noted for their extreme violence. El Salvador's police remain masked to protect their identities at an MS-13 crime scene to avoid gang retribution against them

ABOVE (CIRCLE) MS-13 members have adopted the 'Devil's Horn' hand sign and use it to communicate among themselves

To understand how far the state lost control and how MS-13 now pulls the strings in many places, it's essential to take a look at Ciudad Barrios prison in San Miguel, a city in the eastern part of El Salvador. To prevent complete bloody chaos, the authorities have segregated gangs in the country's prison system. Ciudad Barrios is an MS-13-only jail, one built to house 800 men that is actually home to more than 2,600. When prison guards proved unable to maintain control of the facility, the army was brought in to militarise it. This means that MS-13 now effectively controls the entire jail; the army along with a few remaining prison guards stay outside of the facility for the most part. MS-13 gang members bake their own bread, run their own workshops and even staff their own hospital. With a ratio of 50 inmates to every guard, gang law rules. But even this effective corralling of MS-13 has curtailed the gang's international expansion.

MS-13 is involved in a wide range of criminal activity, including (but not limited to) racketeering, extortion, prostitution, kidnapping, money laundering, contract murder, arms dealing and drug trafficking. But there is one area of illicit activity where the gang has become particularly notorious and shown its infamous prevalence for extreme violence: people trafficking.

MS-13's own history – the migration north from Central America to the U.S. – provides the gang with its largest money-making operation today. The U.S. Department of Homeland Security estimates that there are 11 million illegal immigrants in the U.S. – 15 per cent of whom originally come from Central America. The majority of these people, and many others from all over the world, enter the U.S. (a country with a population of 331.9 million) through the time-worn route of the journey up the Americas to the long and difficult-to-police Mexican-American border. This was MS-13's journey, and now many thousands of hopeful immigrants pay MS-13 to take them over the same ground.

MS-13 have industrialised the process of illegal immigration. In the Mexican town of Matamoros, just south of Brownsville, Texas, the gang has established a major smuggling centre. Matamoros is an industrial town home to many of Mexico's maquiladoras, which are factories producing goods for export to the U.S. in often appalling labour conditions. Among the sprawl of factories, MS-13 holds immigrants from Mexico and other Central American countries such as Guatemala, Honduras, Nicaragua and Costa Rica. MS-13 affiliates find these desperate migrants in their home villages, take their money and ship them to Matamoros. The business has been a highly lucrative and busy one since the early 2000s. However, U.S. Homeland Security has recently begun paying extra attention, as the number of 'border jumpers' from other countries sent across via MS-13-controlled people-smuggling routes is increasing. Nationals from Afghanistan, Indonesia, Iran, Iraq, Jordan, Pakistan and Syria have all been recently found among those being smuggled from Matamoros.

AMERICA'S MOST LETHAL GANG

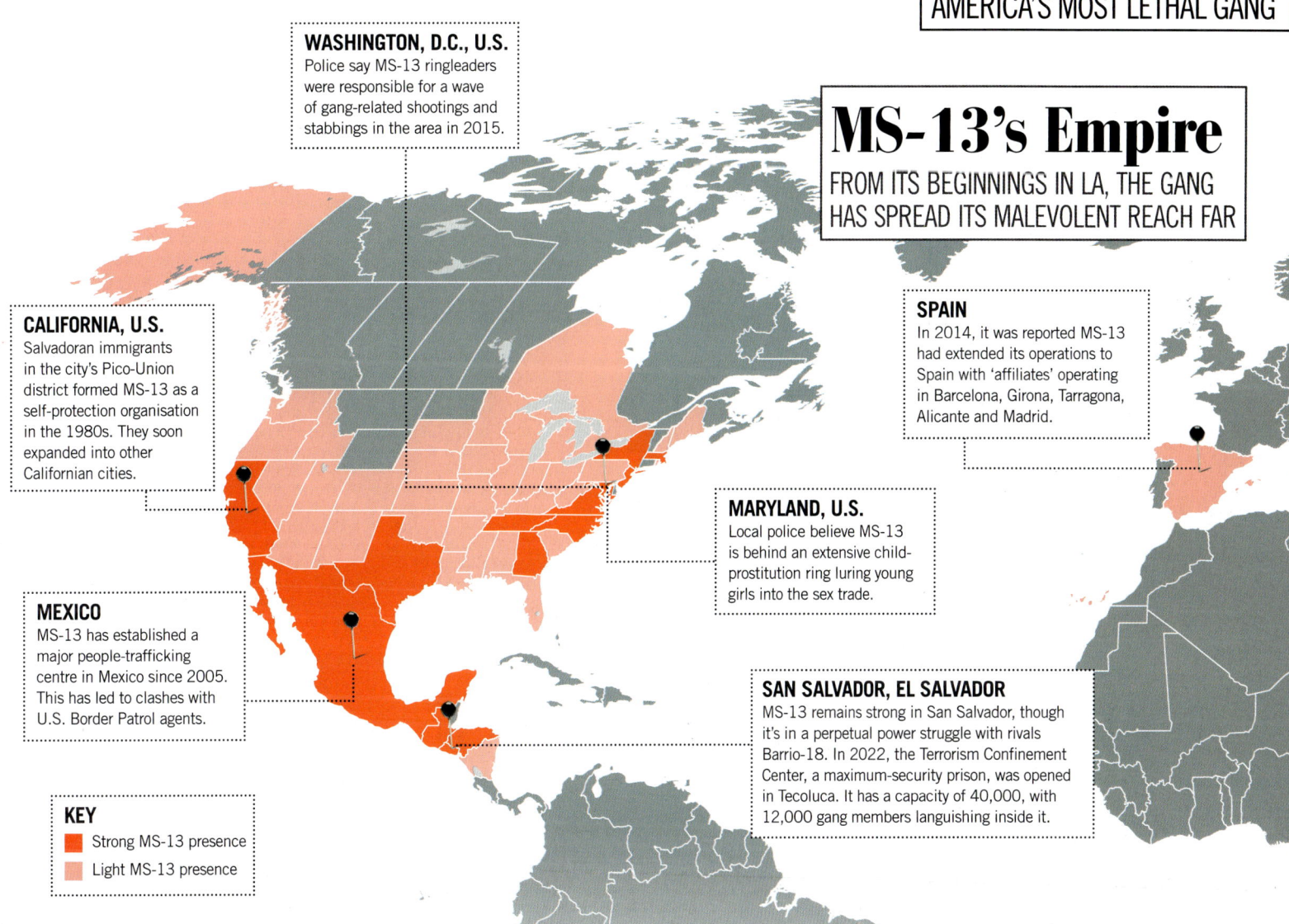

MS-13's Empire
FROM ITS BEGINNINGS IN LA, THE GANG HAS SPREAD ITS MALEVOLENT REACH FAR

WASHINGTON, D.C., U.S.
Police say MS-13 ringleaders were responsible for a wave of gang-related shootings and stabbings in the area in 2015.

CALIFORNIA, U.S.
Salvadoran immigrants in the city's Pico-Union district formed MS-13 as a self-protection organisation in the 1980s. They soon expanded into other Californian cities.

MEXICO
MS-13 has established a major people-trafficking centre in Mexico since 2005. This has led to clashes with U.S. Border Patrol agents.

SPAIN
In 2014, it was reported MS-13 had extended its operations to Spain with 'affiliates' operating in Barcelona, Girona, Tarragona, Alicante and Madrid.

MARYLAND, U.S.
Local police believe MS-13 is behind an extensive child-prostitution ring luring young girls into the sex trade.

SAN SALVADOR, EL SALVADOR
MS-13 remains strong in San Salvador, though it's in a perpetual power struggle with rivals Barrio-18. In 2022, the Terrorism Confinement Center, a maximum-security prison, was opened in Tecoluca. It has a capacity of 40,000, with 12,000 gang members languishing inside it.

KEY
- Strong MS-13 presence
- Light MS-13 presence

Alarm bells started ringing after U.S. intelligence agencies spotted Adnan Gulshair el Shukrijumah, a key Al-Qaeda cell leader with a $5-million bounty on his head, in Honduras in 2005 meeting with leaders of MS-13. Since then, a concerted effort has been made to shut down Matamoros. It's only been a partial success though; more than ten years later, the American authorities believe that MS-13's people-smuggling operations in Mexico and along the Rio Grande Valley are being protected by Mexico's powerful drug cartels in a new alliance with the Salvadoran gangs.

People smuggling is not only lucrative for MS-13, but it is also a way for the gang to replenish its ranks. As well as raiding shelters full of new arrivals to America for young members, MS-13 has established cliques in new cities in the U.S. closely associated with cross-border people trafficking, particularly in Houston and Dallas.

With the arrival of MS-13 in Texas has come their trademark violence. The Texas Department of Public Safety reported that in September 2014, the mutilated body of a 14-year-old school student was discovered in woods near Houston after he had been murdered with a machete. The report indicates that the victim was an MS-13 member and an American citizen who had been killed after trying to leave the gang. A month later, a 16-year-old El Salvadoran member of MS-13 stabbed a 29-year-old Barrio 18 gang member to death in Houston. The young killer had only recently been smuggled into the U.S. and promptly recruited into MS-13. His victim was stabbed multiple times and dumped in a bayou (a boggy creek).

> **"MS-13 MEMBERS SUSPECTED OF CO-OPERATING WITH THE POLICE ARE ROUTINELY EXECUTED BY NEW RECRUITS"**

Texan authorities were not overly surprised by either the rise of MS-13 in their state or the extreme violence that accompanied it. In the early years of the 21st century, MS-13 has spread its tentacles across the U.S. with gang task force reports identifying MS-13 affiliates active in Washington, D.C., Virginia, Maryland, and on into Oregon, Nevada, Utah, Oklahoma, Illinois, Michigan, New York and Georgia. MS-13 offshoots have been identified as far north as Alaska and as far south as Florida.

MS-13 still recruits predominantly from Hispanic communities and typically among young males, with some members being as young as 13. Initiation of new recruits involves being 'jumped' into the gang – beaten by members while others count to 13. Often the initiation is even more extreme; MS-13 members suspected of co-operating with the police are routinely executed by new recruits in a gruesome rite of passage, invariably with a machete.

Recruitment of girls into the gangs is similar. In 2003, 17-year-old Brenda Paz from Virginia sought to leave the MS-13 life and turned informant for the FBI. She was soon found stabbed on the banks of the nearby Shenandoah River. Two other young girls, both friends of Paz who wished to join MS-13, were later convicted of the murder.

ABOVE Graffiti bearing the gang's name can be found across the municipality of San Pedro Masahuat in El Salvador

Nobody it seems is safe from MS-13's reach; not vulnerable young migrants, young men or women in America's Hispanic community, nor even young children.

In 2011, MS-13 hit the headlines in the U.S. once again. They were firmly on the law enforcement radar for drug, people and gun smuggling as well as robbery, extortion and their trademark high-octane violence against innocents and their own. But this time, even those hardened to the criminal nefariousness of the U.S.'s street gangs were shocked by a new level of wickedness – MS-13's deep involvement in child-prostitution rings across the country.

A series of high-profile trials began in 2011 that incriminated MS-13 in the pernicious business of grooming and recruiting girls, often as young as 12 years of age and invariably in protected shelters due to domestic abuse at home, into child prostitution rings. In Fairfax, Virginia, 22-year-old MS-13 member Alonso Cornejo, a.k.a. "Casper", was sentenced to 292 months of jail time. Four other MS-13 members were also sentenced to similar terms for child-prostitution offences. The court heard that men were charged $100 for 15 minutes of sex with the girls in MS-13-controlled brothels. Across the U.S., convictions continued, showing that MS-13 had set up a network of child brothels in what one U.S. attorney called "…an unconscionable crime that reduces young women to indentured sex slaves and may subject them to a lifetime of traumatic memories".

Since 2011, the crackdown on MS-13 by the American authorities has ratcheted up considerably. Deportations of MS-13 members to El Salvador have been increased as well as deportations of convicted members to Guatemala, Honduras, Peru and other home countries. Recently, the U.S. Treasury Department announced a freeze on American-owned assets controlled by the organisation to hit them at the heart of their money-making operations.

Yet still the violence continues. In early 2016, police in the state of Maryland attributed a sudden spike in murders to MS-13. In Montgomery County, a violent murder was attributed to the Locos Salvatruchos, which is a clique of MS-13. In nearby Fairfax County, authorities said that they had investigated three MS-13 related murders in 2015. By January 2016, a total of eight murders had been linked to the gang. Three of the victims were illegal immigrants.

One response by MS-13 to the crackdown in the U.S. appears to have been to 'offshore' its activities, in particular by launching a concerted move into Europe. Following intelligence sharing between the U.S. and Spain, 300 Spanish national police launched raids across the country in 2014 and arrested 35 members of MS-13 in Barcelona, Girona, Tarragona, Alicante and Madrid.

The move seems to be a direct result of the Treasury Department's tougher approach. As well as selling drugs and running prostitution rings, the gangs were opening restaurants and bars as a way to launder money outside of the control of the American authorities.

MS-13 have clearly also enlarged their recruitment pool; as well as Salvadorans, Spanish police have arrested Romanian, Bulgarian and Moroccan nationals in their anti-MS-13 sweep. Spanish police now worry that Barrio-18 are also commencing operations in the country and on the continent, and that the lethal feuds between MS-13 and Barrio-18 that have left a trail of dead from San Salvador to Los Angeles and Washington, D.C., may now continue on the streets of Europe. Just as a 2022 government crackdown in El Salvador is beginning to bear fruit (75,000 people were imprisoned for gang-related crimes across 2022 and 2023 and the murder rate has plummeted by 70 per cent) the battlefield could be shifting across the Atlantic. Only time will tell what damage MS-13 will inflict in their new surroundings.

AMERICA'S MOST LETHAL GANG

What do the Markings Mean?

MS-13 MEMBERS DISPLAY THEIR LIFELONG ALLEGIANCE ON THEIR SKIN

Many street gangs pride themselves on their tattoos and attribute strong significance to them, far beyond the painted bodies that have become fashionable today. But the Mara Salvatrucha take this adornment to another level, covering their faces and torsos with gang 'achievements' and events that tell the story of their loyalty to MS-13. Certain tattoos make individuals instantly recognisable on the street and in prison, where even prison guards will treat them with respect. There are regional variations of the gang's tattoos, but some are common to all of MS-13.

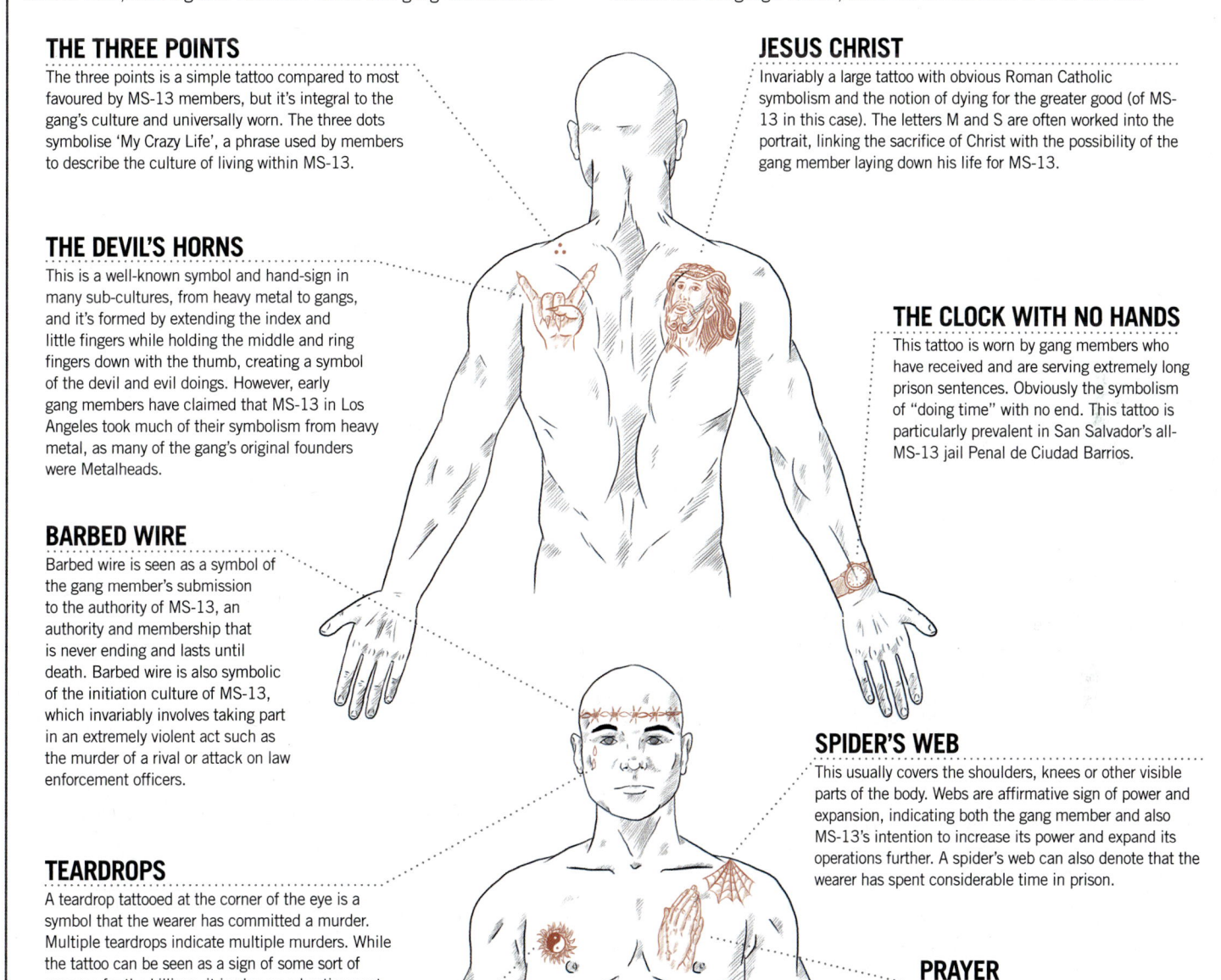

THE THREE POINTS
The three points is a simple tattoo compared to most favoured by MS-13 members, but it's integral to the gang's culture and universally worn. The three dots symbolise 'My Crazy Life', a phrase used by members to describe the culture of living within MS-13.

THE DEVIL'S HORNS
This is a well-known symbol and hand-sign in many sub-cultures, from heavy metal to gangs, and it's formed by extending the index and little fingers while holding the middle and ring fingers down with the thumb, creating a symbol of the devil and evil doings. However, early gang members have claimed that MS-13 in Los Angeles took much of their symbolism from heavy metal, as many of the gang's original founders were Metalheads.

BARBED WIRE
Barbed wire is seen as a symbol of the gang member's submission to the authority of MS-13, an authority and membership that is never ending and lasts until death. Barbed wire is also symbolic of the initiation culture of MS-13, which invariably involves taking part in an extremely violent act such as the murder of a rival or attack on law enforcement officers.

TEARDROPS
A teardrop tattooed at the corner of the eye is a symbol that the wearer has committed a murder. Multiple teardrops indicate multiple murders. While the tattoo can be seen as a sign of some sort of remorse for the killings, it is also an advertisement that the gang member has been "blooded" and is a proven killer.

YIN YANG SYMBOL
The traditional Chinese symbol of duality describes how opposite or contrary forces are actually complementary – the light and the dark. MS-13 members take it to represent the complementarity of good and evil but also, by extension and representative of their gang life, the relationship between violence and death.

JESUS CHRIST
Invariably a large tattoo with obvious Roman Catholic symbolism and the notion of dying for the greater good (of MS-13 in this case). The letters M and S are often worked into the portrait, linking the sacrifice of Christ with the possibility of the gang member laying down his life for MS-13.

THE CLOCK WITH NO HANDS
This tattoo is worn by gang members who have received and are serving extremely long prison sentences. Obviously the symbolism of "doing time" with no end. This tattoo is particularly prevalent in San Salvador's all-MS-13 jail Penal de Ciudad Barrios.

SPIDER'S WEB
This usually covers the shoulders, knees or other visible parts of the body. Webs are affirmative sign of power and expansion, indicating both the gang member and also MS-13's intention to increase its power and expand its operations further. A spider's web can also denote that the wearer has spent considerable time in prison.

PRAYER
Roman Catholic symbolism is integral to much MS-13 tattooing. The prayer image is taken to mean "forgive me mother for my crazy life". This accepts life as a gang member but acknowledges crimes committed. Treacherous gang members have been punished by having their mothers murdered, and so this tattoo is an advance apology and recognition of this harsh punishment.

© Corbis; FreeVectorMaps.com; Getty Images; Kym Winters

123

In 1903, Edwin S. Porter's short film *The Great Train Robbery* ended with an outlaw pointing his pistol point-blank at the camera and emptying the barrel directly at (screaming) viewers. You've seen the shot – Martin Scorsese inserted it at the end of his scintillating 1990 Mob drama *Goodfellas*, right before the credits played out to Johnny Rotten snarling 'My Way'.

The point is, criminals have always been big business in cinema, their dangerous, law-breaking actions offering illicit thrills for viewers. We watch in the dark; they live in it, the shadows pulsing with sex, violence and money as they often propel themselves on upwardly mobile trajectories… and usually crash back down again, often into a yawning grave.

The gangster movie is a subgenre of the crime film. When we think 'gangster', we might immediately think of the Mafia, but it's a mutable subgenre, ranging from loners on revenge missions to small bands of street criminals to large organisations performing crime on an industrial scale. The films can be glamorous or grubby, fictional or factual, kamikaze or coolly calculated.

Here, we pick our ten favourites. Apologies to all those magnificent gangsters we missed out. Please don't march us out to a hole in the desert…

Mobs and the Movies

WORDS JAMIE GRAHAM

THE SHAKEDOWN IS COMPLETE, AND THESE 10 FILMS ARE ALL NUMBER ONE WITH A BULLET

MOBS AND THE MOVIES

The Public Enemy
WILLIAM A. WELLMAN 1931

Warner Brothers made a slew of fast and furious gangster movies in the 1930s, their dangerous thrills and jolting violence distracting viewers from the Great Depression. Set in Chicago, this 74-minute frenzy of a picture tracked the ascent of Tom Powers (James Cagney) from street punk to head of an organised crime operation. With his dizzying rise comes clothes, cars and dames, and though the drama ends with Tom dead in a gutter with his belly full of bullets – followed by a po-faced warning that society must weed out these monsters – it was clearly a case of having your cake and eating it.

"I'll give you the toughest, most violent picture you ever did see!" crowed director William Wellman to producer Darryl Zanuck, and he certainly didn't disappoint.

MGM delighted viewers with toe-tapping musicals. *The Public Enemy* opted for Cagney (in his breakout role) smashing a grapefruit into Mae Clarke's face.

Le Samouraï
JEAN-PIERRE MELVILLE 1967

Influenced by the American film noirs of the 1940s and '50s, French filmmaker Jean-Pierre Melville excelled at fashioning immaculate-looking gangster films shot in muted tones and populated by macho men in trench coats. Theirs was a world of honour, stoicism, treachery, alienation and death, and in movies like *Le Doulos*, *Le Cercle Rouge* and *Un Flic*, a sense of fatalism coated the action like a shroud. And *what* action, for Melville was a master of set-pieces.

Le Samouraï is arguably his masterpiece, tracking loner hitman Jef Costello (an ice-cool Alain Delon) as he's witnessed carrying out a contract and then finds himself pursued not only by cops but his employers. Costello lives in a sparse apartment but mainly in his head, adhering to a rigorous code. He's a mesmerising creation in a stunning film that's influenced a young Martin Scorsese's *Taxi Driver*, John Woo's *The Killer* and Nicholas Winding Refn's *Drive*, to name just three.

The Long Good Friday
JOHN MACKENZIE 1980

Bob Hoskins gives a soaring performance in this British crime classic. He's Harold Shand, an East End crime boss who's determined to oversee the development of the derelict Docklands. On his arm is Helen Mirren, talking him through moments of fretful introspection or stepping up to charm concerned investors. Then, over Easter weekend, a killing spree rubs out Shand's trusted cohorts; our go-getting anti-hero is being out-manoeuvred by the IRA and American mafiosi. Capturing London, and Britain, at a crossroads, Barrie Keeffe's script proved remarkably prescient with regards to approaching Thatcherism ("What I'm looking for is someone who can contribute to what England has given the world," says Shand) and beyond – to now look at Canary Wharf's glimmering skyscrapers is to see what Shand saw in 1980, while the 2012 London Olympics was his dream. *The Long Good Friday* blends glitz and grime, aspiration and violence, and is powered along by Francis Monkman's earworming synth score.

The Godfather
FRANCIS FORD COPPOLA 1972

Paramount didn't want Francis Ford Coppola to direct the screen adaptation of Mario Puza's trashy Mafia novel. Sergio Leone, Peter Bogdanovich, Arthur Penn and more turned it down. Likewise, Laurence Olivier, George C. Scott and Orson Welles, among others, were considered for the Marlon Brando role of Vito Corleone, patriarch of the Corleone crime family. The 'could have beens' and 'what ifs' are endless, but what we got is the one-in-a-trillion combination, like monkeys writing a Shakespeare play. People remember the set-pieces – the horse's head in the bed, Sonny (James Caan) cut down at the toll booth, the baptism crosscut with the murders – but every minute of this luxurious crime saga is a joy, as clean-cut Michael (Al Pacino) is drawn into the family business. *The Godfather* won three Oscars including Best Picture, and took a record-breaking $250 million worldwide. Crime, it seems, does pay after all.

MOBS AND THE MOVIES

The Godfather Part II
FRANCIS FORD COPPOLA 1974

His creative control powered up by the original's success, Coppola decided to work on a larger, darker canvas. *Part II* is at once prequel and sequel, its twin narratives following the arrival of a young Vito Corleone (Robert De Niro) in 1920s New York, striving to protect his own, and the efforts of Michael (Al Pacino) to expand the family empire into Cuba. During the course of the action, Michael loses his elder brother Fredo (John Cazale), his wife Kay (Diane Keaton), and his soul. "The daring of *Part II* is that it enlarges the scope and deepens the meaning of the first film… It's an epic vision of the corruption of America," wrote uber-critic Pauline Kael, and *The Godfather Part II* is one of those rare sequels (see also *The Empire Strikes Back* and *Aliens*) that are frequently cited as surpassing the original. The Academy thought so too: it bagged six of the 11 Oscars it was nominated for.

Scarface
BRIAN DE PALMA 1983

A loose remake of Howard Hawks' 1932 classic of the same name, this savagely thrilling update was scripted by Oliver Stone and directed by Brian De Palma. It shifts the action from Chicago to Miami and makes Tony Montana (Al Pacino) an outlaw from Castro's Cuba. 'The World Is Yours' blinks the message on a Goodyear blimp, and Tony guns for the American Dream, painting the town red as he paves the streets in cocaine. It all ends, of course, with the infamously violent gun battle at Tony's mansion ("Say hello to my leeetle friend!"), De Palma somehow making the previous two-and-a-half hours of bravura camerawork, retina-scorching décor, pummelling profanity, death by chainsaw, incestuous lust, and Pacino bellowing chewed-up vowels seem subtle. But maybe that's the point.

Is *Scarface* a blood-drenched satire on the excesses of Reagan's America? Perhaps. It's certainly a great time at the movies.

Goodfellas
MARTIN SCORSESE 1990

After Coppola gave us aristocratic gangsters, Scorsese gives us street soldiers. Based on Nicholas Pileggi's breathless book *Wiseguys*, *Goodfellas* is 25 years in the Mob through the widened eyes of Brooklyn-born Irish-Italian hoodlum Henry Hill (an electrifying Ray Liotta,). It's all here, from pasta, weddings and date night at the Copacabana, to paranoia, death and betrayal. And it comes at us in a dazzling rush of style: voiceover, freeze frames, crash zooms, whip-pans, slo-mo, time-lapse, and an endless parade of jukebox hits. One of the most wildly entertaining movies ever made, *Goodfellas* is sometimes criticised for a lack of meaning. Hogwash. "You know, they don't think about it a lot," said Scorsese. "They eat a lot and make a lot of money and do the least amount of work possible… If you live for a certain kind of value… you're gonna come smack up against a brick wall. It's materialism versus a spiritual life."

Miller's Crossing
JOEL AND ETHAN COEN 1990

What is the Coen brothers' best film? For many it's the Oscar-winning *Fargo*. For many more, it's stoner-noir classic *The Big Lebowski*. But it's another of their movies indebted to the twisty-turny narratives of 1930s crime writers Dashiell Hammett, Raymond Chandler and James M. Cain that dazzles most brightly. Set in the Prohibition era, this stylish reworking of Hammett's *Red Harvest* charts the gang war between Leo (Albert Finney) and Johnny (Jon Polito), with the action pivoting around Leo's right-hand man Tom (a never-better Gabriel Byrne), who's sleeping with boss' mistress Verna (Marcia Gay Harden), whose brother, Bernie (John Turturro), Johnny wants whacked. Full of Byzantine plotting, tailored suits, abstract motifs, playful artifice and rat-a-tat-tat dialogue ("If you want me to keep my mouth shut, it's gonna cost you some dough. I figure a thousand bucks is reasonable, so I want two."), *Miller's Crossing* is sumptuous treat.

MOBS AND THE MOVIES

Sonatine
TAKESHI KITANO **1993**

No list of the greatest gangster films is complete without a yakuza movie. There are many to choose from – 1960s classics *Pigs and Battleships*, *Youth of the Beast* and *Tokyo Drifter* are all must-sees – but *Sonatine*, by Japanese gameshow host turned world-renowned director Takeshi Kitano, is a singular stunner. In it, world-weary yakuza member Murakawa (a stone-faced Kitano) is assigned to take his clan to Okinawa to help settle a dispute between two factions. Murakawa and his men wind up hanging out on the beach playing frisbee. And with time to contemplate, our man begins to realise that he wants out…

By turns playful, lyrical and soulful, *Sonatine* moves to its own rhythms, a minimalist masterpiece that occasionally erupts into violence. *Chicago Sun-Times* film critic Roger Ebert wrote, "It shows how violent gangster movies need not be filled with stupid dialogue, nonstop action and gratuitous gore." Quite.

Pulp Fiction
QUENTIN TARANTINO **1994**

Quentin Tarantino exploded out of the blocks in the 1990s with three superlative crime films: *Reservoir Dogs*, *Pulp Fiction* and *Jackie Brown*. And while it's the last of these that has perhaps best stood the test of time due to its heartfelt musing on love and ageing, it's *Pulp Fiction* that made the biggest splash, winning the Palme d'Or at the Cannes Film Festival, garnering seven Oscar nominations and entering popular culture to a point that every advert, movie and TV show seemed to steal from it. *Rolling Stone* called it "the new King Kong of crime movies", and its non-linear entwining of three outrageously funny tales involving two Mob hitmen (played superbly by John Travolta and Samuel L. Jackson), a gangster (Ving Rhames), a boxer (Bruce Willis) and a pair of bandits (Tim Roth and Amanda Plummer) is tastier than a Royale with cheese followed by blueberry pancakes. A post-modern masterpiece.

THE HISTORY OF GANGS

Future PLC Quay House, The Ambury, Bath, BA1 1UA

Bookazine Editorial
Editor **Charles Ginger**
Senior Art Editor **Stephen Williams**
Head of Art & Design **Greg Whitaker**
Editorial Director **Jon White**
Managing Director **Grainne McKenna**

Cover images
Getty Images, Alamy

Photography
All copyrights and trademarks are recognised and respected

Advertising
Media packs are available on request
Commercial Director **Clare Dove**

International
Head of Print Licensing **Rachel Shaw**
licensing@futurenet.com
www.futurecontenthub.com

Circulation
Head of Newstrade **Tim Mathers**

Production
Head of Production **Mark Constance**
Production Project Manager **Matthew Eglinton**
Advertising Production Manager **Joanne Crosby**
Digital Editions Controller **Jason Hudson**
Production Managers **Keely Miller, Nola Cokely, Vivienne Calvert, Fran Twentyman**

Printed in the UK

Distributed by Marketforce, 5 Churchill Place, Canary Wharf, London, E14 5HU
www.marketforce.co.uk – For enquiries, please email:
mfcommunications@futurenet.com

History of Gangs First Edition (AHB5751)
© 2024 Future Publishing Limited

We are committed to only using magazine paper which is derived from responsibly managed, certified forestry and chlorine-free manufacture. The paper in this bookazine was sourced and produced from sustainable managed forests, conforming to strict environmental and socioeconomic standards.

All contents © 2024 Future Publishing Limited or published under licence. All rights reserved. No part of this magazine may be used, stored, transmitted or reproduced in any way without the prior written permission of the publisher. Future Publishing Limited (company number 2008885) is registered in England and Wales. Registered office: Quay House, The Ambury, Bath BA1 1UA. All information contained in this publication is for information only and is, as far as we are aware, correct at the time of going to press. Future cannot accept any responsibility for errors or inaccuracies in such information. You are advised to contact manufacturers and retailers directly with regard to the price of products/services referred to in this publication. Apps and websites mentioned in this publication are not under our control. We are not responsible for their contents or any other changes or updates to them. This magazine is fully independent and not affiliated in any way with the companies mentioned herein.

FUTURE Connectors. Creators. Experience Makers.

Future plc is a public company quoted on the London Stock Exchange (symbol: FUTR)
www.futureplc.com

Chief Executive Officer **Jon Steinberg**
Non-Executive Chairman **Richard Huntingford**
Chief Financial and Strategy Officer **Penny Ladkin-Brand**

Tel +44 (0)1225 442 244

Part of the
ALL ABOUT HISTORY
bookazine series

Widely Recycled

ipso. For press freedom with responsibility